WESTERN
MEMORABILIA
IDENTIFICATION AND PRICE GUIDE

WESTERN
MEMORABILIA
IDENTIFICATION AND PRICE GUIDE
FIRST EDITION

WILLIAM C.
KETCHUM

The CONFIDENT COLLECTOR™

AVON BOOKS  NEW YORK

Important Notice: All of the information, including valuations, in this book has been compiled from the most reliable sources, and every effort has been made to eliminate errors and questionable data. Nevertheless, the possibility of error always exists in a work of such scope. The publisher and the author will not be held responsible for losses which may occur in the purchase, sale, or other transaction of property because of information contained herein. Readers who feel they have discovered errors are invited to *write* the author in care of Avon Books so that the errors may be corrected in subsequent editions.

THE CONFIDENT COLLECTOR: WESTERN MEMORABILIA (1st edition) is an original publication of Avon Books. This edition has never before appeared in book form.

AVON BOOKS
A division of
The Hearst Corporation
1350 Avenue of the Americas
New York, New York 10019

Copyright © 1993 by William C. Ketchum, Jr.
Cover photo by Mike Wilson
The Confident Collector and its logo are trademarked properties of Avon Books.
Interior design by Martha Schwartz
Published by arrangement with the author
Library of Congress Catalog Card Number: 93-25879
ISBN: 0-380-77137-3

Library of Congress Cataloging in Publication Data:

Ketchum, William C., 1931–
    Western memorabilia identification and price guide / William C. Ketchum.
    p.   cm.
    Includes index.
    1. Americana—West (U.S.)—Catalogs. I. Title.
F591.K45 1994   93-25879
016.973'075—dc20   CIP

First Avon Books Trade Printing: December 1993

AVON TRADEMARK REG. U.S. PAT. OFF. AND IN OTHER COUNTRIES, MARCA REGISTRADA, HECHO EN U.S.A.

Printed in the U.S.A.

OPM 10 9 8 7 6 5 4 3 2 1

Contents

WESTERN
MEMORABILIA
IDENTIFICATION AND PRICE GUIDE

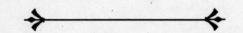

Introduction

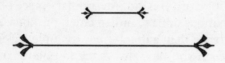

Just as the sheer space of the West, its vastness, and its economic potential attracted nineteenth-century immigrants, so the variety of collectible fields regarded as "Western" has attracted contemporary collectors. Some areas, such as Native American and guns, have long been of interest to a small but knowledgeable group. Others such as cowboy and railroad collectibles are, in the parlance of the antiques marketplace, "hot," while a few such as mining and Western logging, are just beginning to attract a following.

This price guide is designed to provide the collector of modest means with a rough approximation of what is going on in this highly volatile market. Since I believe that a price guide is of little use without some knowledge of the field itself, each section begins with a brief discussion of the history and background of the objects covered. Descriptions of the items priced are as detailed as possible, since identification is essential to valuation.

However, the reader should bear in mind that, unlike the case with many collectibles (toys, dolls, comic books, etc.), most Western pieces are one of a kind. No two Native American baskets, pots, or rugs are quite alike, and much the same is true of Spanish-American, Eskimo, and even many cowboy items. Variations in design, workmanship, quality of decoration, origin, and age can all affect price. A particularly difficult area is that of provenance—who owned it before you did. An ordinary piece once possessed by a famous outlaw, Indian chief, or movie star will often bring more than a much finer example lacking such a history. When you buy, always try to obtain some reliable information (preferably in writing) about where the object originated.

Prices quoted are retail and given as a range based on the most current auction and dealer prices available for items in good/average condition. Readers should bear in mind that exceptional quality or, conversely, serious damage will require sharp adjustments. A damaged piece, for example, may bring anywhere from 20 to 70 percent of what one might expect to pay for the same piece in good condition.

Reproductions and fakes are mentioned throughout, as appropriate, though major problems are confined primarily to the field of Native American crafts, guns, Wells Fargo memorabilia, and some cowboy collectibles. Don't think that you can spot every fake or reproduction. None of us can. The good fake in any field is hard to detect, so your best protection is a written warranty from the seller.

Western collectibles vary widely in availability. Due to their popularity, cowboy and railway items appear frequently at shows and auctions. However, prices here tend to be "top dollar." If you live in the West, you are better off checking out farm and ranch sales or even the local thrift shops. Native American and Eskimo artifacts, which are primarily tourist items, can appear anywhere in the country, while Western logging and mining memorabilia are not usually seen outside their area of origin.

Cowboy
Collectibles

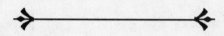

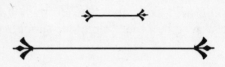

While nostalgia for the "Old West" and for the cowboys who supposedly populated it has been a recurring facet of American mythology, as seen through books, theater, movies, and popular music, it has been within only the past few years that the artifacts of that brief era (c. 1840-1910) have attracted the attention of a large number of collectors. Guns, including those used in the West, have long been of interest to a relatively small group of serious enthusiasts. Items associated with famous lawmen, bad-men, or the movie actors who, at a later date, portrayed them also had their following.

Quite recently, though, this interest has spread to a much broader group. Japanese tourists seek out old Levi's jeans, big-city collectors hanker for Stetsons and "woolly" leather chaps, and drugstore cowboys decorate their apartments with Western saddles and 1930s lamps with cowboy motifs.

All this has led to an unprecedented rise in prices. Such things as metal bits and spurs, once purchased for a few dollars, will now, if made by a well-known manufacturer, command prices in the thousands. However, the market is a highly trendy one driven by a few wealthy collectors and dealers, and prices for similar objects will vary greatly dependent upon where and from whom you are buying. Moreover, little real research on makers and products has been done, so it is hard to determine what is really rare. In this developing field, collectors who do their homework and are not swayed by others' opinions should come out ahead.

Horse Tack

Simply stated, horse tack consists of the objects used by the cowboy in sitting and controlling his horse. These include the saddle, bit and bridle, stirrups, spurs, and quirt. All were important to the ranch hand, and all are collectible.

Cowhands seldom had much money, but what they earned they usually put into horse tack, particularly saddles, spurs, and bits. As a result, manufacturers competed to produce items which would not only do the job but also be appealing to the eye. Saddles were heavily tooled or embossed in floral and figural patterns. Metal spurs and bits would be ingeniously shaped and decorated with contrasting inlays. Manufacturers were proud of their products, so they often stamped or branded their names upon them. Consequently, collectors may seek out the work of well-known manufacturers such as G. S. Garcia or August Buermann and, through research, date their acquisitions, something often impossible in other areas of Western collectibles. All this, however, has a downside. Prices are climbing rapidly, with the better examples bringing thousands of dollars at auction.

Saddles

The Western saddle consists of a leather-covered metal frame, known as a tree, upon which is mounted the seat, whose upward sloping back is termed a cantle. A knoblike protuberance at the front of the seat, known as a fork, terminates in the horn, about which a hand will wrap his lariat when roping cattle or horses.

Desirability in saddles is based primarily on decoration and markings. The finest were nearly covered with embossed patterns, often incorporating Western motifs such as stars, cactus plants, and images of cows, horses, and cowboys. Moreover, many saddles were embellished with silver, chrome, or brass mounts, conchos, and studs. The more of these the higher the price. Another enhancement is the presence of a maker's mark, preferably that of an early and well-known company. Age is also a factor, with many collectors seeking out pre-1900 examples, especially those made when some Western states were still territories.

Condition is important in pricing. A badly worn saddle or one missing the original saddle accoutrements—skirt, straps, fenders, leathers, and stirrups—will bring less. Since these are often replaced at a later date, watch for restorations.

Price Listings—Saddles

Marked by Blake Miller; Cheyenne, Wyoming; c. 1905–1915; tooled leather, silver conchos, pewter and silver mounts; $1,500–2,000.

McClellan type, rare; Midwestern; c. 1840–1860; leather with brass studs, missing accessories; $1,500–1,750.

Miniature or advertising, rare; c. 1915–1925; overall tooled leather decoration, sterling silver mounts; $4,500–5,500.

Early McClellan type saddle, leather and wood; by the Butler Saddlery Co.; c. 1870–1880; $800–950.

Youth saddle, leather, wood and metal; by T. Flynn; Pueblo, Colorado; c. 1915–1925; $500–700.

Mother Hubbard type, marked by V. E. Vaughn; Austin, Texas; c. 1870–1880; undecorated; $2,000–2,750.

Mother Hubbard type; c. 1865–1880; undecorated, silver conchos; $1,600–1,900.

California type, marked by S. Loomis; Santa Barbara, California; c. 1870–1890; elaborate overall tooling, sterling silver mounts and conchos; $15,000–20,000.

Marked by J. S. Collins; Wyoming; c. 1875–1880; simple floral tooling, nickel silver conchos; $5,000–6,000.

Marked by R. T. Frazier; Pueblo, Colorado; c. 1890–1900; simple floral tooling, nickel silver conchos; $900–1,200.

Marked by Edward H. Bohlin; Hollywood, California; c. 1930–1935; overall tooled leather including images of stage coaches and Indians; sterling silver mounts; $11,000–15,000.

Marked by Edward H. Bohlin; Hollywood, California; c. 1920–1940; elaborate overall floral tooling, sterling silver mountings including four gold steer heads; $6,000–8,000.

Slick-fork type; c. 1900–1910; simple floral tooling, nickel silver conchos; $600–700.

Marked by A. W. Maier; Fredricksburg, Texas; c. 1930–1940; simple tooling, nickel silver conchos, restoration; $500–700.

Coggshall type, marked by Miles City Saddlery Co.; Miles City, Montana; c. 1900–1910; undecorated, nickel silver conchos; $700–900.

Marked by F. A. Meanea; Cheyenne, Wyoming Territory; c. 1870–1880; minimal tooling, nickel silver conchos; $1,500–2,000.

Marked by Montgomery Ward & Co.; Chicago, Illinois; c. 1910–1930; minimal tooling, nickel silver conchos; $600–900.

Parade saddle, marked by Nobby Harness Co.; Fort Worth, Texas; c. 1950–1960; elaborate overall tooling, nickel silver mounts and conchos; $600–850.

English style saddle, leather with tooled decoration; c. 1930–1940; $300–450. Though never used by cowboys, these were popular on dude ranches.

Early saddle, leather and wood, attributed to N. Porter Co.; Phoenix, Arizona; c. 1900–1910; $750–950.

Parade saddle, marked by Moss Saddle Co.; Chanute, Kansas; c. 1930–1940; elaborate floral tooling, German silver mounts; $650–950.

Marked by Wade & Co.; San Francisco, California; c. 1910–1930; floral tooling, brass conchos; $700–900.

Oregon style, marked by J. F. Reisacher; Oregon; c. 1890–1900; simple tooling, nickel silver conchos; $950–1,250.

Marked by S. C. Gallup Saddlery Co.; Pueblo, Colorado; c. 1890–1900; minimal tooling, nickel silver conchos; $1,300–1,600.

Marked by Charles P. Shipley; Kansas City, Missouri; c. 1890–1910; overall floral and geometric tooling, nickel silver conchos; $900–1,200.

Stockman's saddle, marked by John M. Drake; Nocona, Texas; c. 1920–1930; tooled decoration, nickel silver conchos; $700–950.

California style saddle, leather, wood, and metal; by J. Jepson and Son; Los Angeles, California; c. 1890–1900; $1,500–1,900.

Woman's sidesaddle, leather with tooled decoration over wood, marked "Jacob's Patent"; c. 1890–1900; $600–750.

Woman's sidesaddle, leather with padded saddle surface and rare slipper type stirrup; c. 1900–1910; $500–750.

Marked by H. H. Schweitzer; Matador, Texas; c. 1910–1930; floral tooling, nickel silver conchos, restoration; $550–750.

Marked by Harpham Brothers; Lincoln, Nebraska; c. 1910–1920; simple tooling, nickel silver conchos; $400–650.

Child's saddle, marked by T. Flynn; Pueblo, Colorado; c. 1910–1920; simple geometric tooling, nickel silver conchos; $450–650.

Woman's saddle, marked by Roberts-Dearborn Hardware Co.; Carlsbad, New Mexico; c. 1920–1940; overall floral tooling, nickel silver conchos; $550–750.

Woman's sidesaddle, marked by T. Flynn; Pueblo, Colorado; c. 1900–1920; geometric tooling, nickel silver conchos; $650–900.

Bits

The bit and attached bridle are the means by which a rider controls his mount. The bridle, of leather or, less often, woven horsehair, fits harnesslike over the horse's head and is secured to a roughly H-shaped metal bit which fits in the animal's mouth. The reins, by which the rider directs the horse, are also attached to the bit.

There are several variations in the form of the bit including snaffle, bar, curb, ring, and spade types. To some these distinctions are important, while other collectors focus their interest more on the remarkable workmanship lavished on these small bits of metal. Their shanks may be shaped like a woman's leg (the so-called "gal leg" type), a snake, an arrow, the American eagle, or even a pair of "six-shooters." The iron or chrome steel bodies are often inlaid in silver, brass, copper, or even gold; the lip bar may take the form of a fish, a duck, or a pair of dolphins.

Such miniature works of art were costly, and the manufacturers, who usually were also spur makers, proudly marked them with their names. Consequently, makers' logos and decoration (the more the better!) are the keys to value here. Condition is important. Breaks, repairs, or missing parts will devalue a piece. Reproductions have been reported, and as with all metal pieces, watch out for old but unmarked bits which have been given a new bogus mark of a respected maker.

Price Listings—Bits

Gal leg form, chrome steel, marked by August Buermann; Newark, New Jersey; with 1877 patent date; $90–135.

With shanks embossed with horse heads and buffalo horns, marked by August Buermann; Newark, New Jersey; with 1914 patent date; $300–450.

Gal leg form, wrought iron, marked by L. D. Stone; San Francisco, California; c. 1860–1880; $400–600.

Miniature or salesman's sample gal leg type, stainless steel; engraved details, unmarked; c. 1900–1920; $750–950.

With shanks in the shape of rearing horses, chrome steel, marked by North & Judd; New Britain, Connecticut; c. 1900–1910; $150–225.

California type half-breed bit, silver and silver overlay on brass, 8 inches long; by G. S. Garcia; Elko, Nevada; c. 1920–1925; $1,600–2,100.

Pistol form bit, engraved nickel silver overlay on brass with abalone shell inlay, 8.5 inches long; by prisoner "9647"; state prison, Canyon City, Colorado; c. 1900-1920; rare and desirable; $1,500–2,000..

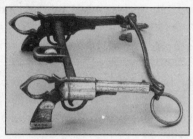

With shanks in form of dolphin and concho, chrome steel, marked by G. S. Garcia; Elko, Nevada; c. 1900–1915; $500–750.

With shanks in shape of American eagle, lip bar in form of ducks feeding from bowl, chrome steel, marked by G. S. Garcia; Elko, Nevada; c. 1910–1920; $2,000–2,500.

Spade bit, floral shaping and engraving, wrought iron with copper ferrules, marked by Jose De Jesus Mardueno; Carpenteria, California; c. 1865–1870; $1,500–2,000.

Grazing bit, engraved cheeks, chrome steel, marked by J. O. Bass; Tulia, Texas; c. 1910–1930; $275–375.

Loose-jaw type light spade bit, silver and engraved silver overlay, 9 inches long; by Raphael Gutierrez; Cheyenne, Wyoming, or San Francisco, California; c. 1930–1945; $950–1,450.

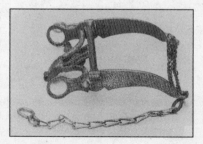

Port bit, undecorated wrought iron, marked by J. O. Bass; Tulia, Texas; c. 1900–1915; $150–225.

La Cruz style straight shank bit, engraved chrome steel with copper, marked by Scott Silver; Carmel, California; 1948; $1,000–1,250.

With floral and star inlay and engraving, chrome steel, marked with his number by prisoner at Canyon City, Colorado, prison; c. 1920–1930; $175–325.

Port bit, undecorated wrought iron, marked by Bianchi; Victoria, Texas; c. 1900–1920; $150–250.

Port grazing bit, undecorated wrought iron, attributed to Bianchi; Victoria, Texas; c. 1900–1920; $75–100.

Half-breed type, shanks in form of woman's body, nickel plate, unmarked; c. 1880–1900; $300–450.

Straight shank bit with inlaid floral decoration, chrome steel, marked by A. L. Hunt; Caliente, California; c. 1910–1920; $250–375.

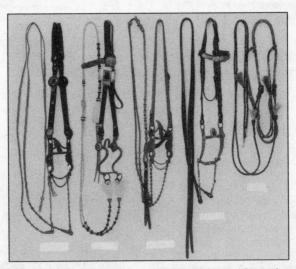

A group of bits and bridles in leather and metal by various Western makers; hackamore at right is of woven horsehair; all date c. 1900–1930 and price range is $300–750 each.

Rare S-shaped shank spade bit with chevron inlay, wrought iron, marked by C. E. Irwin; California; 1862; $400–650.

California type spade bit, floral and geometric silver inlay, wrought iron, marked by D. H. Fox; Los Angeles, California; c. 1910–1930; $400–550.

Half-breed type, heart-form shanks, floral and geometric inlay in silver on chrome steel: lip bar in form of snakes; unmarked; c. 1900–1920; $850–1,250.

Homemade bit with place for photographs and heart cutouts, chrome steel, unmarked; c. 1930–1940; $65–100.

Half-breed bit, floral engraving on monel metal, marked by Western Bit & Spur Co.; California; c. 1920–1940; $85–145.

Half-breed bit, silver overlay, shanks in form of United States shield, wrought iron, marked by Miguel Morales; Portland, Oregon; c. 1935–1940; $1,000–1,400.

Bridles

Most bridles were made of cut and braided leather, often embellished with tooled decorative patterns augmented by nickel or German silver conchos, bosses, and studs. Occasionally, they were made from braided horsehair, a time-consuming task (four inches per hour!), but one which produced highly desirable examples. Most leather bridles were produced by the same firms which made saddles and similar goods, and marked examples will be found. However, due to their relatively fragile nature, bridles in collectible condition are not as common as bits.

Price Listings—Bridles

Lightweight all leather, unmarked and undecorated; c. 1920–1940; $90–120.

Rawhide leather with silver mounts, unmarked, possibly South American; c. 1900–1920; $200–250.

Rolled and stitched leather, undecorated but marked by R. T. Frazier; Pueblo, Colorado; c. 1910–1920; $500–650.

Stitched leather decorated with German silver conchos and studs and marked by the Miles City Saddlery Co.; Miles City, Montana; c. 1920–1940; $600–750.

Knotted and braided leather, unmarked but prison made; c. 1890–1910; $200–300.

Stitched leather with tooled floral decoration and nickel silver conchos, unmarked; c. 1910–1930; $275–350.

Stitched leather with cheek straps embellished by German silver studs and conchos. Unusual polychrome-painted German silver bosses; unmarked; c. 1920–1940; $300–450.

Bridle and reins, leather and chrome steel, typical of the plain equipment used by most cowboys; c. 1910–1930; $75–125.

Bareback rodeo rider's bridle with characteristic single thick rein, leather and chrome steel; c. 1915–1935; $90–140.

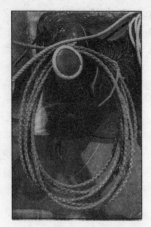

Cowboy's rope or lariat, woven rawhide; c. 1890–1900; $250–400.

Two elaborate headstalls, leather with brass and nickel silver decoration, Western; c. 1920–1940; $600–850 each.

Horsehair in three colors creating sophisticated diamond patterns, unmarked but prison made; c. 1920–1930; $700–950.

Horsehair in two colors creating chevron pattern; unmarked but prison made; c. 1910–1930; $550–700.

Two-color braided horsehair in chevron pattern and stitched leather with nickel silver bosses, unmarked; c. 1910–1930; $350–500.

Complex polychrome geometric horsehair decoration applied to stitched leather, conchos and buckles of nickel silver, unmarked; c. 1900–1920; $800–950.

Twisted and knotted rawhide with nickel silver ferrules, unmarked; c. 1890–1910; $200–275.

Horsehair braided in black and white creating attractive rope and diamond patterns, unmarked but prison made; c. 1900–1920; $900–1,200.

Horsehair braided in two colors creating a variety of decorative patterns, unmarked but attributed to Walla Walla, Washington, prison; c. 1900–1910; $3,000–3,500.

Headstall (portion of bridle that fits over horse's head), stitched leather embellished with German silver diamonds, hearts, clubs, and spades: attributed to G. S. Garcia; Elko, Nevada; c. 1920–1930; heavily restored; $700–900.

Headstall, stitched leather decorated with silver mountings of butterflies, acorns, and grizzly bears as well as large conchos: attributed to G. S. Garcia; Elko, Nevada; c. 1920–1930; $1,000–1,500.

Spurs

Wishbone-shaped spurs have been used by horsemen for over three thousand years. Readily recognizable to all collectors, they consist of the U-shaped heel band and a long shank terminating in a rowel which may be of varying size and simply a round disk or, more often, star-shaped with anywhere from five to eighteen points. While often fearsome-looking, these were designed not to punish a horse but to direct and instruct it.

Though small, spurs have always been big in the eyes of horsemen, and finely decorated examples will command a good price today. Elaborate inlay in silver and even gold on an iron, brass, monel metal, nickel silver, or aluminum frame is frequently accompanied by engraving and by the name of the manufacturer, often a firm which also made bits and other metallic horse gear.

Value in spurs is primarily dependent upon decoration and manufacturer. Condition is always a factor, and buyers should always check for restoration, replaced rowels being, perhaps, most common. And watch out for bogus makers' marks added to older unmarked examples.

Price Listings—Spurs

Art Deco style, unmarked and of undecorated aluminum; c. 1930–1945; $50–75.

Heel band decorated with engraved and embossed representations of two Southern California Catholic Missions; silver overlay on chrome steel, marked by Edward H. Bohlin; Hollywood, California; c. 1920–1935; $3,500–4,000.

With gal leg shanks, inlay in silver and copper on iron, marked by Kelly Brothers & Parker (K.B. & P.); Delhart, Texas; c. 1910–1920; $800–950.

With steer head inlay on heel band, shanks with arrow motif, silver on iron, marked by Kelly Brothers & Parker; Delhart, Texas; c. 1910–1920; $750–900.

Spurs, brass with Texas star design and tooled leathers, 7.5 inches long; by August Buermann; c. 1910–1920; $450–600.

Spurs, silver and engraved silver overlay, tooled leathers, 8 inches long; by G. S. Garcia; Elko, Nevada; c. 1915–1925; $2,500–3,200.

Unmarked and undecorated wrought iron; Colorado; c. 1890–1910; $275–350.

Shanks and heel bands, silver engraved in floral designs on iron, marked by J. O. Bass; Tulia, Texas; c. 1900–1920; $1,200–1,500.

Gal leg shanks with silver chevron overlay on heel band, by Andy Anderson; Fort Worth, Texas, 1973. The work of Anderson and other contemporary artists will bring high prices; $1,750–2,250.

Gal leg form, copper and silver overlay and banding on iron, unmarked; c. 1880–1900; $200–250.

Nevada style with spurred shanks, plain silver inlay and buttons on iron, unmarked; c. 1900–1910; $450–600.

With applied embossed silver spur buttons in the form of buffalo heads, brass, unmarked; c. 1920–1940; $600–800.

Heel band with applied silver hearts, diamonds, clubs, and spades; knife blade shanks, silver on iron, unmarked; c. 1900–1910; $300–400.

Spurs, double gal leg type, brass and engraved silver overlay, tooled leathers, 7 inches long; by Kelly Brothers; Delhart, Texas; c. 1915–1925, $700–900.

Spurs, California type with bird head shanks, engraved silver inlay, and concho button covers, 8 inches long; by Qualey Brothers; c. 1895–1900, $3,000–3,500.

Spurs, early steel and leather "gut hooks," 6.5 inches long, Western; c. 1880–1890; $200–275.

Heel band with floral and heart engraving, large buttons engraved with ranch brand on iron, marked by G. S. Garcia; Elko, Nevada; c. 1910–1920; $1,600–2,000.

Heel bands and shanks with overall silver inlay and engraving on iron, marked by G. S. Garcia; Elko, Nevada; c. 1905–1915; $6,500–7,000.

Heel bands and shanks in nickel silver inlay in "crisscross" pattern on iron; made at Canyon City, Colorado, state prison; c. 1890–1900; $375–550.

Simple geometric engraving on chrome steel, marked by Harpham Brothers; Lincoln, Nebraska; c. 1910–1930; $275–350.

Simple floral engraving on chrome steel, marked by August Buermann; Newark, New Jersey; patented 1877; $450–650.

Complex sculptured heel bands and shanks with floral engraving, marked by August Buermann; Newark, New Jersey; c. 1900–1915; $1,000–1,400.

Snake inlay in silver on shanks, iron, marked by August Buermann; Newark, New Jersey; c. 1900–1920; $5,000–5,750.

Serpentine shanks with simple floral engraving on wrought iron, marked by R. L. Causey of Safford, Arizona; c. 1905–1910; $550–750.

Floral engraving on nickel steel, marked "Pat'd"; c. 1900–1920; $200–300.

Spurs, three types of steel spurs, 6.5 to 7.5 inches long, Western; c. 1900–1920; left to right; $125–165, $225–275, $250–300 per pair.

Chevron form brass inlay on chrome steel, marked by L. G. Grubb; Tulia, Texas; c. 1910–1930; $275–375.

Brass with chrome bosses, undecorated and unmarked; c. 1920–1940; $50–75.

Double mounted with large silver conchos on iron, unmarked; attributed to California; c. 1910–1930; $700–800.

Cowboy Clothing

The image of the cowhand clad for the trail brings to mind such things as boots, a large, distinctive hat, Levi's, chaps, and a leather vest. Indeed, these—along with smaller items such as roping cuffs or gauntlets, belts, and a bandanna— were standard issue on the plains. However, it is important to keep in mind that many others—sheepherders, farmers, and even townsmen—dressed in a very similar way. Since relatively few items of clothing were marked by their manufacturers or have a reliable history of cowboy use, it is inevitable that much that is bought and sold as "cowboy" is that in look only. Collectors should be wary of undocumented tales connecting an article of clothing with a particular cowboy or ranch. Also, as in all areas, condition is important. Watch for damage or restoration. With the exception of the ubiquitous repro brass belt buckles, fakes and reproductions are not a problem.

Hats

Though varying in form, Western hats were designed primarily to provide a cool sunshade. Their wide brims and high crowns were useful on horseback amid the open plains, whereas they would have been quite impractical in forested areas. Several forms include the Montana Peak, the Sugar-Loaf Sombrero, and the Plainsman. The first, with its high four-sided peak and stiff brim, is familiar to us as the hat of the Canadian Mounted Police. The Sugar-Loaf had a very wide brim and a rounded peak reminiscent of the loaf form in which bulk sugar was sold during the 1800s. The Plainsman, with its soft, sometimes rolled rim, low crown, and tie strings, is the prototypical "cowboy hat." All three have a hatband running around the crown just above the brim, and if this is made of an unusual material such as rattlesnakeskin or leather studded with silver conchos, it greatly augments the hat's desirability.

Western hats were subject to hard use, and few pre-1900 examples can be documented. On the other hand, prices are on the modest side for these modest collectibles.

Price Listings—Hats

Sugar-Loaf type, gray suede leather, beadwork band reads MONTANA; c. 1930–1940; $130–175.

Sugar-loaf type cowboy hat, black suede with silk band; c. 1920–1930; $165–215.

Sombrero type cowboy hat, black suede with ropework band; c. 1900–1910; $200–275.

Sugar-Loaf type, tan suede leather, tooled leather band with tassels; c. 1850–1870; $200–275.

Sugar-Loaf type, tan suede leather, silk band; c. 1870–1890; $175–225.

Sugar-Loaf type, early Stetson, tan suede leather, silk band; c. 1860–1880; $200–275.

Sugar-Loaf type, black suede leather, rattlesnake skin band; c. 1910–1920; $225–300.

Sugar-Loaf type, gray suede leather, band missing; c. 1910–1930; $35–55.

Sugar-Loaf type, tan suede leather, wide leather band; c. 1910–1930; $75–125.

Sugar-Loaf type, gray suede leather, band of woven horsehair; c. 1880–1910; $275–350.

Plainsman type, black suede leather, leather band decorated with small silver buttons; c. 1900–1920; $275–350.

Plainsman type, tan suede leather, narrow silk band, leather tie strings; c. 1910–1940; $180–220.

Plainsman type, gray suede leather, rim bound in silk, silk band; c. 1880–1900; $200–250.

Plainsman type, tan suede leather, lizard skin band; c. 1900–1920; $225–275.

Plainsman type, gray suede leather, silk band, woven fabric tie strings, Stetson; c. 1920–1940; $135–185.

Plainsman type, black suede leather, thin leather band; c. 1900–1910; $150–200.

Plainsman type, tan suede leather, leather band with silver conchos; c. 1890–1910; $250–325.

Plainsman type, tan suede leather, braided leather band, braided leather tie strings; c. 1900–1920; $175–225.

Plainsman type, dark gray suede leather, silk band; c. 1910–1930; $75–100.

Plainsman type, brown suede leather, braided band of silver tinsel cloth, four silver tinsel stars on crown; c. 1900–1910; $150–200.

Plainsman type, tan suede leather, silk band, woven fabric tie strings; c. 1920–1940; $65–85.

Sombrero type cowboy hat shaped in the manner popularized by Tom Mix, tan suede with silk band; c. 1920–1930; $125–175.

Plainsman type cowboy hat, dark gray suede with silk band; c. 1940–1950; $80–120.

Plainsman type, gray suede leather, silk band, curled brim; c. 1920–1940; $75–100.

Plainsman type, off-white suede leather, silk band, cloth ties; type popular on dude ranches; c. 1940–1960; $35–50.

Montana Peak type, brown suede leather, wide leather band; c. 1900–1920; $100–135.

Montana Peak type, brown suede leather, beadwork band; c. 1890–1910; $200–250.

Montana Peak type, tan suede leather, narrow silk band; c. 1920–1940; $75–100.

Montana Peak type, tan suede leather, wide leather band decorated with nickel silver studs; c. 1910–1930; $125–175.

Montana Peak type, brown suede leather, leather band with tooled floral decoration; c. 1900–1920; $175–250.

Montana Peak type, gray suede leather, braided leather band; c. 1910–1930; $100–135.

Montana Peak type, brown suede leather, knife blade rim, wide silk band; c. 1900–1910; $90–130.

Bandannas

Factory-made bandannas appeared in the West after the Civil War and soon became standard range wear. They were printed in a variety of patterns but in few colors; red and white and blue and white were by far the most common. Useful not only as handkerchiefs but also as a covering for the head or the mouth during a dust storm, as a makeshift bandage, or as a blindfold for animals, bandannas were used and discarded. Today there are few examples that can be said with certainty to have seen use on the Western plains.

Price Listings—Bandannas

Floral and geometric patterns in white on a red ground; cotton; c. 1920–1940; $15–25.

Band of flowers and Greek key pattern in red on white ground; cotton; c. 1910–1930; $20–30.

Overall floral design in white on red ground; cotton; c. 1910–1930; $15–25.

Floral border in red on white, central pattern of bull's-eyes in white on red ground; cotton; c. 1900–1920; $25–40.

Sparse floral border in red on white, central pattern of white rectangles on red ground; cotton; c. 1900–1920; $25–40.

Red with two bordering bands of white; cotton; c. 1890–1910; $35–50.

Blue with wide border checkered in white and central pattern of white dots on blue ground; cotton; c. 1900–1920; $25–40.

Blue with design of cowboys and horses in white; cotton; c. 1935–1950; $15–20.

Blue with overall floral design in white; cotton; c. 1930–1950; $10–15.

Overall pattern of blue and white checks; cotton; c. 1920–1940; $15–25.

Blue with large central floral medallion in white; cotton; c. 1900–1920; $15–25.

Shirts

Western shirts, used by both cowboys and other residents of the area, were typically of cotton, cotton flannel, or wool, the latter usually being reserved for winter use. Often collarless, they came in a limited range of hues. For work there were shades of blue, gray, brown, and black. Fancier striped or checkered patterns might also be found, but these were often saved for Sunday or visits to town. As with so much clothing, early shirts are hard to date and harder to associate with a given locality.

After 1900 the fancier shirts associated with "dudes" and dude ranches became popular. These were usually decorated in braiding and whipstitch and might often be of silk rather than of wool or cotton. For most collectors, these are "Western" shirts.

Price Listings—Shirts

Cotton flannel pullover blouse form, light gray with brass buttons; c. 1880–1910; $125–150.

Cotton flannel pullover blouse form, brown with mother-of-pearl buttons, collarless; c. 1870–1900; $150–200.

Cotton, Levi's type, blue with brass buttons; c. 1920–1940; $65–85.

Cotton, Levi's type, gray with brass buttons; c. 1920–1940; $50–75.

Pullover blouse form, striped light and dark brown, with mother-of-pearl buttons; c. 1880–1900; $125–175.

Wool check, red and black, with hardwood buttons; c. 1900–1920; $60–90.

Wool check, blue and black, brass buttons, single breast pocket; c. 1910–1930; $50–75.

Wool, black, brass buttons; c. 1900–1920; $35–50.

White cotton, with braided whipstitch decoration at shoulders and breast; lariats, cactus plants, and flowers; nickel silver buttons; c. 1920–1940; $135–185.

White cotton, braided whipstitch decoration including representation of cowboy on horse covering entire back; mother-of-pearl buttons; c. 1930–1950; $150–225.

Blue satin, braided whipstitch decoration in floral motifs at shoulders, around pockets, and down arms; mother-of-pearl buttons; c. 1930–1950; $100–150.

Golden silk with overall braided whipstitch decoration; horses, cowboys, cattle, cactus, etc.; mother-of-pearl buttons; c. 1930–1940; $300–400.

Woman's, pale blue silk with floral braided whipstitch decoration at shoulders and over breast; mother-of-pearl buttons; c. 1940–1955; $175–250.

Red silk with braided whipstitch decoration at shoulders and braided logo, TEXAS, across back; mother-of-pearl buttons; c. 1940–1960; $200–275.

Vests

Most early vests were of cotton, with denim examples appearing on the plains in the late nineteenth century. Examples in wool and leather will also be encountered. All are hard to date, though cotton prints and checks often denote a pre-1910 era. Again, most American men wore vests, so it is usually difficult to associate a given example with the West, much less with a Westerner. Prices are generally moderate, other than for twentieth-century denim, which has attracted attention from the Japanese. Pre-1971 denim jackets in good condition may bring prices in the high hundreds, but they are of little interest to most collectors of Western memorabilia.

Price Listings—Vests

Brown sharkshin, silk lined, small hardwood buttons; c. 1900–1920; $75–100.

Cotton plaid, checkered in brown, tan, and cream, silk lined, mother-of-pearl buttons; c. 1890–1910; $150–200.

Cotton, brown with geometric diamond pattern in off-white, satin lined; c. 1900–1910; $125–175.

Cotton, overall polka dot decoration in white against a dark gray ground, silk lined; c. 1860–1880; $200–275.

Cotton, dark gray, satin lined, back with early cotton laces; c. 1850–1870; $175–250.

Wool plaid, red and black check, satin lined, brass buttons; c. 1910–1930; $125–175.

Brown wool, cotton lined, with bone buttons; c. 1890–1910; $110–160.

Brown suede leather, silk lined, leather-laced back, brass buttons; c. 1870–1900; $250–350.

Black suede leather, silk lined, sterling silver buttons; c. 1890–1910; $225–275.

Blue cotton denim, chrome buttons, red tag on pocket marked LEVI'S, short belt at back; c. 1940–1950; $200–250.

Blue cotton denim, chrome buttons, no tag, short belt at back, Levi's; c. 1900–1930; $350–500.

Blue cotton denim, copper-colored metal buttons, blue bell insignia on label, by Wrangler; c. 1940–1960; $150–225.

Blue cotton denim, copper-colored metal buttons, label marked "Union Made," by Lee Manufacturing Co.; c. 1940–1960; $125–175.

Pants

The cowboy is popularly associated with Levi's, the blue cotton denim pants first manufactured in 1853. As a result, even though other materials, such as wool and leather, were frequently worn, many collectors seek only denims; and prices for these have escalated. Regardless of material, clues to early manufacture include loose, baggy fit, back strap and buckle for size adjustment, and buttons instead of zippers.

Price Listings—Pants

Wool twill, red and black check, back strap and buckle, brass button fly; c. 1900–1920; $150–200.

Dark gray, heavy wool, bone button fly, no pockets; c. 1880–1900; $75–125.

Black wool twill, shaped for riding, back strap and buckle, brass button fly; c. 1900–1920; $125–175.

Brown hide or raw leather with leather fringe, cotton lined, bone button fly; c. 1850–1875; $550–750.

Brown linen, back strap and buckle, brass button fly, no pockets; c. 1870–1880; $250–350.

Tan linen, back strap and buckle, bone button fly, single back pocket; c. 1880–1900; $200–275.

Blue cotton denim, back strap and buckle, brass button fly, suspender buttons; c. 1880–1900; $200–275.

Blue cotton denim, red Levi's tag on hip pocket, brass button fly; c. 1940–1960; $100–125.

Blue cotton denim, brass button fly, rivets on back pockets, attributed to Levi's; c. 1900–1930; $135–185.

Blue cotton denim, brass button fly, Lee label; c. 1950–1960; $35–50.

Blue cotton denim, brass button fly, Wrangler label; c. 1950–1970; $25–40.

Belts and Buckles

Belts worn in the West did not differ significantly from those worn throughout the United States. Much the same may be said of belt buckles. Wells Fargo and a few other concerned did produce distinctly Western buckles for their employees. However, collectors should be aware of the huge number of reproductions of these as well as other fanciful "Western" buckles which appear regularly at flea markets and antiques shows. The great majority of these cast and stamped brass buckles are recent reproductions.

There are, however, a substantial number of brass and nickel silver buckles from the 1920–1950 period which have a Western theme and which are collectible. Also, there are the heavy brass-studded leather belts worn during the same period by those competing at rodeos. The latter are uncommon and can bring good prices.

Price Listings—Belts

Light brown leather with tooled representations of cowboys on horseback, cattle, and cacti; plain brass buckle; c. 1930–1950; $35–55.

Dark brown leather, openwork weave, cast brass buckle with embossed "Texas Star" motif; c. 1920–1940; $65–95.

Light brown leather with tooled representations of long-horned cattle skulls and cacti, plain brass buckle; c. 1940–1960; $30–50.

Brown leather with tooled representations of wagon and settlers, plain brass buckle; c. 1930–1950; $30–50.

Light brown leather with tooled representations of cowboys and long-horned cattle; c. 1930–1950; $35–55.

Black and white leather with tooled floral designs, plain brass buckle; c. 1930–1950; $25–40.

White leather with tooled representations of cacti and desert flowers, large Art Deco type brass buckle; c. 1930–1950; $60–85.

Red and white leather with tooled floral and geometric designs, cast brass buckle with large "T" (for Texas?); c. 1930–1950; $40–70.

Bronco-busting or rodeo belt, brown leather; broad back studded with brass rivets in various geometric designs, narrow belt with plain brass buckle; c. 1910–1930; $200–350.

Bronco-busting or rodeo belt, brown leather; broad back with decorative brass studs in form of long-horned cow head, narrow belt with plain brass buckle; c. 1920–1940; $250–375.

Bronco-busting or rodeo belt, black leather; broad back with decorative nickel silver studs in geometric patterns enclosing name JIM, narrow belt with plain silver buckle; c. 1930–1940; $250–350.

Bronco-busting or rodeo belt, white leather; broad back with nickel silver studs in floral pattern, narrow belt with plain nickel silver buckle; c. 1930–1950; $175–250.

Price Listings—Buckles

Nickel silver with embossed representation of rearing stallion; c. 1930–1945; $50–75.

Nickel silver with embossed representation of long-horned cow head; c. 1935–1955; $40–60.

Brass with embossed representation of jackrabbit; c. 1930–1950; $35–55.

Belt buckle, nickel silver and brass, 3.5 inches long; by Chambers Belt Co.; Phoenix, Arizona; c. 1930–1940; $45–65.

Brass with embossed representation of cactus plants; c. 1930–1950; $30–45.

Brass with embossed representation of the Alamo; c. 1940–1955; $40–65.

Gauntlets and Cuffs

For protection, heavy leather riding gloves with wide cuffs were worn by most cowboys prior to 1875. These were adapted from military models and were often Indian-made of deerskin with beadwork designs. Examples are shown in the section on Native American beadwork. By the 1880s, gauntlets had been largely replaced by cylindrical leather cuffs, 5 to 7 inches long, which were worn with thick leather roping gloves. Cuffs were sometimes made by saddle manufacturers, and a maker's mark as well as tooled decoration or studding increases a pair's value. Both cuffs and gauntlets are relatively uncommon.

Price Listings—Gauntlets (pairs)

Heavy suede leather, brown with fringing at cuffs; c. 1870–1880; $75–100.

Leather, black, cuffs outlined with nickel silver studs; c. 1880–1900; $125–185.

Leather, brown, cuffs with tooled floral decoration; c. 1880–1890; $100–135.

Leather, white sheepskin; c. 1890–1910; $85–125.

Leather, brown wolf hide with hair; c. 1860–1870; $150–200.

Price Listings—Cuffs (pairs)

Heavy black leather, secured with brass buckles; c. 1900–1920; $100–135.

Brown leather, secured with brass buckle and lacing, edged with three rows of nickel silver studs; c. 1910–1930; $110–150.

Brown leather, secured with brass snaps and buckle, decorated with brass studs in form of five-pointed star; c. 1900–1920; $175–250.

Black leather, secured with lacing, tooled floral border ; c. 1890–1910; $150–200.

Dark brown leather, secured with nickel silver buckle and lacing, band of geometric tooling top and bottom, nickel silver studs; c. 1880–1900; $200–300.

Brown leather, secured with lacing, brass studs in form of five-pointed star; c. 1900–1920; $175–275.

Boots

The Western boot, now often an elaborate status symbol, was originally an important piece of working gear. Adapted from the cavalry boot, its sharp toe helped to pick up the near stirrup on a wheeling horse, while the high heel prevented a rider's foot from sliding through the stirrup. Built high to protect the leg from brush and contact with the stirrup leathers, the boot was stiffened with stitchwork that over the years became more elaborate, resulting in the gaudy dude boots of the 1930–1960 period.

While early working boots were monochromatic, made of calfskin dyed brown or black, later examples came in a variety of colors with complex overlaid and cutout decorative patterns. Interestingly enough, some of the latter bring higher prices than the much-harder-to-find nineteenth-century examples.

Price Listings—Boots

Very high black calfskin with long "mule ear" pulls to facilitate removal; c. 1870–1880; $275–375.

Low-cut tan calfskin with suede uppers and short fabric pulls to facilitate removal; c. 1860–1880; $235–285.

High black calfskin with early square toe and no pulls; c. 1850–1870; $300–400.

High brown calfskin with suede uppers and leather pulls to facilitate removal; c. 1870–1885; $200–275.

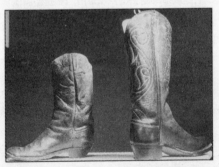

Boots: left, short work boot, undecorated tan calfskin; c.1910–1925, $165–235; right, high riding boot, embossed tan calfskin; c. 1920–1930; $200–285.

Boots: left, black calfskin with stitchwork decoration; c.1915–1925; $225–325; right, tan calfskin with stitchwork decoration; c. 1920–1930; $190–240.

Boot, elaborately decorated red, white, and blue calfskin with pictorial inserts; c. 1930–1940; $400–550 pair.

Black calfskin with blue floral inserts; attributed to Acme Boot Co.; c. 1935–1945; $250–300.

Black calfskin with elaborate overall floral inserts in red and white, cloth pulls to facilitate removal; c. 1940–1960; $300–400.

Brown calfskin with white uppers, overall tooled floral decoration; c. 1935–1945; $175–275.

Tan calfskin with white inserts of long-horned cattle heads; c. 1940–1960; $275–375.

Tan calfskin with overall floral tooling and leather pulls to facilitate removal; by the Frye Boot Co.; c. 1940–1950; $200–275.

Black and tan calfskin with white inserts in form of five-pointed star; c. 1930–1940; $300–400.

Child's size, white calfskin with floral inserts in red and blue; c. 1950–1965; $90–120.

Child's size, brown calfskin with overall tooling of cattle and lariats; c. 1940–1960; $125–175.

Coats

Bad weather on the plains meant rain and wind and, in winter, freezing cold and blizzard conditions. To combat these, the horsemen employed heavy coats and rain gear. The former might be of heavy blanketlike wool, but more often a warm if smelly buffalo coat was utilized. For rainy stretches there were raincoats or "slickers" of rubberized fabric. Both were fragile. Few examples survive, and these are usually in poor condition.

Price Listings—Coats

Buffalo coat, knee length with wide collar, button front, tan with red and black check woolen blanket lining, two flap front pockets; c. 1880–1900; $900–1,200.

Buffalo coat, knee length with wide collar, button front, dark brown with brown woolen lining, two open front pockets set at angle; c. 1890–1910; $750–1,000.

Buffalo coat, knee length with narrow collar, button front, dark brown with soft leather lining, two slit pockets above two flap pockets; c. 1880–1910; $600–950.

Buffalo jacket, waist length with beaver collar, metal hook-and-eye front, brown with untanned hide lining, two slit side pockets; c. 1870–1890; $700–950.

Buffalo jacket, waist length with wide collar, button front, brown with gray woolen blanket lining, two slit side pockets; c. 1880–1900; $550–750.

Slicker, boot-top length with button band collar, brass snap front, rubberized fabric originally yellow, now light brown; lined with gray wool, two flap side pockets; c. 1900–1910; $950–1,350.

Slicker, boot-top length with button band collar, nickel silver button front, rubberized fabric originally yellow, now light brown; unlined, two flap front pockets; c. 1880–1900; $800–1,200.

Chaps

Without a doubt, the most popular of cowboy clothing collectibles is chaps, the seatless leather pants or leggings worn by riders to protect the legs from the thorny brush often encountered in the West. The earliest form, termed "shotgun chaps" because of their straight legs—which some likened to the barrels of a double-barrel shotgun—was pulled on like a pair of pants. Since this involved removing the boots, a later innovation, "bat wings" (named for its resemblance to a splayed bat), became popular. These had leggings which snapped on in the back, as well as a back-fastening buckle. Yet another variation is "hair pants" or "woollies," chaps made from goat or sheep hides with the hair left on. These were favored for cold-weather work on the northern ranges, but when wet they gave off an exceedingly unpleasant odor.

Chaps were often made and marked by the same manufacturers that produced saddles and bridles. Marked examples are highly desirable, as are those decorated with fringe, metal conchos, studs, and tooling. Watch for restoration, which is common to such hard-used wearing apparel.

Price Listings—Chaps

Shotgun form, reddish brown leather, two front pockets, inexpensive type advertised in Montgomery Ward catalog for just $4.75!; c. 1895–1900; $200–250.

Shotgun form, dark brown leather, fringed legs, single front pocket; marked by Visalia Stock Saddle Co.; Visalia, California; c. 1880–1890; $650–900.

Shotgun form, gray leather, nickel silver studs and front pocket each side, marked by P. A. Monroe; Alva, Oklahoma Territory; c. 1870–1880; $750–1,000.

Shotgun form, brown leather with fringing and silver conchos down each leg, marked by R. T. Frazier; Pueblo, Colorado; c. 1900–1930; $1,000–1,400.

Shotgun form, dark and light brown leather, fringed legs, tooled floral border, marked by Frank A. Meanea; Wyoming Territory; c. 1870–1880; $2,750–3,750.

Shotgun form, black leather with nickel silver conchos and fringed legs; c. 1910–1930; $600–750.

Bat wing form, black leather with edging of silver conchos, marked by Edward H. Bohlin; Hollywood, California; c. 1920–1930; $2,500–3,000.

Bat wing form, reddish brown leather, basket weave tooling, outlined in nickel silver studs, two front pockets, marked by Fred Mueller; Denver, Colorado; c. 1900–1910; $700–900.

Bat wing form, brown leather, outlined in nickel silver studs and decorated with conchos in same material, two front pockets; c. 1900–1920; $450–650.

Bat wing form, black leather with silver conchos and dozens of nickel silver studs, marked by Charles P. Shipley; Kansas City, Missouri; c. 1910–1930; $900–1,250.

Bat wing form, dark brown leather with silver concho border and decorated with silver studs in form of horseshoes, stars, and half-moons; c. 1920–1940; $1,200–1,600.

Chaps, bat wing form, brown leather decorated with nickel silver conchos and the owner's initials, "TG"; c. 1920–1930; $400–550.

Chaps, "woolies" or "hair pants," angora wool and tooled tan leather; c. 1890–1910; $1,000–1,500.

Bat wing form, light brown leather, elaborately hand-painted decoration with word ARIZONA, large snake, and motifs such as swastikas, hearts, diamonds, spades, and dice; silver conchos, two front pockets, marked by N. Porter; Phoenix, Arizona; c. 1910–1930; $5,000–7,500.

Bat wing form, light brown leather with band of silver conchos down each leg, marked by Stelz Saddlery Co.; Houston, Texas; c. 1920–1935; $550–700.

Bat wing form, dark brown leather, three nickel silver conchos on each leg, a single front pocket; c. 1890–1910; $800–950.

Bat wing form, so-called California style, brown leather with elaborate overlaid and pierced tooling, two silver conchos each leg; c. 1850–1870; $1,500–2,200.

Bat wing form, light brown leather with nickel silver conchos, two front pockets, marked by Marfa Saddlery Co.; Marfa, Texas; c. 1900–1920; $700–900.

Shotgun-form woollies, in pinto brown and white, marked by Lawrence; Portland, Oregon; c. 1910–1930; $900–1,300.

Shotgun-form woollies of gray angora with nickel silver hearts on tooled belt; c. 1900–1920; $1,400–1,800.

Shotgun-form woollies in brown, undecorated;
c. 1900–1920; $750–900.

Shotgun-form woollies in black angora with tooled belt;
c. 1900–1910; $1,200–1,600.

Guns of the West

Guns have long had a fascination for American (primarily
male) collectors. This is due in part to our history, which
is unlike that of Europe and Asia, where only the noble
and wealthy were allowed the use of weapons. From the
beginning Americans owned guns and used them in a dan-
gerous society where law enforcement was often a matter
of self-help.

The West is particularly a part of that history with
weapons such as the Colt .45 "Peacemaker," the Colt .41
"Thunderer," and the Winchester .44/.40, the gun that
"won the West," mirroring a story of violence that has
become greatly romanticized over the years.

The hobby of gun collecting is much older than the
interest in Western Americana, and its enthusiasts form a
large and extremely knowledgeable group. For the most
part, they seek weapons that either are rare (usually
because few examples were made) or are associated with
well-known owners such as Billy the Kid or Buffalo Bill.
For such examples they have paid well over $500,000. On
the other hand, relatively common nineteenth-century
handguns and rifles in average condition may sell for a few
hundred dollars or even less.

Collectors should also bear in mind that, although
almost every adult male (cowboy, farmer, or storekeeper)

in the West owned at least one gun until well into the twentieth century, few guns were made exclusively for sale and use in that area. Most, in fact, were produced by Eastern factories, and a Colt .45 could as easily have been owned by a Southern planter as by a Montana cowpoke. Since so many needed guns, many different models were produced by numerous manufacturers. The field is a broad one.

Also, because of the long history of gun collecting in this country and the high prices sometimes obtainable, there are many pieces on the market which have been cleverly repaired, have parts which are not original, or are complete fakes or reproductions (the latter are now also bringing good prices). Beginning collectors should study the many books on this field and should buy only from dealers who guarantee their merchandise.

Handguns

The category of handguns includes a wide range of single-shot pistols, tiny derringers, and multi-shot revolvers. Western collectors for the most part are interested in revolvers, the first of which was patented in 1835 by Samuel Colt. These are the famous "six guns" of Western lore, produced by a variety of makers including Colt, Savage, Remington, Smith & Wesson, and Whitney.

Since the value of a handgun is often closely associated with who owned it, collectors should be leary of fabricated stories. Had Wild Bill Hickok, for example, actually carried all the six-shooters he is claimed to have owned, he would not have been able to walk, much less fire a gun!

When buying, demand written documentation for such claims.

Be on the lookout for desirable rarities such as presentation pieces or pairs of revolvers which may be inscribed and sometimes have gold or silver inlay, ivory handles, and the like. And remember, condition is very important. Factory-fresh, never-fired weapons bring the highest prices. Restorations, pitted metal parts, and worn-out barrels all affect value.

Price Listings—Handguns

Colt Paterson percussion revolver, presentation model, .34 caliber with ivory grips and silver banding, with extra 12–inch barrel, all in mahogany case; c. 1836; $750,000–800,000.

Colt Bisley model 1875, six shot revolver; $700–1,000.

Cased pair of deluxe Colt Third Model Dragoon percussion revolvers, in rosewood case with all loading and cleaning implements and Colt family history; c. 1856; $500,000–600,000.

Pair of silver-plated Colt .41 caliber single action presentation revolvers with elaborate engraving; c. 1870–1880; $40,000–43,000.

Pair of Colt silver-plated single action, .44 caliber presentation revolvers with elaborate engraving; c. 1935–1937; $55,000–65,000.

Pair of twentieth-century Colt .41 caliber commemorative percussion revolvers, unfired condition; $800–950.

Colt model 1961, factory engraved, .44 caliber percussion Navy model revolver with carved ivory grips, twentieth century; $1,400–1,800.

Colt model 1851, Navy single action percussion revolver, six shot, .36 caliber, near mint condition; $4,500–5,000.

Colt model 1878, six shot, double action revolver, an elabo-

Percussion type .44 caliber revolvers, both by Remington Arms Co.: above, c. 1870–1880, $150–200; below, modified to rimfire, c. 1880–1890; $225–325.

Colt Peacemakers, .45 caliber; by the Colt Manufacturing Co.; c. 1875–1885: above, Bisley model with extended handle, $850–1,250; below, Standard model, $1,100–1,400.

rately engraved presentation piece presented by Colt to poet Jack Crawford; $150,000–200,000.

Colt Frontier model, six shot, single action revolver, .44/.40 caliber; c. 1870–1885; $700–800.

Colt gold-plated six shot, .45 caliber single action presentation revolver with elaborate engraving; c. 1870; $30,000–33,000.

Colt fluted Army issue revolver, from famous collection; c. 1860–1865; $1,300–1,700.

Colt pocket revolver, .41 caliber, percussion converted to cartridge; c. 1862; $850–1,000.

Colt single action Frontier Scout revolver, .22 caliber, early twentieth century; $200–275.

Colt single action, .45 caliber Peacemaker long barrel revolver with ivory grips; c. 1870; $3,300–3,700.

Forehand & Wadsworth .32 caliber five shot, double action revolver; c. 1890–1900; $225–275.

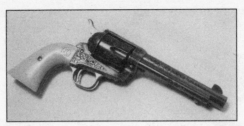

Short barrel, single action, .45 caliber presentation model silver-plated Peacemaker with mother-of-pearl grips and elaborate engraving; by the Colt Manufacturing Co.; c. 1873–1880, $9,000–12,000.

So-called Philadelphia derringer, cap and ball, engraved steel and hardwood body; a concealed or "boot" pistol; by Derringer Co.; c. 1865–1875; $800–950.

Forehand & Wadsworth .32 caliber double action, six shot revolver; c. 1890–1895; $135–185.

Harrington & Richardson .32 caliber double action, six shot revolver; c. 1880–1895; $200–275.

Harrington & Richardson .38 caliber double action, six shot bayonet revolver; c. 1890–1900; $300–400.

Hopkins & Allen .38 caliber five shot, double action revolver; c. 1890–1895; $100–200.

Hopkins & Allen .32 caliber hammerless double action, five shot revolver; c. 1885–1895; $150–225.

Iver Johnson .32 caliber double action, five shot, snub nose revolver; c. 1900–1910; $100–175.

Iver Johnson .38 caliber long barrel, double action, five shot revolver; c. 1900–1910; $135–185.

Remington model 1875, .44 caliber six shot revolver; $300–450.

Six shot revolver, .44 caliber New Model #3; by Smith & Wesson; one of the guns favored by Buffalo Bill Cody; c. 1875–1900; $650–850.

Smith & Wesson .357 caliber six shot revolver, early twentieth century; $200–275.

Smith & Wesson .44 caliber six shot American revolver with ivory grips; c. 1870–1880; $900–1,200.

Smith & Wesson .32 caliber six shot No. 2 Army revolver, engraved and silver-plated, in mahogany case; c. 1860; $12,000–15,000.

Smith & Wesson .32 caliber six shot No. 2 Army revolver; c. 1861–1863; $550–700.

Smith & Wesson .44 caliber six shot, single action revolver, Charles King patent; c. 1869–1871; $1,300–1,800.

Smith & Wesson .44 caliber Russian model six shot, single action revolver; c. 1870–1875; $750–1,000.

Double action, .45 caliber presentation model revolver with gold and silver plating and mother-of-pearl grips; by Smith & Wesson; c. 1875–1890; $6,500–8,000.

Starr Arms Co. model 1858, double action, six shot, .45 caliber revolver; $400–500.

Whitney .36 caliber five shot, single action pocket revolver; c. 1871; $1,500–2,000.

Rifles

Technically, the rifle is a shoulder-held arm with a spiral-grooved barrel bore which causes the bullet to spin, while a musket has a smooth bore. The latter was the older form and largely out of date by the time the West was settled. As a consequence, collectors of Western memorabilia are concerned only with rifles.

The rifle was the working weapon of the West. Unlike handguns, which were useful only to kill people at short range, rifles served as hunting weapons. Then as now, few rural households were without one. There are, consequently, a great variety from which to choose; however, most collectors seek out the top brands: Winchester, Remington, Springfield, Henry, and Sharps.

As with handguns, collectors should seek out unusual examples in good condition and be wary of heavily restored rifles or the numerous reproductions which are on the market.

Price Listings—Rifles

Colt New Lightning magazine rifle, .38 caliber, octagonal barrel; c. 1885–1895; $400–550.

Gallager's patent carbine, .50 caliber, marked Richardson & Overman; Philadelphia; c. 1850–1860; $800–950.

Henry rifle, .44 caliber, rare iron frame; c. 1855–1865; $32,000–37,000.

Henry rifle, .44 caliber, rare presentation piece with factory engraving, c. 1875; $475,000–500,000.

Henry rifle, .44 caliber lever action repeater; c. 1860–1866; $1,300–1,800.

Hotchkiss experimental third model, .44 caliber bolt action carbine; c. 1870–1880; $2,000–2,400.

Marlin model 1895, repeating rifle, .38/.56 caliber; $350–450.

Marlin model 1893, takedown repeating rifle, .40/.65 caliber; $275–350.

Marlin model 1891, side ejector repeating rifle, .32 caliber; $325–400.

Remington No. 4 New Model single shot rifle, .32 caliber; c. 1880–1890; $175–250.

Remington .45/.70 caliber long-range repeating rifle; c. 1885–1890; $350–500.

Sharps model 1853, deluxe carbine with factory-engraved

Rolling block, .44 caliber carbine; by Remington Arms Co.; c. 1890–1895; $350–550.

Cap and ball carbine, .40 caliber; by J. Henry & Son. The well-regarded Henry rifles were among the first to appear in the West; c. 1855–1865; $750–1,000.

Single shot, .32 caliber rifle; by unknown manufacturer;
c.1870–1880; $200–300.

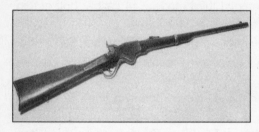

"Indian Model,"
.52 caliber lever
action rimfire
carbine; by
Spencer Arms Co.;
c.1865–1875;
$850–1,150.

hunting scene, marked "Patented 1848," .50 caliber;
$12,500–15,000.

Sharps model 1874 Sporting Rifle, .45 caliber single shot;
$3,000–3,700.

Sharps dropping block, breech loading rifle, .41 caliber;
c. 1860–1870; $1,800–2,200.

Sharps & Hankins .52 caliber rimfire carbine; c. 1862–1865;
$1,500–1,800.

Spencer lever action, .52 caliber repeating rifle; c. 1860;
$2,000–2,400.

Springfield military model 1864, muzzle loading percussion
rifle, .58 caliber; $900–1,100.

Springfield model 1873, .45/.70 caliber trapdoor carbine;
$600–750.

Springfield model 1884, trapdoor carbine, .45 caliber;
$400–550.

Stevens Sure Shot, .22 caliber single shot rifle; c. 1890–1895;
$200–275.

Stevens Favorite take-apart rifle, .32 caliber; c. 1890–1895;
$250–325.

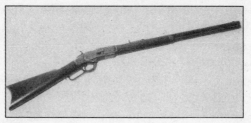

Repeating rifle, Winchester model 1873, .44/.40 caliber by
Winchester Arms Co.; c. 1873–1885; $600–800.

Stevens New Ideal, model 1894, .32/.40 caliber rifle;
$400–550.

Whitney .69 caliber Navy issue percussion rifle; c. 1862–1863;
$1,000–1,200.

Winchester model 1873, lever action repeating rifle, .44/.40
caliber, octagonal barrel; $550–700.

Winchester model 1895, lever action repeating rifle, .30/.40
caliber; $250–325.

Winchester model 1906, pump action rifle, .30 caliber, near
mint condition; $600–700.

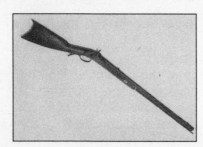

Muzzle-loading, cap and
ball rifle with octagonal
barrel, .52 caliber; by
Sharps; c. 1850–1860;
$1,000–1,300.

Reloading equipment for cap and
ball rifle, all c. 1840–1870: lead
melting pot, cast iron, $35–50;
explosive caps, $30–45 per box;
ball molds, $70–95.

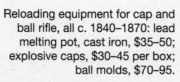

Winchester model 1886, takedown rifle, .38 caliber; $1,000–1,300.

Winchester model 1886, deluxe sporting rifle, .30 caliber, mint condition; $2,400–2,800.

Winchester model 1876, .50/.95 caliber Express, once owned by Buffalo Bill Cody; $200,000–275,000.

Winchester model 1890, repeating rifle, .22 caliber, unfired condition; $1,500–1,800.

Winchester model 1900, single shot rifle, .22 caliber, unfired condition; $2,000–2,300.

Winchester model 1873, .44 caliber repeating rifle with octagonal barrel; $1,700–2,000.

Winchester model 1876, .40/.60 caliber lever action rifle with octagonal barrel; $1,400–1,700.

Cowboy Kitsch

Also referred to by collectors and dealers as "Cowboy Funk," this category embraces two distinct areas of collectibles. First, there are the articles of clothing, equipment, and horse tack which were made for or owned by rodeo riders, performers in Western movies or Wild West shows, radio personalities, and prominent persons who affected a Western look. With the exception of rodeo gear, most of these items were made for show rather than for work on the range. However, associations with people such as Buffalo Bill or Gene Autry can result in values far higher than those ascribed to much earlier and more authentic Western memorabilia.

Needless to say, provenance is a key to value here. Since a saddle used by John Wayne will bring much more than an identical one used by nobody in particular, it is essential that a buyer be furnished with proof of origin.

A second and much larger category encompasses all the objects made with a Western or cowboy theme, including the many items sold or given away in connection with radio, movie, and television shows having a Western theme. From bucking bronco bookends to cowboy clocks, this is a huge field and, equally important, an area where collectors can buy reasonably. From the 1920s up to the present time, our fascination with the West has resulted in the production of thousands of objects, including toys and the numerous premiums given away to promote radio programs featuring cowboy figures like Tom Mix and the Lone Ranger. Unlike the case with most Western collectibles, such cowboy kitsch can often be bought for very little at tag sales, yard sales, and secondhand or thrift stores. Since most items are so inexpensive, there has been little incentive to make reproductions. The beginning collector can buy with confidence.

Hollywood, Wild West, and Rodeo Memorabilia

Price Listings

Advertising movie poster for *The Squaw Man*, an early Western movie, lithographed cardboard; c. 1915–1925; $450–650.

Mounted head of a bison or
buffalo, 39 inches high;
Montana; c. 1870–1880;
$650–900.

Advertising movie flyer for *Blue Blazes Rawden* with early
cowboy star William S. Hart, printed paper; c. 1920–1925;
$75–100.

Advertising lobby card for *Rustlers of Red Dog* starring Johnny
Mack Brown, lithographed cardboard; c. 1930–1935;
$50–75.

Advertising movie poster for *Saddle Pals* starring Gene Autry
and Champ, Jr., lithographed cardboard; 1947; $60–90.

Advertising movie poster for *Range War* starring Hopalong
Cassidy and his horse, Topper; 1938; $100–150.

Elaborately tooled parade saddle, chaps, bridle, martingale,
and headstall, all with silver mounts; made c. 1930–1940
by F. Fredholm, Los Angeles, California, for Leo F. Ecord,
an important Los Angeles politician; $23,000–28,000.

Woman's rodeo costume of blue silk sateen with leather
fringe and nickel silver studs; c. 1910–1920; $750–1,000.

Leather gun belt and holster decorated with nickel silver
conchos and studs; owned by Dale Truman, stand-in for
actor Hopalong Cassidy; c. 1930–1940; $2,250–2,750.

Saddle, heavily floral tooled brown leather with silver studs
and conchos; made by Bob Brown of Hollywood,
California, for actor Leo Carillo ("Pancho" in the "Cisco
Kid" series); c. 1950–1960; $5,500–6,000.

Coat or hat rack, long-horned steer horns and woolen upholstery material, 27 inches long, Western; c. 1880–1900; $200–280.

Hat, Plainsman type, black suede leather with silk band; made by Stetson for cowboy movie star Hoot Gibson; c. 1925–1935; $400–550.

Hat, Plainsman type, tan suede leather, beaded band; worn by Texas Bill, a rodeo star; c. 1920–1930; $350–450.

Spurs, wrought iron with engraved sterling silver overlay in form of hearts and crowns and impressed initial "M"; once owned by cowboy star Tom Mix; c. 1930–1940; $4,000–4,750.

Rodeo poster advertising appearance of Tom Mix, lithographed cardboard; c. 1930–1940; $150–200.

Circus poster advertising appearance of cowboy star Tim McCoy, lithographed paper; c. 1930–1950; $80–120.

Circus poster advertising appearance of Hopalong Cassidy, lithographed cardboard; c. 1950–1955; $125–165.

Sterling silver money clip with engraved Western scene and logo of Gene Autry, cowboy star; by Tiffany & Co. of New York; c. 1930–1940; $250–300.

Carte de visite of the Wild West Show star and sharpshooter Prairie Flower; c. 1885–1895; $40–55.

Armchair made from Texas long-horned steer horns with velvet upholstery, 46 inches high, Western; c.1880–1900; $900–1,200.

Couch made of steer horn and ironwood with leather upholstery tooled in Western motifs; once owned by cowboy star Gene Autry, c. 1930–1940; $2,500–3,000.

Bronze equestrian statue of the cowboy movie star John Wayne, c. 1960–1970; $1,800–2,300.

Rodeo poster, "King Brothers Championship Rodeo," lithographed cardboard with illustrations of horsemen roping cattle, etc.; c. 1910–1920; $275–350.

Rodeo souvenir program featuring Roy Rogers, picture of Rogers and horse Trigger; lithographed paper; 1947; $45–65.

Wild West Show poster, "101 Ranch Real West," lithographed cardboard with images of cowboys and Indians; produced by Miller & Arlington; c. 1890–1910; $750–1,000.

Letter signed by Buffalo Bill Cody along with first edition of book, *The Last of the Great Scouts: The Life Story of Col. W.F. Cody "Buffalo Bill";* Helen C. Wetmore; London; 1903; $9,000–11,000.

Poster for "Buffalo Ranch: Real Wild West," lithographed cardboard with many Western illustrations (cowboys, horses, cattle, etc.); c. 1910–1915; $650–750.

Program for Buffalo Bill's Wild West Show & Congress of

Light wagon or "pony break," painted wood and iron, leather upholstery; used at Buffalo Bill's ranch; Cody, Wyoming; c. 1900–1910; $20,000–25,000.

Rough Riders, lithographed cardboard in shape of bison head; c. 1890–1900; $200–250.

Booklet form program for Buffalo Bill's Wild West Show, lithographed paper; c. 1880–1900; $150–200.

Booklet form program of lithographed paper for the Buffalo Bill Rough Rider Show featuring Buffalo Bill Cody and Pawnee Bill; 1912; $125–175.

Photograph, cabinet card, of Buffalo Bill; by photographer E. Stacy; Brooklyn, New York; c. 1900–1905; $250–300.

Photograph, identical to above but with autograph of Buffalo Bill Cody; dated 1895; $450–650.

Photograph, cabinet card, of Buffalo Bill with Chief Sitting Bull of the Sioux; by William Notman & Son, photographers; c. 1884; $200–275.

Photograph, cabinet card, of the sharpshooter Annie Oakley; c. 1900–1910; $175–250.

Photograph of two women at a Western dude ranch, treated paper, 5 x 7 inches; c.1900–1910; $50–70.

Photograph of Lone Star Harry ("The Revolver King"), a popular Wild West Show figure; c. 1890–1910; $100–175.

Photograph, nearly four feet long, of the members of the 101 Ranch wild west show troupe; c. 1915; $2,000–3,000.

Photograph of Hopalong Cassidy, inscribed "Good Luck—Your Friend Hoppy"; c. 1945–1950; $15–25.

Promotional pamphlet, lithographed paper, for Lone Star Harry, The Revolver King; c. 1890–1910; $85–135.

Gold-filled pocket watch owned by Lone Star Harry and presented to him by members of the Wild West Show in which he appeared; c. 1900–1910; $1,000–1,500.

Promotional materials in black and white on paper for Bronco Billy, a rodeo star; c. 1913-1915; $125–175.

Lithographed metal trade sign for "Al Furstnow . . . Sole Maker of the Saddle That Made Miles City Famous"; c. 1900–1920; $800–1,000.

Trade sign in form of Winchester rifle, polychromed wood and metal; Phoenix, Arizona; c. 1895–1900; $1,500–2,000.

Trade sign for boot seller and repairer, polychrome-painted wood, 29 inches long; Boulder, Colorado; c. 1910–1920; $450–650.

Trade sign for a butcher shop, cast iron. Most of the Western steers ended up in shops like this; 25 inches long; Denver, Colorado; c. 1910–1930; $350–475.

Concord stagecoach, polychrome-painted wood, iron, and leather; used on the Mendocino, California, line; c. 1855–1875; $9,000–12,000.

Trade sign, lithographed tin, for White Rye, featuring cowboy offering toast at saloon bar, great detail and color; c. 1900–1910; $24,000–28,000.

Butcher's rack of cast iron, featuring representation of cowboy on horseback chasing a steer; made by Gus V. Brecht Co.; St. Louis, Missouri; 1892; $2,500–2,750.

Set of life-size plaster death masks of outlaws Cherokee Bill, Lonny Logan, and Bob Dalton; late nineteenth century; $2,750–3,250.

Stagecoach, extremely rare polychrome wood and iron nine-passenger Overland Stage; made by Abbott & Downing; Concord, New Hampshire; c. 1870–1890; $45,000–55,000.

Stagecoach, polychromed wood and iron, active on the Deadwood, South Dakota line; c. 1880–1895; $25,000–30,000.

Cowboy Kitsch

Price Listings

Door knocker, brass, in the form of a long-horned steer head; made and marked by the Gorham Silver Co.; Connecticut; c. 1910–1930; $125–175.

Dinner bell in form of long-horned steer head, cast and sheet iron; c. 1900–1920; $135–185.

Clock in brass-studded leather case, decorated with buffalo horns and hoofs and having bronze statuette of buffalo mounted on top; c. 1915–1925; $750–1,250.

Cigarette box, rectangular with hinged top and made of plastic wood (a glue-and-sawdust compound), with embossed representation of cowboy on horse; c. 1930–1940; $15–25.

Cigarette tobacco pouch, cotton, with lithographed paper label, STUD SMOKING TOBACCO, featuring rearing

Highly detailed miniature representation of a Western saddle, bronze, 8 inches high; c. 1960–1970; $550–750.

Tobacco advertising poster, lithographed paper mounted in wooden frame, 18 x 14 inches; Colorado; c. 1870–1890; $600–800.

Cowboy accessories: left, shoulder bag, leather; c.1880–1900; $165–225; right, canteen, leather-covered glass bottle; c.1870–1890; $130–180.

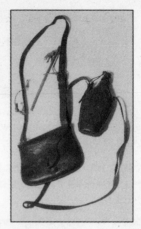

horse; made by R. J. Reynolds Tobacco Co.; c. 1910–1930; $20–30.

Salt and pepper shakers in form of cowboy boots and saddle, polychrome white earthenware; c. 1935–1945; $10–15.

Souvenir spoon, state of Colorado, handle with embossed representation of cowboy roping steer; c. 1940–1950; $25–30.

Whiskey bottle, figural, representation of cowboy in colored milk glass; by Lionstone; 1969; $15–25.

Whiskey bottle, figural, representation of the sharpshooter, Annie Oakley in colored milk glass; by Lionstone, 1969; $20–30.

Cosmetics bottle, boots and saddle, colored glass; by Avon Products; 1968; $15–20.

Cosmetics bottle, bucking bronco, colored glass; by Avon Products; 1971; $5–10.

Cosmetics bottle, Western style saddle, colored glass; by Avon Products; 1971; $7–12.

Mantel clock in form of cowboy on a horse, bronze-colored white metal on a bakelite base; c. 1940–1950; $20–35.

Mantel clock in form of cowboy hat, silver-colored white metal; c. 1930–1945; $25–40.

Weathervane in the form of a cow, tin and cast iron, 18 inches long; found in Colorado; c. 1900–1920; $150–225.

Pair of cast bronze bookends in form of cowboy on rearing horse, marked "1930, Cowboy And Broncho [sic]"; $45–65.

Songbook, *Cowboy Songs and Mountain Ballads*, printed and lithographed paper; 1932; $18–27.

Buffalo Bill long barrel cap pistol, cast iron; made by Kenton Manufacturing Co.; c. 1923-1930; $65–100.

Night light in the form of pistol holster and embossed "Hopalong Cassidy," white metal; c. 1935–1945; $175–250.

Hopalong Cassidy lead pencil, inscribed "Good Luck From Hoppy," painted wood; c. 1950–1955; $12–18.

Picture frame, embossed picture of Cassidy, rope, and gun; heavy color-lithographed cardboard; c. 1950–1960; $23–30.

Family album, cattle baron's family, treated paper, leather and cardboard with gilded metal fittings, 12 x 9.5 inches; Texas; c.1890–1920; $100–150.

Hopalong Cassidy plate, picture of Hoppy on horse Topper and salutation "To My Friend—Hoppy," color-lithographed white earthenware; c. 1950–1960; $25–35.

Hopalong Cassidy box camera, picture of Cassidy on horseback, lithographed plastic and metal; c. 1955–1965; $40–60.

Hopalong Cassidy deputy badge, stamped tin with inset photograph; c. 1945–1955; $50–75.

Hopalong Cassidy spurs, leather and silver-colored pot metal, c. 1950–1955; $55–85.

Hopalong Cassidy flashlight gun, black plastic with Cassidy's name in white; c. 1950–1960; $45–85.

Lone Ranger game including Lone Ranger figure, horse Silver, and blacksmith tools, all of polychrome molded plastic; c. 1967–1970; $45–65.

Lone Ranger badge, "Deputy," cast brass with secret compartment; c. 1940–1950; $25–40.

Lone Ranger "Hiyo Silver" pin, silvered pot metal; c. 1938–1940; $10–15.

Lone Ranger compass in form of pot metal "silver bullet," with secret compartment; c. 1940–1945; $25–45.

Toothbrush holder, figural form with Lone Ranger and horse Silver, colored composition; c. 1935–1940; $30–45.

Board game, "The Scout," lithographed cardboard, 7 x 14 inches; by Clark & Sowdon; New York; c. 1890–1900; $200–275.

Lone Ranger "Six Shooter" ring, in form of plastic and pot metal pistol; c. 1940–1950; $45–75.

Lone Ranger doll, composition with leatherette and cotton clothing including hat, 20 inches high; c. 1938–1942; $200–350.

Lone Ranger outfit, child's size hat, vest, shirt, and chaps; cotton and leatherette, all with Lone Ranger logos; c. 1940–1960; $55–80.

Lone Ranger book bag, canvas with applied plastic head of Lone Ranger; c. 1950–1960; $35–45.

Gene Autry book bag, cloth with lithographed representation of Autry; c. 1950–1970; $30–45.

Gene Autry store display, color-lithographed cardboard with representation of Autry, his horse in background; c. 1930–1945; $60–90.

Gene Autry toy six-gun, silvered pot metal with plastic grips, in original color-lithographed cardboard box; c. 1950–1960; $70–95.

Arcade card for Gene Autry movie *Gene Autry & Champ*, color-lithographed cardboard; c. 1940–1945; $10–15.

Gene Autry and Champ at Melody Ranch lunchbox, color-lithographed tin; c. 1940–1950; $35–45.

Bandanna, overall Western motifs including Gene Autry and horse Champ, color-lithographed rayon; c. 1935–1940; $20–30.

Toy sheriff's badge, embossed "Member Gene Autry Riders," stamped tin; c. 1935–1945; $10–15.

Gene Autry children's boots, color-lithographed picture of Autry and horse Champ, rubberized fabric; c. 1940–1950; $30–45.

Cisco Kid face mask, polychrome plastic with elastic band; c. 1952–1955; $13-18.

Cisco Kid picture ring, enameled white metal; c. 1950–1955; $50–65.

Lobby poster for movie *The Daring Caballero* starring Cisco

Kid and Pancho, color-lithographed cardboard, 1949; $50–75.

Cisco Kid toy six-gun, color-lithographed cardboard; premium for Tip-Top bread; c. 1940–1950; $35–50.

Writing tablet, cover imprinted "From your good Amigo, Duncan Reynaldo—Cisco Kid", c. 1940–1950; $5–10.

Matt Dillon (*Gunsmoke*) marshal's badge, bronzed pot metal; c. 1960–1970; $10–20.

Knitted wool cowboy doll stuffed with kapok and having a lariat of twisted twine; c. 1940–1960; $20–35.

Cast composition body Shirley Temple cowgirl doll with mohair wig and leather vest, chaps, and boots, plaid shirt and felt hat; c. 1935–1940; $65–95.

Cap gun, white metal with plastic grips, "Texan Jr."; by Hubley Manufacturing Co.; c. 1940–1955; $30–45.

Bedspread, multicolored chenille, with Roy Rogers, Double R bar logo, and numerous illustrations of Western life; c. 1935–1950; $350–425.

Roy Rogers ring, silvered pot metal in form of Western hat; c. 1940–1950; $15–25.

Roy Rogers deputy badge, bronze-colored pot metal; c. 1950–1955; $5–10.

Rubber horseshoe, for Trigger, Roy Rogers' horse, full size; c. 1950–1960; $8–16.

Horseshoes, wrought iron, reflecting wide variety in sizes and forms, 4.5 to 6.5 inches long; all c. 1880–1920; $3–5 each.

Buffalo robe of the sort often used by cowboys sleeping out on the plains, 5 x 6 feet, Western; c. 1880–1900; $250–350.

Roy Rogers bandanna, printed cotton with Western scene; c. 1950–1960; $12–18.

Roy Rogers "Quickshooter" hat, child's colored felt hat with Roy Rogers logo; c. 1955–1965; $25–50.

Roy Rogers store advertising display, large round color-lithographed cardboard sign with picture of Rogers; c. 1945–1950; $75–100.

Roy Rogers bank, boot on horseshoe base, embossed Rogers and horse Trigger, bronzed pot metal; c. 1950–1960; $30–40.

Tom Mix arm patch, blue cotton with TM logo on checkerboard ground; c. 1933–1947; $25–45.

Tom Mix badge, silvered pot metal; c. 1935–1945; $30–55.

Tom Mix toy branding iron of black cast iron; c. 1935–1940; $35–55.

Tom Mix bandanna, multicolored cotton with TM logo; c. 1935–1945; $40–70.

Tom Mix medal embossed "Straight Shooters," glow-in-dark bakelite with cloth ribbon; c. 1935–1940; $45–60.

Tom Mix six-shooter, wooden pistol painted black with Tom Mix signature and TM logo on white-painted grips; c. 1933–1938; $55–95.

Cowgirl skirt, marked with Tom Mix's TM logo, lithographed cotton and leatherette; c. 1935–1940; $40–55.

Tom Mix jigsaw puzzle, picture of Tom Mix on horse, color-lithographed paper on cardboard; c. 1935–1940; $60–80.

Salesman's sample kit for Red Ryder promotional items, fiberboard case with picture of Red Ryder; c. 1945–1950; $75–100.

Red Ryder cork firing carbine, black metal barrel, brown plastic stock; manufactured by Daisy; c. 1950–1960; $50–75.

Red Ryder BB gun, black metal barrel, brown wood stock; made by Daisy Manufacturing Co.; c. 1940–1950; $90–150.

Wall plaque featuring Red Ryder and Little Beaver on horseback, molded colored plaster; c. 1950–1960; $10–15.

Hoot Gibson child's cowboy suit, leatherette and printed cotton; by Wornova Clothing Co.; c. 1935–1940; $65–95.

Hoot Gibson lariat, woven rope; c. 1935–1940; $35–65.

Wild Bill Hickok marshal's badge, pot metal star with inset picture of Hickok and his sidekick, Jingles; c. 1950–1965; $25–45.

Wild Bill Hickok, Western Bunkhouse kit, lithographed paper cutouts of ranch building and contents; premium for Vornado air circulators; c. 1955–1965; $20–30.

Wyatt Earp, milk glass bowl with decalcomania picture of Wyatt Earp in gun battle; c. 1970–1980; $5–10.

Pecos Bill, plastic windup toy, cowboy with lariat on horse, polychrome plastic and iron wire; c. 1950–1960; $150–250.

Windup toys: left, cowboy, lithographed tin; c. 1950–1955; $75–100; right, Indian, polychrome-painted composition and lithographed tin; c. 1960–1965; $35–50.

Red Ranger clicker type pistol, black sheet steel; manufactured by Wyandotte; c. 1938–1941; $15–25.

Paladin, wallet with pictures of Paladin, lithographed plastic; c. 1960–1970; $15–20.

Paladin checkerboard with star's picture, lithographed cardboard with plastic checkers; c. 1960–1970; $20–25.

Shaving mug, white earthenware decorated with polychrome glaze representation of long-horned steer and name of Western rancher; c. 1900–1910; $500–600.

Coffee can, Golden West Coffee, tin with lithographed picture of cowgirl; c. 1925–1930; $30–45.

Chalkware figure of cowboy on horse, colored red, blue, yellow, and black with gilt glitter; c. 1935–1950; $25–45.

Chalkware figure of standing cowboy with pistol in hand, colored green, yellow, brown, and black; c. 1935–1950; $20–35.

Ashtray in form of cowboy hat, white earthenware highlighted in pink and brown; c. 1940–1960; $5–10.

Ashtray in form of cowboy hat, brass; c. 1935–1945; $5–10.

Child's mug with lithographed picture of cowboy on rearing horse, white earthenware; c. 1960–1980; $10–15.

Matching child's plate with lithographed picture of cowboy on rearing horse, white earthenware; c. 1960–1980; $5–8.

Native American Art and Crafts

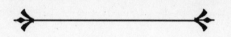

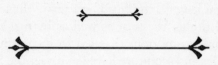

Interest in American Indian artifacts is of long standing. This is due in part to the wide variety of objects available and the high artistic quality of many, but it also reflects the important role that Native Americans have played in the development of our country. Fascination with Indians and Indian-made objects can be traced back at least to the first quarter of the nineteenth century, and by 1850 many whites were forming collections of weapons, textiles, basketry, and pottery.

As white traders, settlers, and tourists moved into the West, they provided a market for native crafts and also influenced those crafts. Plains Indian beadwork, which had previously been primarily geometric in decoration, began to feature European-style floral motifs and the Europeans themselves, as well as elements like the American eagle and flag. The owners of trading posts, which came to be an important outlet for Indian products, encouraged craftsmen to adopt forms and decoration more familiar to white buyers. Indian wearing blankets were replaced by rugs and table mats, and motifs utilized in Oriental and hooked rugs were transferred to Navajo weavings.

Despite all this, it was not until the last decade that Indian collectibles really took off. Prior to that time many major collections had been formed, usually through buying on the reservations or at trading posts, but prices remained moderate. However, those days seem gone forever. A veritable collector "feeding frenzy," fueled by the craze for all things Western as well as by magazine and clothing-store promotions, has led to increasingly high prices. Textiles and sculpture have gone over the $100,000 plateau, while prices in the tens of thousands for basketry and pottery are not regarded as unusual.

Under these circumstances, it might seem difficult for the average collector to break into the field. However, not all Indian craft objects have fallen into the hands of auction houses and expensive dealers. During the past century hundreds of thousands of Americans visited the West, and they all seem to have brought back Indian "souvenirs." It is possible to find artwork, silver, rugs, beadwork, pottery, and basketry in attics and storerooms throughout the United States, often at prices far below those of the prevailing market. It only requires knowledge of what to look for and persistence in seeking it out.

Moreover, there is also that field of pseudo-Indian artifacts referred to by dealers as "kitsch." These objects, which utilize Indians or Indian motifs in their design, range from ashtrays to playing cards. Most are not only inexpensive but also readily available, frequently from your local secondhand shop, flea market, or yard sale.

On the other hand, it should be noted that escalating prices have led to fraud, with numerous fakes appearing on the market, especially in the fields of art, sculpture, beadwork, and weaponry. Collectors must know the field and be particularly suspicious of anything that is offered to them at a price substantially below that of the going market.

Indian Basketry

Though it is believed that Native Americans were making baskets over ten thousand years ago and examples dating to the sixth century A.D. are known, almost all available to collectors were made within the past 100 years. However, this relative lack of antiquity has not hurt the market for Western basketry. Prime examples have brought over $100,000, and many other pieces sell in the $1,000-and-up range. Fortunately though, since baskets have continued to be made in the traditional manner, many examples dating from the 1930s to the present day are often found within the $50-200 price range.

All authentic Western Indian baskets are handwoven from native materials such as grass, rush, roots, and bark. These substances may be dyed in appealing patterns or enhanced with materials like feathers, abalone or other shells, glass beads, silk thread, and bits of metal.

Keys to value are condition, decoration, and size. Most collectors are very concerned about condition. Damage such as large cracks, missing pieces, and fading will reduce

Basket, Pima; Arizona; c. 1920–1925; 8 inches in diameter, 5.5 inches high. The varied geometric pattern in brown on tan is typical of Pima basketry; $200–275.

Jar or olla, Pima; Arizona;
c. 1915–1925; 8.5 inches in diameter,
11 inches high. Jars were typically
used for storage; some were so
tightly woven as to hold water;
$600–850.

Three baskets, Hopi; Arizona; c. 1930–1945. Left to right:
4 inches in diameter, 5 inches high; 6.5 inches in diameter,
8 inches high; 7 inches in diameter, 9.5 inches high. Values,
respectively: $70–90; $250–350; $125–175.

the value of an otherwise important piece from 20 to 90 percent.

Decoration is very important. Plain baskets in natural colors usually bring far less than those which show sections dyed red, black, or yellow with natural dyes. Better yet are vessels into which have been woven (usually in dark material such as the black seedpod, called "devil's claw," against a white ground like bleached bear grass) geometric or pictorial patterns. Diamonds, triangles, crosses, stars, circles, and ovals may be found. The more different forms and the more space they occupy, the more valuable the basket.

Even more desirable are pictorial decorations. Abstract human figures as well as birds and animals such as horses, deer, and rabbits are found on a relatively small number of baskets. All will bring good prices.

Most Indian baskets seen today range in diameter from 5 to 8 inches and in height from 3 to 6 inches. Larger and smaller ones will bring a premium. A rare decorated

Covered basket, Ute; Nevada; c. 1910–1930; 15 inches in diameter, 14 inches high. Despite its age and large size, lack of decoration assures that this piece will be reasonably priced; $200–275.

miniature only 2 inches in diameter can bring $1,000 per inch, while the large and elaborately patterned ollas and burden baskets as much as 3 feet high are likely to sell in the $10,000-plus range.

Fakes are not usually a major problem for basket buyers. The complexity of weaving and the difficulty in duplicating the wear and fading resulting from age have discouraged fraud. However, bear in mind that many native basket makers continue to work in the traditional manner. Older vessels should show wear along the bottom, tiny breaks in the rim wrapping, a nut-brown patina, and an overall feeling of brittle dryness.

Southwestern Baskets

The ancient "basket makers" of the Southwestern pueblos were first in the field, and today pueblo peoples such as the Hopi, Santo Domingo, and Cochiti follow their craft. Better known, however, are the wares of the neighboring Pima, Papago, and Apache. The pictorially decorated examples from the latter tribe can bring especially high prices.

Price Listings—Southwestern Baskets

Olla or vase, Apache; New Mexico; c. 1890–1910; 13 inches in diameter, 20 inches high; all-around vertical diamond pattern with interspersed crosses; $9,000–14,000.

Olla or vase, Apache; New Mexico; c. 1920–1935; 8 inches in diameter, 15 inches high; horizontal bands of animal and geometric designs; $1,500–2,000.

Olla or vase, Apache; New Mexico; c. 1890–1910; 11 inches

Pima basketry; Arizona; c. 1920–1940. Left to right: Tray, 13 inches in diameter, 3 inches high; bowl, 4.5 inches in diameter, 4 inches high; bowl, 11.5 inches in diameter, 6 inches high. Prices: $350–450; $75–95; $300–400.

Southwestern basketry, left to right: Covered basket, Pima; Arizona; c. 1940–1950; 8 inches long, 4 inches high. Handled basket, Papago; Arizona; c. 1955–1965; 4 inches high, 5 inches in diameter. Tray, Apache; Arizona; c. 1955–1965; 10 inches diameter. Prices from left: $175–250; $50–75; $200–275.

Water jars, Apache; Arizona; c. 1910–1940. Left: 10 inches in diameter, 14 inches high; right: 8.5 inches in diameter, 12 inches high. Prices: left, $350–500; right, $200–300.

Water jars: Left: Ute; Nevada; c. 1920–1930; 5 inches in diameter, 8.5 inches high. Right: Walapai; Arizona; c. 1910–1920; 10 inches in diameter, 14.5 inches high. Prices, respectively: $125–165; $275–375.

in diameter, 18 inches high; large horse and dog figures in reserves surrounded by triangular geometric patterns; $6,000–7,000.

Olla or vase, Apache; New Mexico; c. 1890–1900; 18 inches in diameter, 27 inches high (very large); random decoration of human figures interspersed with triangles set into diamond patterns; $20,000–25,000.

Olla or vase, Apache; New Mexico; c. 1900–1910; 16.5 inches in diameter, 14.5 inches high, narrow neck, globular form; vertical diamond bands interspersed with human and animal figures; $3,500–5,500.

Tray, Apache; New Mexico; c. 1900–1910; 23 inches in diameter, 2.5 inches high; band of human and deer figures surrounded by overall geometric banding; $10,000–15,000.

Tray, Apache; New Mexico; c. 1900–1910; 20 inches in diameter, 2.5 inches high; central seven-point star, scattered human and animal figures; $8,000–11,000.

Tray, Apache; New Mexico; c. 1900–1920; 21 inches in

diameter, 3 inches high; alternating bands of stylized parrots and plants; $7,000–10,000.

Tray, Apache; New Mexico; c. 1920–1930; 24 inches in diameter, 3.5 inches high; complex pattern of humans and dogs set within crossed necklaces; $9,000–10,500.

Tray, Apache; New Mexico; c. 1910–1930; unusual oval form, 22 inches long, 17 inches wide; central lizard motif surrounded by equestrian figures and geometric border; $2,700–3,200.

Covered basket, Apache; New Mexico; c. 1920–1940; oval form, 26.5 inches long, 13 inches wide; two simple triangular bands on body, one on lid; $650–850.

Tray, Hopi; Arizona; c. 1930–1950; 11.5 inches in diameter, 1 inch high; in part checkerboard pattern, in part concentric bands of triangles; $90–135.

Olla or jar, Papago; Arizona; c. 1920–1930; 13.5 inches in diameter, 14 inches high; random motifs including hands, roosters, and scorpions (rare); $1,500–1,900.

Bowl, Papago; Arizona; c. 1950–1970; 5 inches in diameter, 2 inches high; simple geometric patterns along lower body; $30–50.

Turtle effigy, Papago; Arizona; c. 1930–1940; 18.5 inches long, 10 inches wide; oval body with checkered design, banded legs, and tail; $400–750.

Burden basket, Apache; Arizona; c. 1940–1950; 16 inches in diameter, 20 inches high. These were carried on the back and supported by a band worn across the forehead; $400–600.

Left: Wedding basket, Navajo; Arizona; c. 1950–1965; 13 inches in diameter, 2.5 inches high; woven for Navajo by Ute and other tribes. Right: Handled jar or pitcher, Paiute; Arizona; c. 1960–1970. Prices: left, $100–135; right, $70–95.

Olla or vase, Papago; Arizona; c. 1915–1930; 8 inches in diameter, 21 inches high; cylindrical vessel with flaring rim, decorated with vertical bands of female figures and triangles; $1,400–1,900.

Bowl, Papago; Arizona; c. 1900–1920; 12.5 inches in diameter, 9 inches high; six stylized representations of splayed-out lizards running completely around vessel; ticked rim; $900–1,400.

Bowl, Pima; Arizona; c. 1920–1930; 7 inches in diameter, 10.5 inches high; center band of figures on horseback, men and deer, "key" motifs above and below; $1,000–1,750.

Tray, Pima; Arizona, c. 1910–1920; 6 inches in diameter, 1 inch high; covered with strong geometric meander pattern radiating out from dark, central bull's-eye; $600–800.

Winnowing basket or tray, Pima; Arizona; c. 1910–1920; 2 inches high, 15 inches in diameter; overall checkered pattern radiating out from dark, central bull's-eye; $750–1,000.

Winnowing basket or tray, Pima; Arizona; c. 1900–1920; 3 inches high, 22.75 inches in diameter; complex decoration of concentric bands connecting columns of triangles; solid center; $1,000–1,500.

Bowl, Pima; Arizona; c. 1920–1930; 2.5 inches high, 4.5 inches in diameter; diagonal bands of triangles cover body from top to bottom; rim trimmed with blue glass beads; $250–400.

Bowl, Pima; Arizona; c. 1900–1920; 9 inches high, 12 inches in diameter; dark, radiating whirling log pattern against lighter ground; $2,200–2,600.

Jar, Pima; Arizona; c. 1920–1935; 13 inches high, 12.5 inches in diameter; globular form with flaring rim; overall criss-cross pattern of checkered diamonds; $900–1,200.

Western Baskets

Basket makers range throughout the far West from Southern California to the coasts of Washington and Alaska. The variations in style are very great, from the geometrically patterned Washo vessels to the feather-and-shell-covered Pomo "treasure baskets" to the painted bark-and-root hats produced by Haida and Tlingit craftsmen.

Price Listings—Western Baskets

Seed jar, California Mission; c. 1900–1920; 4.5 inches high, 6.2 inches in diameter; bands of terraced diagonals across body; tiny crosses above base; $400–500.

Seed jar, California Mission; c. 1920–1940; 7.5 inches high, 11.5 inches in diameter; shouldered jar decorated with wide spiked band enclosing large diamonds and random small crosses; $700–950.

Bowl, California Mission; c. 1910–1930; 5 inches high, 12.5 inches in diameter; low, flaring sides embellished with checkered snake design spiraling up around body; $750–1,000.

Root basket, Salish; Washington; c. 1950–1960; rare octagonal shape, 16 inches at widest point, 9 inches high; simple geometric decoration; $90–135.

Tray, California Mission; c. 1915–1935; 3 inches high, 11.5 inches in diameter; central swirling abstract "pinwheel" or floral design in dark and light; $650–950.

Bowl, California Mission; c. 1925–1940; 4 inches high, 6 inches in diameter; vertically alternating human figures and geometric devices; $700–900.

Cap, Hupa; California; c. 1920–1930; 5 inches high, 7 inches in diameter; bowl-shaped "Maiden's Cap" with concentric bands of stepped triangles, diagonal ticking above and below; $200–275.

Basket, Hupa; California; c. 1930–1940; 5 inches high, 9.25 inches in diameter; polychrome decorated with two bands of stacked boatlike motifs and banding below rim; $800–1,200.

Cradle, Yokuts; California; c. 1920–1940; 12 inches wide, 19 inches long; woven roots; basketry cradles are rare; $200–275.

Left to right: Bowl, Modoc; California; c. 1905–1915; 7 inches in diameter, 5 inches high. Strainer, Klamath; Oregon; c. 1910–1925; 13 inches in diameter, 3 inches high. Bowl, Quinault; British Columbia; c. 1920–1930; 9 inches in diameter, 7 inches high. Prices, left to right: $200–300; $150–225; $175–300.

Bowl, Hupa; California; c. 1930–1940; 3.75 inches high, 6.5 inches in diameter; broad bands of triangles alternating with random smaller triangles; $500–750.

Bowl, Klamath; California; c. 1930–1940; 6 inches in diameter, 4 inches high; scalloped rim, decorated with dark, fencelike pattern encircling body; $175–250.

Bowl, Maidu; California; c. 1920–1940; 20 inches in diameter, 13 inches high; bold fringed zigzag pattern covering most of body; $1,400–2,200.

Bowl, Maidu; California; c. 1915–1930; 8 inches in diameter, 9.5 inches high; images of bats and butterflies in black against lighter ground; $2,500–3,500.

Basket, Mono; California, c. 1910–1930; 6.5 inches in diameter, 3.5 inches high; bands of dark, serrated triangles running diagonally from bottom to top against lighter ground; $450–600.

Basket, Mono; California; c. 1910–1920; 7 inches in diameter, 5 inches high, globular form; overall pattern of vertically stacked triangles alternating with vertical bars; $200–275.

Covered bowl or basket, Mono; California; c. 1915–1930; 12.2 inches in diameter, 7.5 inches high; overall abstract

Burden basket, Klamath; Oregon; c. 1900–1910; 14 inches wide, 16 inches long; tightly woven conical vessel with complex geometric design; $700–950.

foliate decoration, lid knob beaded in red, white, and blue; attributed to famous maker Maggie Howard; $9,000–12,000.

Bowl, Nootka; Vancouver Island; c. 1900–1920; 12.3 inches in diameter, 9 inches high; polychrome decoration; encircling bands of brown chevrons and blue beading; $350–500.

Bowl, Paiute; Nevada; c. 1900–1910; 7 inches in diameter, 4 inches high; three simple geometric bands encircle body; $100–125.

Water jar, Paiute; Nevada; c. 1900–1920; 9 inches in diameter, 14 inches high, cone-shaped with narrow neck; two thin lines of chevrons against darker tweedlike weave; $250–350.

Basket, Pomo; California; c. 1900–1920; 11 inches in diameter, 8 inches high; fully decorated with alternating large and small diagonal "lightning bolt" patterns; checkered band at rim; $3,000–4,500.

West Coast basketry; left to right: Bowl, Pit River, California; c. 1910–1920; 5 inches in diameter, 4 inches high. Basket, Pit River, California; c. 1910–1920; 11 inches in diameter, 13 inches high. Covered basket, Makah; Washington; c. 1940–1960; 5.5 inches diameter, 4 inches high. Prices, left to right: $275–375; $600–850; $100–150.

Basket, Pomo; California; c. 1920–1940; 7.5 inches in diameter, 3 inches high; overall "hourglass" pattern enclosing serrated "quail plume" motifs; rectangular pattern around rim; $1,300–1,700.

Jewel or "gift" basket, Pomo; California; c. 1920–1930; 7.75 inches in diameter, 3.5 inches high; exterior covered with concentric rows of bird feathers; clamshell disks around rim; $2,000–2,500.

Miniature basket, Pomo; California; c. 1900–1910; 2 inches in diameter, 1 inch high; 10–point star pattern on top and bottom; $700–900.

Miniature basket, Pomo; California; c. 1920–1950; 2.6 inches in diameter, 1.3 inches high; oval form, decorated with glass beads in red, white, and yellow; $275–450.

Basket, Pomo; California; c. 1920–1930; boat-shaped, 5 inches maximum diameter, 8 inches long; geometric and stylized whirlwind decoration; $600–800.

Basket, Pomo; California; c. 1900–1920; boat-shaped, 18 inches maximum width, 27 inches long; overall geometric stepped pyramid decoration; $9,000–13,000.

Basket, Pomo; California; c. 1900–1930; boat-shaped, 13 inches maximum width, 17 inches long; encircling ring of simple diamond motifs at base; $1,400–1,900.

Burden basket; Salish; Washington; c. 1900–1910; 11.75

California basketry, left to right: Water bottle, Mono; c. 1920–1940; 4.5 inches in diameter, 8 inches long. Cooking basket, Bannock; c. 1910–1920; 9 inches in diameter, 13 inches high. Burden basket, Mono; c. 1910–1925; 9.5 inches in diameter, 14 inches long. Prices, left to right: $140–190; $225–300; $400–650.

inches high, 13 inches wide, deep oval form; human figures and trees on one side, columns of right triangles on
other; $1,800–2,500.

Bowl, Salish; Washington; c. 1900–1920; 3.5 inches high, 5
inches in diameter; concentric stepped columns around
flaring sides; base with checkered circles; $650–1,000.

Bowl, Salish; Washington; c. 1910–1930; 8 inches high, 16.5
inches in diameter; terraced triangles interspersed with
small crosses running around body; scalloped rim;
$900–1,400.

Bowl, Tulare; California, c. 1900–1920; 10 inches in diameter, 3 inches high; encircling diamond pattern; 10–pointed
star in base; $250–400.

Bowl, Tulare; California, c. 1920–1930; 7 inches in diameter,
3.5 inches high; diagonal bands, zigzags flanked by
stepped triangles; $750–1,100.

Jar, Tulare; California; c. 1910–1920; 8 inches in diameter,
5.5 inches high; wide shoulder, narrow neck with vertical
banding; body with two bands of "diamondback rattlesnake" motif; $1,300–1,700.

Bowl, Panamint; California; c. 1920–1930; oval or boat
shape, 7 inches wide, 11 inches long; dyed polychrome
with butterflies, arrows, and pair of bows; $6,500–9,500.

Bowl, Panamint; California; c. 1920–1940; 6 inches high, 17
inches in diameter; encircling decoration of large (8 inches) male figures and geometric devices, central fleur-de-
lis; famous collection; $16,000–19,000.

Seed jar, Panamint; California, c. 1915–1925; 9 inches high,
12 inches in diameter, globular form with narrow neck;
serrated columns terminating in tree forms radiate from
base; $4,500–7,000.

Bowl, Panamint; California; c. 1910–1920; 4.5 inches wide, 9
inches long; oval vessel encircled by thin, abstract human
figures and having a ticked rim; $250–350.

Bowl, Chumash; California; c. 1890–1920; 5 inches high, 20
inches in diameter; rare polychrome geometric decoration

including "Greek Key" design and stair-step pattern; $25,000–30,000.

Tray, Chumash; California; c. 1880–1900; 3.75 inches high, 21 inches in diameter; complex concentric geometric pattern; finely woven and famous collection; $30,000–40,000.

Basket, Mono; California; c. 1890–1900; 3 inches high, 9.5 inches in diameter; two concentric bands of diamonds crossed by three single bands curving into center; $800–1,200.

Basket, Maidu; California; c. 1880–1900; 2.5 inches high, 8 inches in diameter; central motif of abstract seven-petal flower surrounded by smaller flowers; $600–750.

Gambling tray, Shasta; California; c. 1890–1910; 2 inches high, 24 inches in diameter; central "exploding star" surrounded by bands of geometric devices; $1,500–2,000.

Bowl, Skohomish; British Columbia; c. 1915–1925; 9 inches high, 12.5 inches in diameter; three rows of abstract human figures running completely around the body; row of dogs at rim; $1,250–1,700.

Basket, Tlingit; Alaska; c. 1890–1910; 17 inches high, 25 inches in diameter; polychrome decoration of crosses within diamonds, stripes, steps, and banding (rare and very large); $7,500–12,500.

Basketry utensils: Top: drying tray, Washoe; California; c. 1910–1930; 16 inches wide, 18 inches long: Bottom: seed beater used in preparing food, Yokuts; California; c. 1920–1930. Prices: top, $475–675; bottom, $100–165.

Covered "rattle" basket, Tlingit; Alaska; c. 1900–1920; 5 inches high, 7 inches in diameter; polychrome geometric decoration in red, green, and yellow; seeds in lid create "rattle"; $1,600–2,200.

Tubular container, two-piece, Tlingit; Alaska; c. 1910–1930; 6 inches high, 2 inches in diameter; interior with polychrome decoration of diamonds in yellow, orange, and brown; $650–900.

Basket, Tlingit; Alaska; c. 1900–1920; 7 inches high, 6.5 inches in diameter; flaring cylinder with two horizontal bands of diamonds against a latticework ground; $550–800.

Basket, Tlingit; Alaska; c. 1900–1920; 10 inches high, 7.5 inches in diameter; two horizontal polychrome bands of crosses within lozenges, all in red, green, yellow, and orange; $1,400–1,900.

Basket, Tlingit; Alaska; c. 1920–1930; 9 inches high, 7.5 inches in diameter; three bands of polychrome chevrons, rectangles, and parallelograms; $1,200–1,600.

Basket, Tlingit; Alaska; c. 1920–1940; 6.5 inches high, 6 inches in diameter; circled by horizontal terraced elements set within two crenulated bands in black and white; $1,000–1,350.

Basket, Tlingit; Alaska; c. 1910–1930; 7.5 inches high, 5 inches in diameter, flattened oval form; central band of crosses, bands of chevrons at base and rim; $900–1,300.

Hat, Tsimshian; British Columbia; c. 1900–1920; 12 inches high, 16 inches in diameter; in form of truncated cone and painted in red and black with abstract totemic elements; $750–1,000.

Covered basket, Aleutian; Attu; c. 1920–1930; 8.5 inches high, 5 inches in diameter; bands, diamonds and semicircular patterns embroidered in colored wool on grass ground; $600–800.

Covered basket, Aleutian; Attu; c. 1920–1940; 6.75 inches high, 4.25 inches in diameter; three polychrome flowers embroidered in pink, red, green, purple, yellow, and orange silk thread; $900–1,200.

Covered basket, Aleutian; Attu; c. 1920–1940; 7 inches high, 4.5 inches in diameter; encircled by four quartered diamonds with two checkered bands of pink, gray, and orange silk thread; $750–900.

Basket, Aleutian; Attu; c. 1920–1940; 4 inches high, 5.5 inches in diameter; scalloped rim; body covered with alternating checked bands and widely spaced polychrome floral motifs; $800–1,100.

Wallet, Aleutian; Attu; c. 1920–1940; width 4 inches, length when folded 5.2 inches; embroidered with bands of terraced diamonds in orange, red, purple, and blue; $1,200–1,500.

Basket, Washo; Nevada; c. 1900–1930; 6 inches high, 9.5 inches in diameter; encircling bands of triangles; $650–850.

Winnowing tray, Washo; Nevada; c. 1900–1920; 19 inches long, 14 inches wide; triangular form with simple geometric banding; $500–750.

Basket, Yokuts; California; c. 1890–1900; 9 inches high, 16 inches in diameter; so-called "friendship basket" with two bands of stylized female (rare) figures holding hands; $12,000–16,000.

Basket, Yokuts; California; c. 1900–1920; 7.5 inches high, 14 inches in diameter; "friendship basket" with band of male figures holding hands beneath "diamondback rattlesnake" border; $3,000–4,000.

Covered bowl, Yokuts; California; c. 1920–1930; 11 inches high including lid, 13.5 inches in diameter; three tiers of "diamondback rattlesnake" pattern encircle body, another on lid; $2,500–4,000.

Bowl, Yokuts; California; c. 1900–1910; 9.75 inches high, 15.5 inches in diameter; three "diamondback rattlesnake" bands encircle body; random vertical lines of triangles; $1,200–1,800.

Jar or olla, Yokuts; California; c. 1900–1920; 16 inches in diameter, 13.5 inches high; traditional "diamondback rattlesnake" decoration; $750–1,000.

Miniature bowl, Yokuts; California; c. 1930–1940; 1.75 inches high, 3.5 inches in diameter; encircled by polychrome "diamondback rattlesnake" motif; $250–325.

Basket, Yokuts; California; c. 1900–1910; 4.3 inches high, 9.75 inches in diameter; so-called "treasure basket" in bottleneck form with encircling bands of hourglass motifs; $750–950.

Bowl, Yurok; California; c. 1910–1930; 4 inches high, 7 inches in diameter; terraced bands zigzag from top to base; narrow banding about rim; $800–1,300.

Basketry-covered glass; left to right: Jar, Paiute; Arizona; c. 1950–1960; 3.75 inches in diameter, 6 inches high. Wine bottle, Pit River, California; c. 1950–1970; 4 inches in diameter, 12 inches high. Covered bowl, Tlingit; Alaska; c. 1950–1960. Prices, left to right: $100–140; $200–300; $265–385.

Indian Pottery

Colorful Indian pottery is one of the most popular of all Western collectibles and one of the most available. It has been made in large quantities for the tourist trade since the late nineteenth century, primarily in the Southwestern states of Arizona and New Mexico. There is a great price range. Large, spectacularly decorated nineteenth-century pots have sold for over $100,000. Ordinary examples from the 1940–1970 period can often be found for $50–100 apiece.

Technically, there are two distinct ceramic categories: "pre-contact" or pre-European wares made prior to the arrival of whites in the sixteenth century, and everything else. The former category, including examples from the important Hohokam and Mimbres cultures, is rare and costly. The latter category includes both wares made, primarily prior to 1900, for community use and those turned out for sale to whites. Since many of the items in the latter category were made to sell through gift shops such as those run from 1870 on by the Fred Harvey Company, the items show a much broader range of form and decoration than the traditional wares. Where the former might be limited to such utilitarian items as bowls, canteens, and seed or storage jars, the latter typically encompasses such Anglo forms as ashtrays, tiles, vases, figurines, and plates.

Decoration remained traditional and remarkably similar until the 1950s, when some Native American potters began to experiment with new techniques, often reflecting their adaptations of contemporary mainstream ceramics styles. Such recent ware has a loyal following, though most collectors seek more recognizable examples.

Another later innovation, and an important one in terms of the current market, is the craftsman's signature.

Early Indian wares were never signed. However, from the 1920s on, creative artists such as Marie and Julian Martinez from San Ildefonso Pueblo and Leah Nampeyo of Hano began to sign their products. Today, most larger pieces are so marked, and the signature of a respected potter can substantially increase the value of a piece.

Age affects value, as relatively few pre-1900 pieces have survived. However, it is less a factor than decoration. Elaborate decoration featuring human and animal figures is in great demand, particularly if it is rendered in several colors.

Size is another consideration. As with baskets, very large examples can bring a premium. On the other hand, smaller (3 inches high and less) pots do not command the prices one would pay for basketry of a comparable size. It is much easier to make a small pot, and thousands have been turned out, often originally sold for 10 to 50 cents each!

Many different Southwestern tribal groups have produced pottery. Among the more desirable examples are those from the New Mexican pueblos of San Ildefonso, Santa Clara, Santo Domingo, Acoma, Cochiti, Tesuque, and Zia, as well as the Hopi village of Hano in Arizona.

An important thing for collectors to keep in mind is how Native American pottery was—and usually still is—made. Unlike white potters, who have for centuries employed brick or stone kilns, Indians fire their ware out in the open beneath piles of dried animal dung, wood, or charcoal. The low temperature thus achieved results in an extremely fragile body. Moreover, colored slip decoration is often applied after firing. As a consequence, water or even damp can seriously affect this ware. Collectors should check pieces offered to them for restoration, which may include extensive inpainting to restore areas of decoration destroyed by water damage.

Collectors of earlier, pre-1860 wares should also bear in mind that much of what is on the market has been dug up, often from graves where it was traditionally buried with the deceased. Native Americans have become increasingly concerned about what they regard as grave robbery, and they have, in some cases, attempted to reclaim artifacts that they felt were unlawfully obtained. Anyone buying pre-contact or even pre-1900 pottery should obtain a warranty of title from the seller.

Price Listings—Indian Pottery

Mimbres culture bowl, 10 inches in diameter; New Mexico; c. 950–1150; large polychrome decoration of dancing anthropomorphic figure surrounded by geometric designs; $60,000–65,000.

Mimbres culture bowl, 9 inches in diameter; New Mexico; c. 950–1150; black on white overall geometric zigzag pattern; $6,000–8,000.

Mimbres culture bowl, 7 inches in diameter; New Mexico; c. 1000–1200; sparse black on white geometric zigzag pattern; $600–850.

Mimbres culture shallow bowl, 10 inches in diameter; New Mexico; c. 1050–1200; complex black-on-white geomet-

Bowl, earthenware, 8 inches in diameter; Mimbres culture; c. 950–1150; interior with black on white zigzag or "lightning" pattern, $1,500–2,000.

Jar or olla, earthenware, bird and rain cloud motifs in black on white, 9.5 inches high; Cochiti Pueblo, New Mexico; c. 1895–1905; $2,000–3,000.

Bowl,
earthenware,
7.5 inches in
diameter; Santo
Domingo Pueblo,
New Mexico;
c. 1920–1930;
$250–325.

ric border incorporating stylized fish form; plain center; $4,500–6,500.

Mimbres culture bowl, 8 inches in diameter; New Mexico; c. 1100–1200; black-on-white decoration including large central fish with plaid body and concentric ring border around rim; $3,500–5,000.

Mimbres culture bowl, 6 inches in diameter; New Mexico; c. 1100–1250; black-on-white decoration including central armadillo type animal with checkerboard body; $2,500–4,000.

Mimbres culture bowl, 6 inches in diameter; New Mexico; c. 1150–1250; bordering checkerboard pattern in black on white; $700–950.

Sikyatki culture jar or olla, 12 inches high; Arizona; c. 1400–1650; elaborate red, yellow, and black polychrome geometric and figural decoration; $70,000–80,000.

Sikyatki culture bowl, 5 inches high; Arizona; c. 1400–1500; polychrome decoration in red and yellow on white includes human busts; $25,000–35,000.

Sikyatki culture bowl, 5 inches high; Arizona; c. 1400–1500; polychrome decoration in red and yellow on white includes human busts; $25,000–35,000.

Sikyatki culture shallow bowl, 12 inches in diameter; Arizona; c. 1375–1450; central representation of large birdlike creature against white ground; $9,000–12,000.

Sikyatki culture bowl, 6 inches high; Arizona; c. 1400–1600;

overall geometric decoration in red, yellow, and black against a white ground; $12,000–15,000.

Hohokam culture bowl, 8 inches high; Arizona; c. 900–1100; overall complex swirling design in white on a red ground; $7,500–9,500.

Hohokam culture bowl, 9 inches high; Arizona; c. 900–1200; overall complex geometric decoration in white on a red ground featuring triangles and rectangles; $9,000–12,000.

Hohokam culture bowl, 5 inches high; Arizona; c. 700–900; overall geometric design in white on red with central star motif; $6,000–7,500.

Gila culture bowl, 8 inches high; Arizona; c. 1300–1400; abstract geometric design with squares, diamonds, and oblong banding in black and white on red covers upper half; $2,500–4,000.

Gila culture tray, 13 inches in diameter; Arizona; c. 1300–1400; overall abstract swirling geometric design in black and white on red; $7,000–9,500.

Gila culture jar or olla, 10 inches high; Arizona; c. 1300–1400; overall geometric design in black and white on red includes stepped patterns and circular banding; $5,000–6,500.

Mesa Verde culture mug, 5 inches high; Arizona; c. 1200–1300; rows of sawtooth banding in black on white; $900–1,200.

Mesa Verde culture mug, 5.5 inches high; Arizona; c. 1200–1300; concentric banding surrounding stepped pattern in black on white; $750–950.

Mesa Verde culture bowl, 4.5 inches high; Arizona; c. 1200–1300; concentric bands of black on white slip surround abstract Greek Key pattern; $1,300–1,700.

Mesa Verde culture bowl, 5.5 inches high; Arizona; c. 1200–1300; concentric bands of black on white surround abstract lightning pattern; $1,100–1,500.

Salado culture jar or olla, 14 inches in diameter; Arizona; c. 1350–1500; blocks of geometric decoration in black and white on red ground; $5,500–7,500.

Kinishba culture tray, 13 inches in diameter; Arizona or New Mexico; c. 1300–1400; overall polychrome geometric decoration in black and red on white ground; $4,000–6,500.

Fourmile area bowl, 8 inches in diameter; Arizona; c. 1300–1400; polychrome decoration of Kachina-like head surrounded by geometric banding; $20,000–25,000.

Polacca jar or olla, Hopi, 10 inches high; Arizona; c. 1880–1890; abstract decoration in red, yellow, orange, and black on white featuring large Kachina figures; $13,000–17,000.

Polacca ceremonial rattle, Hopi, 8 inches long; Arizona; c. 1860–1880; stylized frog in yellow, gray, and black on a red ground; $3,500–5,500.

Left: Jar or olla, roadrunner motif in red and brown on white, 7 inches high; Zia; c. 1960–1965; $300–450. Right: Plate, 8 inch diameter, geometric pattern in red, black, and brown on cream; Isleta Pueblo; c. 1965–1970; $100–135; both pieces from New Mexico.

Jar or olla, earthenware, parrot motif in red, black, and tan on white, 10 inches in diameter; Acoma Pueblo, New Mexico; c. 1960–1970; $3,500–4,200.

Left: Bowl, earthenware in red and gray, 5 inches high; Santa Clara Pueblo, New Mexico; c. 1930–1940; $125–185. Right: Bowl, earthenware in tan and black on white, 4 inches high; Hopi; Arizona; c. 1925–1935; $175–235.

Polacca bowl, Hopi, 4 inches high; Arizona; c. 1870–1890; abstract floral and bird designs on a white ground; $900–1,200.

Polacca tray, Hopi, 11 inches in diameter; Arizona; c. 1870–1900; interior covered with abstract swirling geometric pattern in red and black on white; $2,000–2,800.

San Ildefonso Pueblo bowl, 6 inches high; New Mexico; c. 1923–1925; signed Marie; polished and matt black with simple abstract design; $900–1,250.

San Ildefonso Pueblo bowl, 9 inches in diameter; New Mexico; c. 1923–1925; signed Marie; polished and matt black with simple floral and geometric designs; $550–675.

San Ildefonso Pueblo plate, 11 inches in diameter; New Mexico; c. 1923–1925; signed Marie; polished and matt black with encircling feather design; $1,800–2,400.

San Ildefonso Pueblo bowl, 10.5 inches in diameter with terraced rim; New Mexico; c. 1925–1930; signed Marie; polished and matt black with geometric decoration; $2,300–2,800.

San Ildefonso Pueblo plate, 11 inches in diameter; New Mexico; c. 1955–1970; signed Marie & Popovi (Martinez); polished and matt black with encircling feather design; $4,000–5,500.

Left: Bowl, earthenware with floral pattern in red and black on cream, 3.5 inches high; San Ildefonso Pueblo, New Mexico; c. 1910–1920; $350–550. Right: Jar or olla, earthenware in black on white, 8 inches high; Cochiti Pueblo, New Mexico; c. 1950–1960; $250–325.

San Ildefonso Pueblo plate, 12 inches in diameter; New Mexico; c. 1955–1970; signed Marie & Popovi (Martinez); polished and matt red with encircling feather design; $5,500–6,500.

San Ildefonso Pueblo vase or olla, 7.5 inches high; New Mexico; c. 1955–1970; signed Marie & Popovi (Martinez); polished and matt sienna and black with geometric designs; $10,000–12,000.

San Ildefonso Pueblo vase or olla, 10 inches high; New Mexico; c. 1925–1943; signed Marie & Julian (Martinez); polished and matt black; $5,000–5,700.

San Ildefonso Pueblo jar, 9 inches high; New Mexico; c. 1925–1943; signed Marie & Julian (Martinez); polished and matt black with geometric design over upper body; $2,000–2,500.

San Ildefonso Pueblo pot, 6 inches high; New Mexico; c. 1960–1970; signed Tonita & Juan; polished and matt black with geometric design over upper body; $250–350.

San Ildefonso Pueblo miniature pot, 2 inches high; New Mexico; c. 1950–1970; signed Blue Corn; polished and matt red with simple geometric designs; $75–100.

San Juan Pueblo gourd form jar, 7 inches high; New Mexico; c. 1920–1940; polished red glaze; $175–235.

San Juan Pueblo wedding vase, 9 inches high; New Mexico; c. 1920–1940; polished red glaze, shaped pouring spouts; $200–275.

San Juan Pueblo jar or olla, 8 inches high; New Mexico; c. 1930–1940; upper half polished red, lower half matt orange with simple geometric designs; scalloped rim; $100–175.

Santa Clara Pueblo pot, 7 inches high; New Mexico; c. 1940–1960; signed Margaret Tafoya; polished black, heavily carved in geometric designs; $2,500–3,000.

Santa Clara Pueblo bowl, 6 inches high; New Mexico; c. 1940–1960; signed Margaret Tafoya; polished black with four bear paw imprints; $1,700–2,100.

Santa Clara Pueblo wedding vase, 10 inches high; New Mexico; c. 1940–1960; polished red, upper body carved with simple geometric patterns; $750–1,250.

Santa Clara Pueblo wedding vase, 4 inches high; New Mexico; c. 1950–1970; polished black, upper body carved with simple geometric patterns; $65–95.

Santa Clara Pueblo bowl, 4 inches high; New Mexico; c. 1925–1945; red bowl with band of blue and gray triangles encircling neck; $100–175.

Bowl, earthenware with geometric decoration in red and black on white, 9 inches in diameter; Zuni; New Mexico; c. 1930–1940; $900–1,200.

Earthenware, Zuni; New Mexico; c. 1945–1955. Left to right: Bowl, black on orange-white, 5 inches in diameter; $75–100. Bowl, bird in black on white, 13 inches in diameter; $600–900. Vase in black and red on orange-white, 9 inches high; $165–245.

Earthenware, Acoma; New Mexico; c. 1950–1970. Left to right: Turtle form canteen, black on white, 7 inches in diameter; $325–400. Vase, red-orange and black on white, 9.5 inches high; $175–250. Bowl, brown and black on white, 3.5 inches high; $90–120.

Santa Clara Pueblo bowl with rope twist handle, 6 inches high; New Mexico; c. 1950–1970; polished black body deeply carved with geometric patterns; $150–250.

Santa Clara Pueblo bowl, 3 inches high; New Mexico; c. 1955–1975; polished black with simple scratch decoration; $55–75.

Cochiti Pueblo storyteller figure, 8 inches high; New Mexico; c. 1940–1960; by Helen Cordero; female figure covered with smaller figures of children, all in red and black on white; $600–750.

Cochiti Pueblo storyteller figure, 6.5 inches high; New Mexico; c. 1940–1960; male figure beating drum in red and blue on white; $350–550.

Cochiti Pueblo canteen, 8 inches in diameter; New Mexico; c. 1890–1900; applied frog figures, simple floral decoration in black on off-white, loops for carrying line; $1,750–2,500.

Cochiti Pueblo jar or olla, 7 inches high; New Mexico;l c. 1880–1900; sparse abstract floral pattern in black on off-white ground; $1,000–1,500.

Cochiti Pueblo pitcher, 8 inches high; New Mexico; c. 1965–1975; signed Laurencita Herrera; in form of duck-like bird, body details in brown on white, handle in red and black; $250–400.

Acoma Pueblo jar or olla, 14 inches high; New Mexico; c. 1900–1910; elaborate four-color decoration: red, black, and brown on white including parrot and flowers; $25,000–29,000.

Acoma Pueblo jar or olla, 12 inches high; New Mexico; c. 1920–1940; black and red decoration of flowers and parrots on white; $11,000–13,000.

Acoma Pueblo jar or olla, 9 inches high; New Mexico; c. 1910–1925; overall geometric decoration in red and black on white; $2,500–2,800.

Acoma Pueblo miniature bowl, 2.75 inches high; New Mexico; c. 1950–1960; overall geometric decoration in red and black on white; $75–100.

Acoma Pueblo bowl, 3.5 inches high; New Mexico; c. 1960–1970; paper label ACOMA/PUEBLO; simple geometric decoration in red and black on white; $125–175.

Acoma Pueblo, miniature turkey figurine 3 inches high; New Mexico; c. 1955–1965; signed M. Z. Chino (Marie Chino); red with touches of black; $50–75.

Acoma Pueblo jar or olla, 12 inches high; New Mexico; c. 1960–1970; signed M. Z. Chino; unglazed rough corrugated surface gives the impression piece is wrapped in rope; $175–275.

Bowl, earthenware, polished red on darker red dragon design, 10 inches in diameter; signed by Margaret Tafoya; Santa Clara Pueblo, New Mexico; c. 1960–1970; $2,000–2,700.

Plate, earthenware, polished black feather design on black, 11 inches in diameter; signed by Maria Martinez; San Ildefonso Pueblo, New Mexico; c. 1940–1950; $1,400–1,900.

Earthenware, polished black on black. Left: Bowl, 5 inches high; signed Jeanette Martinez; c. 1940–1955; $600–850. Right: Jar with feather design, 10 inches high; signed by Maria and Julian Martinez; c. 1934–1943; both San Ildefonso Pueblo, New Mexico; $1,800–2,400.

Hopi gourd form canteen with two handles, 4.5 inches high; Arizona; c. 1950–1965; signed Edith Nash; Kachina figure design in red and black on off-white; $150–250.

Hopi tile, 5 x 3.5 inches; Arizona; c. 1950–1965; signed Edith Nash; roadrunner bird design in red and black on off-white; $90–135.

Hopi bowl, 8 inches in diameter; Arizona; c. 1950–1965; signed Edith Nash; elaborate geometric design featuring central Kachina figure; $400–600.

Hopi bowl, 10 inches in diameter; Arizona; c. 1905–1915; by Nampeyo; abstract bird forms in red and black on off-white ground; $12,000–17,000.

Hopi seed jar, 11 inches in diameter; Arizona; c. 1905–1915; by Nampeyo; overall decoration of geometric pyra-

Bowl, earthenware, heavily carved, polished black on black, 6.5 inches in diameter; Santa Clara Pueblo, New Mexico; c. 1925–1940; $300–400.

mid-like forms in red and black on off-white ground; $9,000–12,000.

Hopi vase, 7 inches high; Arizona; c. 1950–1970; signed Jeanette (Nampeyo); abstract bird wing decoration in red and black on white; $200–300.

Hopi bowl, 4.5 inches high; Arizona; c. 1950–1970; signed Nellie Nampeyo; abstract bear claw design in red and black on white; $225–325.

Mohave jar or olla, 12 inches high; Arizona; c. 1970–1975; signed Elmer Gates; applied rattlesnake form curls around body decorated in diamond pattern, all in red on orange; $300–500.

Mohave jar or olla, 6 inches high; Arizona; c. 1960–1970; delicate stair-step design in red on orange ground; $200–300.

Mohave water bottle, 9 inches high; Arizona; c. 1960–1970; signed Annie Fields; three-spout bottle of humanlike form is decorated in abstract red designs on white ground; $350–500.

Mohave effigy bottle, 6 inches high; Arizona; c. 1960–1975; signed Annie Fields; vessel in form of frog with red details and yellow eyes, all on white slip ground; $275–375.

Earthenware. Left: Bowl, geometric black and red designs on white, 9.5 inches in diameter; Hopi; Arizona; c. 1940–1945; $400–550. Right: Bowl, red, tan, and cream, 5.5 inches high; San Juan Pueblo, New Mexico; c. 1960–1965; $125–175.

Earthenware, Maricopa; Arizona; c. 1950–1965. Left to right: Bowl, red and black, 8 inches in diameter; $125–175. Bowl, red, black, and white with "swastika" design, 8 inches in diameter; $165–235. Jar or olla, red and black, 7.5 inches high; $180–240.

Maricopa long-neck vase, 13 inches high; Arizona; c. 1950–1960; abstract Greek Key design in black runs around shoulder of polished red vessel; $90–140.

Maricopa wedding vase, 9 inches high; Arizona; c. 1965–1975; signed Grace Monahan; abstract Greek Key design in black encircles neck of polished red vessel; $200–275.

Maricopa bowl, 8 inches in diameter; Arizona; c. 1950–1970; band of white below rim is decorated with triangular pattern in black, all on polished red body; $150–250.

Maricopa bowl, 4 inches high; Arizona; c. 1960–1970; scalloped rim; polished red body decorated with concentric looping in black; $100–175.

Navajo jar or olla, 12 inches high; Arizona; c. 1940–1960; rough brown surface covered with piñon pitch for waterproofing; $50–80.

Navajo jar or olla, 10 inches high; Arizona; c. 1960–1970; signed Fae Tso; brown surface covered with piñon pitch and decorated with abstract sticklike human figures; $250–350.

Navajo jar or olla, 14 inches high; Arizona; c. 1940–1960; bulbous vessel, brown surface covered with piñon pitch and decorated with necklace of applied wheat-sheaf form tassels; $200–275.

Santa Ana Pueblo jar or olla, 11 inches high; New Mexico; c. 1870–1890; red base, upper body decorated with bands and geometric forms in red on white ground; $4,500–5,500.

Santo Domingo Pueblo bowl, 9 inches high; New Mexico; c. 1900–1920; overall abstract floral patterns in red on a white ground; $5,000–6,000.

Santo Domingo Pueblo bowl, 4 inches high; New Mexico; c. 1930–1940; bold floral decoration in black on white, red base; $250–325.

Santo Domingo Pueblo bowl, 5 inches high; New Mexico; c. 1920–1940; abstract arrow pattern in black on white, red base; $375–475.

Santo Domingo Pueblo jar or olla, 10 inches high; New Mexico; c. 1910–1920; red base, upper body decorated with abstract floral patterns in red and black on white ground; $1,600–2,100.

Tesuque Pueblo "rain god" figure, 9 inches high; New Mexico; c. 1910–1930; seated clay figure holding pot, touches of red and blue paint; $650–900.

Tesuque Pueblo "rain god" figure, 6 inches high; New Mexico; c. 1900–1920; seated clay figure covered with gray slip; $350–500.

Earthenware; San Ildefonso Pueblo, New Mexico. Left: Double-lobed canteen, black and red on cream, 6.5 inches high; c. 1950–1955; $200–275. Right: Effigy pitcher with deer and birds, black on red, 9.5 inches high; c. 1910–1920; $1,300–1,800.

Figure of rain god, earthenware, red and black on white, 5 inches high; Tesuque Pueblo, New Mexico; c. 1940–1950; $90–130.

Tesuque Pueblo bowl, 10 inches in diameter; New Mexico; c. 1900–1910; elaborate geometric decoration in black on white with abstract bird forms, inside and out; $8,500–10,000.

Tesuque Pueblo jar or olla, 8 inches high; New Mexico; c. 1880–1900; red base, upper body decorated with abstract floral motifs in black on white; $7,000–9,500.

Tesuque Pueblo bowl, 6 inches high; New Mexico; c. 1940–1950; applied human and animal figures on a gold-colored micaceous body; $140–190.

Taos Pueblo bowl, 12 inches in diameter; New Mexico; c. 1960–1970; signed Virginia Romero; glittering gold body color produced by use of micaceous (mica-bearing) clays; $175–250.

Bowl, earthenware with applied frog and snake figures, black and white on red, 5 inches high; probably Zuni; New Mexico; c. 1910–1930; $1,800–2,300.

Earthenware, Zuni; c. 1950–1970. Left to right: Melon-shaped musical instrument, red and cream, 6 inches long; $70–95. Pot with effigy figure handle, red, brown, and yellow, 8 inches long; $155–195. Turtle form canteen, red, black, and white, 5.5 inches long; $190–240.

Taos Pueblo jar or olla, 10 inches high, New Mexico, c. 1940–1960; applied frog figures on gold body produced by use of micaceous clays; $150–225.

Zia Pueblo jar or olla, 12 inches high; New Mexico; c. 1950–1960; by Juanito Pino; abstract brown border, two large birds in red and black, and red base on white; $750–950.

Zia Pueblo jar or olla, 13.5 inches high; New Mexico; c. 1935–1940; by Serafina Bell; large birds and scrollwork in red on white ground; $2,700–3,300.

Zia Pueblo jar or olla, 12 inches high; New Mexico; c. 1895–1905; red base, upper body decorated with abstract floral patterns and two well-executed deer; $8,000–10,000.

Zia Pueblo tile, 6 x 3.5 inches; New Mexico; c. 1940–1950;

Earthenware, Mohave; Arizona; c. 1890–1910; all with geometric designs in orange on tan. Left to right: Pitcher, 4.5 inches high; $150–225. Bowl, 10 inches in diameter; $300–425. Cup, 4 inches in diameter; $175–250.

Earthenware, all having golden surface produced by use of mica-bearing clays; New Mexico. Left to right: Porringer, 3.5 inches high; San Juan Pueblo; c. 1940–1950; $140–180. Candlestick, 4 inches high; Taos Pueblo; c. 1960–1970; $60–85. Cooking pot, 8 inches in diameter; San Lorenzo Pueblo; c. 1970–1975;

depiction of the roadrunner bird in red and black on white; $90–120.

Zia Pueblo canteen, 8 inches in diameter; New Mexico; c. 1910–1920; abstract floral designs in red and brown on white; loops for carrying line; $2,500–4,000.

Zuni jar or olla, 12.5 inches high; New Mexico; c. 1900–1920; elaborate overall geometric designs in red and black on white ground; $9,000–10,000.

Zuni pot, 10 inches high; New Mexico; c. 1910–1920; overall geometric decoration in red and black on white featuring deer with "heart-line" motif; $6,500–8,000.

Earthenware pictorial tiles, all in reddish brown and black on orange-white ground; Hopi; Arizona; c. 1935–1945. Left to right: Bird motif, 4 x 5.5 inches; $110–140. Kachina mask, 7 x 6.5 inches; $100–130. Kachina mask, 4 inches square; $90–130.

Zuni bowl, 4 inches high; New Mexico; c. 1930–1960; zigzag or lightning-bolt pattern in red and brown on an off-white ground; $125–175.

Zuni platter, 9 inches square; New Mexico; c. 1910–1920; rare terraced sides and central motif of froglike figure surrounded by snakes in brown on white ground; $2,300–2,900.

Zuni ovoid ceremonial pot, 8.5 inches high; New Mexico; c. 1860–1880, applied frog figures cling to shoulder of pot, neck and sides of which are decorated with abstract patterns in red on white ground; $13,000–14,000.

Native American Drawings and Paintings

━━◆━━━◆━━

Like almost all other peoples, Western Indians have long employed pictorial imagery as a means of communication. Petroglyphs, or rock carvings, have been found throughout the West, and these simple stick-figure representations are thought to have not only had religious significance but also to have been employed to mark territorial boundaries.

Though some petroglyph-bearing rocks have been removed and sold, it is clear that these important records are not a proper subject for the collector. Enthusiasts for Indian art, instead, seek out hide and ledger art, the majority of which has been produced by Plains and Pueblo Indians.

The former consists of drawings done in locally available vegetable colors, usually on buffalo hide robes, shields, tipis, tipi liners, and smaller items like knife sheaths and pipe bags. While to the untutored eye these may appear to be childlike scratchings, they actually are important pictorial records of tribal history: annual calendars or "winter counts," battle tales, buffalo hunts, or personal visions.

One may best understand them by realizing that each piece—shield, robe, etc.—may encompass several days' or even a year's events. The stick figures of men and animals are identified by clothing or other characteristics and the action is read from right to left, top to bottom.

The earliest-known hide drawing dates to 1805, and there are few authentic post-1900 examples due to extermination of the bison and to the plains wars, during which Indian villages and possessions were regularly burned or abandoned. Unfortunately, however, there are fakes. During the past decade numerous dubious pieces, primarily shields, robes, and smaller items, have appeared on the market. Collectors should always be suspicious of examples without a clear history, and especially those done either on buffalo hide which does not appear old or on material other than such buffalo hide.

Buffalo hide was also used, as was buckskin, in the making of small cases and bags with polychrome abstract decoration. These are often referred to as "parfleche," because all hair was removed from the hide prior to painting it. Unlike hide drawings, parfleche decoration usually has no documentary function.

As their sources of hide dried up, Indian artists turned to paper supplied by whites, usually in the form of small notebooks or ledgers (hence the collector term "ledger drawings") such as those used by students and storekeepers. They continued to employ their traditional artistic conventions, but figures became more fully developed, and ink, watercolors, pencil, and crayons replaced natural pigments and deer-hair brushes.

Though the earliest ledger drawings date to the 1820s, the great majority are from the post-1870 period. Unlike the case with hide paintings, quite a few of the ledger artists are known. The work of men such as Squint Eye, Old White Woman, and Roan Eagle will often bring prices in the thousands.

Unfortunately, fakes can be a problem here as well, particularly since the basic material, nineteenth-century ledger paper, is far more easily obtained than old buffalo hide. Collectors should always obtain a warranty of authenticity when buying these pieces.

Northwest Coast tribes also practiced the arts of drawing and painting, creating highly original abstract totemic representations of birds, animals, and men. These were painted in natural colors on ritual items such as blankets, capes, dance aprons, and hats, and resemble in content carvings from the same area. Unlike Plains Indian art, this work had no record-keeping function. Northwest coastal examples are rare and costly.

Price Listings—Native American Drawings and Paintings

Buffalo hide, polychrome pictorial decoration, battle scene with braves on horseback and afoot, wounded and dead, 74 x 85 inches; Sioux or Cheyenne; Central Plains; c. 1880–1900; $16,000–20,000.

Buffalo hide, polychrome pictorial decoration, group of warriors on horseback, 72 x 81 inches; Central Plains; c. 1890–1900; $9,000–12,000.

Elk hide, spectacular polychrome pictorial decoration showing buffalo hunt and celebration following the hunt, 70 x 77 inches; Central Plains; c. 1870–1890; $40,000–55,000.

Buffalo robe, polychrome decoration of hunting scene with Indians on horseback, deer, and bison, 60 x 50 inches; Plains Indians; c. 1880–1900; $14,000–19,000.

Buffalo robe, child's size, polychrome abstract geometric decoration, primarily rectangles, 46 x 36 inches; Northern Plains; c. 1890–1900; $8,000–9,500.

Poncho, buffalo hide, polychrome decoration representing deities and suns in abstract geometric forms, 46 x 31 inches; Apache; c. 1870–1890; $12,000–17,000.

Tipi liner (partial), buffalo hide decorated in red, green, black, and yellow with bands of complex geometric designs, 48 x 59 inches; Northern Plains; c. 1860–1880; $11,000–15,000.

Miniature tipi, buckskin painted with geometric devices including quartered circles in red, yellow, green, and brown, 30 inches high; Central Plains; c. 1900–1920; $700–950.

Miniature tipi, buckskin with sparse decoration in red, brown, and black of bison and deer, 27 inches high; Central Plains; c. 1890–1910; $2,200–2,900.

Miniature tipi, cowhide with polychrome images of sun and moon and buffalo, 12 inches high; Central Plains; c. 1930–1945; $65–95.

Shield, buffalo hide painted green and yellow with group of circles in white, 22 inches in diameter; Jemez Pueblo, New Mexico; c. 1860–1865; from the William Bell Collection; $14,000–19,000.

Shield, cowhide decorated with sunburst design in red, pink, yellow, green, and black, 20.5 inches in diameter; Pueblo; Arizona or New Mexico; c. 1880–1890; $3,000–4,000.

Shield, cowhide with bold abstract representation in red and black of bear and bear tracks within geometric grid, 19 inches in diameter; Kiowa; Oklahoma; c. 1900–1909; $30,000–45,000.

Shield, buffalo hide, polychrome-painted with large central eaglelike bird, eagle feather attachment, 25 inches in diameter; Sioux; Dakotas; c. 1880–1890; said to have been found at Wounded Knee; $80,000–90,000.

Shield, buffalo hide, polychrome-painted representation of

fight between Sioux and Crow warriors, 22 inches in diameter; Sioux; South Dakota; c. 1850–1870; $60,000–75,000.

Shield, cowhide miniature, polychrome-painted with image of Indian on horseback, 9 inches in diameter; Plains Indians; c. 1930–1950; $75–100.

Drum, buffalo hide and wood, drumhead decorated with white cross against red and green ground, 14 inches in diameter; Northern Plains; c. 1880–1900; $1,200–1,600.

Drum, cowhide and wood, decoration of two polychrome Kachina-like figures on drumhead, 10.5 inches in diameter; Pueblo; Arizona or New Mexico; c. 1890–1910; $1,700–2,500.

Drum, cowhide and wood, polychrome decoration of eagle on one side, tipi on the other, 9 inches in diameter; Plains Indians; c. 1940–1950; $65–90.

Drum, cowhide and wood, polychrome decoration, bust of Indian on one side, abstract geometric drawing on the other, 8 inches in diameter; Plains Indians; c. 1950–1970; $50–75.

Parfleche case, buffalo hide, abstract geometric decoration, primarily linked diamonds, in blue, brown, red, and black, 16 inches long; Crow; Northern Plains; c. 1870–1890; $9,500–10,500.

Drum, rawhide over hardwood frame, 11 inches in diameter; California; c. 1930–1940; $700–950.

Parfleche container, rawhide painted in geometric designs, red, black, blue, and yellow, 16 x 25 inches; Northern Plains Indians; c. 1880–1900; $1,800–2,200.

Parfleche berry bag, buckskin with checkered red and green pattern, 12 x 16 inches; Sioux; Dakotas; c. 1880–1900; $2,200–2,600.

Parfleche envelope form carrying case, buffalo hide decorated with vertical bands alternating with elongated diamonds, all in red, pink, yellow, and blue, 20 x 12 inches; Northern Plains; c. 1890–1910; $3,500–4,300.

Parfleche envelope form carrying case, buffalo hide decorated with bands of diamonds and arrowheads in blue, pink, brown, and green, 18 x 12 inches; Cheyenne; Dakotas, c. 1895–1905; $2,000–2,700.

Parfleche envelope form carrying case, buckskin decorated in pink, blue, and green with simple rectangular designs, 12 x 8 inches; Central Plains; c. 1900–1910; $600–850.

Dance blanket, woven wool and cedar bark, polychrome abstract decoration featuring "diving whale" motif, 41 x 25 inches; Tlingit; Alaska; c. 1880–1890; $18,000–22,000.

Dance blanket, woven wool and cedar bark, abstract decoration with "Sea-Grizzly" motif in yellow, white, black, and green, 60 x 43 inches; Tlingit; Alaska; c. 1890–1900; $15,000–20,000.

Dance blanket, woven wool with unusual abstract design featuring repetition of Killer Whale motif in yellow, white, black, and green, 64 x 54 inches; Tlingit; Alaska; c. 1920–1930; $17,000–22,000.

Cape, woven cedar bark, abstract decoration in red, pink, and black with Killer Whale designs and stylized human figure, 44 x 30 inches; Northwest Coat; c. 1870–1890; $20,000–25,000.

Cape, woven wool, abstract decoration in yellow, white, green, and black with "Sea-Grizzly" motif, 32 x 40 inches; Tlingit; Alaska; 1938; $7,000–9,500.

Harpooner's cape, woven sea grass with painting in red, green, and black of two totemic birds, 47 x 35 inches; Kwakiutl; British Columbia; c. 1880–1900; $11,000–16,000.

Tunic, woven wool with abstract representations of birds and animals in yellow, white, green, and black, 51 x 23 inches; Tlingit; Alaska; c. 1900–1910; $18,000–22,000.

House mat, cedar bark woven in a checkered pattern, painted in red and black with horned totemic figures, 44 x 21 inches; Northwest Coast; c. 1900–1920; $6,700–7,800.

Drum, buckskin and wood, drumhead decorated with painted representation of totemic bird figure, 11 inches in diameter; Northwest Coast; c. 1900–1920; $4,500–6,000.

Ledger drawing, watercolor and ink on paper, many Indians gathered in council with the caption, "These men are going to read the law. They are all Arapahoes," approx. 8 x 14 inches; Arapaho; c. 1880–1890; $11,000–14,000.

Ledger drawing, watercolor and ink on lined paper, hunting scene, approx. 6 x 8 inches; by the well-known artist Squint Eye; Cheyenne; 1887; $6,000–8,000.

Ledger drawing, watercolor and ink on lined paper, hunting scene with artist and his friend Col. Z. W. Bliss of the U. S. Army, approx. 6 x 8 inches; Squint Eye; Cheyenne; 1887; $7,500–9,000.

Ledger drawing, pencil and crayon on lined paper, birds and animals, approx. 6 x 8 inches; Lakota Sioux; c. 1880–1900; $2,500–3,000.

Ledger drawing, watercolor and ink on lined paper, of Indian chasing buffalo, approx. 6 x 8 inches; by Old White Woman; Cheyenne; c. 1880–1890; $4,500–5,500.

Ledger drawing, watercolor, ink, and pencil, of Indian brave taking part in the Sun Dance ceremony, approx. 6 x 8 inches; Cheyenne; c. 1880–1900; $1,800–2,200.

Ledger drawing, watercolor, of a mounted Indian brave, approx. 6 x 8 inches; by Roan Eagle; Sioux; c. 1890–1895; $3,000–4,000.

Ledger drawing, Indian courting scene with young man and woman, watercolor and crayon, approx, 6 x 8 inches; Old White Woman; Cheyenne; c. 1880–1890; $4,000–5,000.

Native American Sculpture

For most collectors of Western Indian artifacts, the term sculpture is associated with the brightly colored Kachina figures produced by the Hopi people of Arizona. However, some of the most sophisticated and, today, most expensive carving was done by the Northwest Coast tribes whose extraordinarily sophisticated work rivals the finest sculpture of Europe or Africa. A limited amount of collectible sculpture was also produced by the Plains Indians and in California.

Reproductions can be a problem in this field. The Hopi continue to make Kachina figures both for ceremonial use and for sale to tourists and collectors. While technically these are not "reproductions," some examples for the tourist trade are of inferior quality. Moreover, "look-alikes," often of plastic, have been produced in Taiwan.

Though it is not likely that many will be fooled by these, their presence tends to degrade the whole field.

Contemporary Northwest Coast sculpture is often of high quality; however, the collector should be aware of Japanese-made reproductions, primarily of animal form bowls, which have been entering the country. These are hand-carved and decorated in the same manner as authentic pieces. They look good and can fool the unwary.

Kachinas

Kachinas are small, doll-like figures, 6 to 18 inches high, carved from cottonwood, brightly painted, and often adorned with beads, feathers, yarn, straw, and fabric. They have been made since at least the mid-1800s by men of the various Hopi villages located in northeastern Arizona. To the Hopi they represent the hundreds of supernatural beings and ancestors which they (and some Zuni) regard as capable of controlling weather, crops, and the lives of men and women.

In this context Kachina figures are employed to instruct women and girls (who are not initiated into the various Kachina cults) in their religion. They are not, as some whites think, toys.

The earliest Kachina figures, c. 1860–1880, were flat with featureless torsos and heads carved in the half round. They were lightly colored in two or three hues. Over the years the modern, three-dimensional form with lifelike pose, great detail, and polychrome surface has evolved. While classic pieces from the 1880–1920 period tend to bring the highest prices, modern examples by well-known carvers may sell for thousands of dollars.

Kachina, Hopi; Eototo, or "father of the Kachinas," carved cottonwood, traces of polychrome decoration, 6 inches high; c. 1870–1910; $1,000–1,500.

Some Kachinas are hard to distinguish, but most have distinct features, such as dress and accessories (bows, drums, etc.), which enable the collector to recognize them. Among the better known are Chaveyo with his dragonlike teeth and feather headdress, the black-and-white-striped Hano clowns, the Koyemsi or Mudheads with their brown gingerbread-man bodies, and the beaked Mongwa or Great Horned Owl. It should be noted, though, that carvers employ great artistic license, and a Chaveyo created by one may bear little resemblance to that made by his neighbor.

Price Listings—Kachinas

Wakas or Cow, carved cottonwood with highly detailed polychrome-painted body and characteristic forward curving horns, 14.5 inches high; Hopi; c. 1895–1905; $7,000–8,000.

Lakone Mana, carved cottonwood with polychrome-painted body, a single horn at side of head, and painted tableta or headdress, 12 inches high; Hopi; c. 1890–1910; $3,500–4,200.

Palhik Mana or Corn-Grinding Maiden, carved cottonwood with large geometric tableta or crest across head and shoulders, 11 inches high; Hopi; c. 1895–1905; $2,300–3,000.

Tukwinong or Cumulus Cloud, shallow carved polychrome-painted cottonwood body with two-tiered headdress resembling banks of clouds, 13 inches high; Hopi; c. 1870–1890; $6,000–8,000.

Patung or Squash, cottonwood body carved and painted with stripes to resemble a gourd, 16 inches high; Hopi; c. 1960–1980; $200–300.

Snake Dancer, carved cottonwood with polychrome-painted body, outstretched arms, and snake held crosswise in mouth, 8 inches high; Hopi; c. 1900–1920; $1,500–2,100.

Eototo or "father" of the Kachinas, carved cottonwood, predominantly white body and conical mask, skirt with polychrome geometric trim, doughnutlike ruff around neck, 12 inches high; Hopi; by carver Jimmy Kewanwytewa; c. 1960; $2,000–2,5000.

Koyemsi or Mudhead, carved cottonwood with brown-painted body, knob on top of head, and cookie-cutter eyes and mouth, 5 inches high; Hopi; c. 1920–1930; $450–600.

Kachina, Hopi, possibly Hemis; carved cottonwood, polychrome paint, feathers, and cloth, 9.5 inches high; c. 1920–1930; $1,200–1,600.

Kachina, Zuni; bear dancer, carved cottonwood, polychrome paint, dyed wool, and vegetable fiber, 17 inches high; c. 1910–1925, $1,700–2,400.

Koyemsi or Mudhead, carved cottonwood with brown body, black skirt, rattle in one hand, feather in the other, cookie-cutter eyes and mouth, 12 inches high; Hopi; c. 1920–1930; $600–850.

Koyemsi or Double Mudheads, two figures, one on the other's shoulders, carved cottonwood with brown bodies, white scarves, and black skirts, cookie-cutter eyes and mouth, 15 inches high; Hopi; c. 1900–1910; $4,000–5,500.

Paiyakyamu or Hano clown, carved cottonwood with black-and-white-striped body, two short horns on head, brass bells in ears, 8 inches high; from important Fred Harvey Collection; Hopi; c. 1890–1900; $5,500–7,000.

Paiyakyamu or Hano clown, carved cottonwood with black-and-white-striped body, long horns on top of head, 7 inches high; Hopi. c. 1920–1930; $350–500.

Paiyakyamu or Hano clown, carved cottonwood with black-and-white-striped body, wearing cloth hat and wrists wrapped in woolen yarn. Body marked "Peace" and "Clown Power," 11 inches high; Hopi; dated 1971; $100–150.

Huhuwa or Cross-Legged, carved cottonwood with polychrome body, legs carved to twist across each other;

wears cloth cape and skirt, 11 inches high; Hopi; from important Fred Harvey Collection; c. 1890–1900; $3,000–4,000.

Mongwa or Great Horned Owl, carved cottonwood with polychrome body; owl face and beak surrounded by owl feathers; carries spear in hand, 20 inches high; Hopi; c. 1950–1960; $1,200–1,600.

Mastop (Hopi fertility figure), carved cottonwood with polychrome body, painted hand print on chest, cloth skirt, straw collar, holds black and white rod in hand, 13 inches high; Hopi; c. 1960–1965; $350–450.

Soyok Wuhti or Ogre Woman, carved cottonwood body wrapped in cotton dress, straw hair with feathers, protruding rodlike mouth, carries stick in each hand, 11 inches high; Hopi; c. 1920–1930; $900–1,300.

Chaveyo or Ogre Man, carved cottonwood with polychrome body, protruding lips and big teeth, feather headdress, carries bow in one hand, 15 inches high; Hopi; c. 1955–1965; $750–950.

Wiharu or White Ogre, carved cottonwood with polychrome body, protruding ducklike mouth and fringed crest, large, bulbous eyes, wears canvas tunic and leggings, 10 inches high; Hopi; c. 1935–1945; $225–300.

Kachinas, both in carved cottonwood and polychrome paint, cloth, and feathers. Left: Wakas or cow Kachina, Zuni; 13 inches high; c. 1915–1925; $1,300–1,800. Right; Citoto; Hopi; 12.5 inches high; c. 1920–1930; $850–1,250.

Group of miniature Kachina dancers, Hopi; Sakw-A'Hote, carved cottonwood with polychrome paint, cloth, and feathers, 4 inches high; c. 1925–1935; $450–650.

Angwusnasomtaka or Crow Mother, carved conical cottonwood body painted in geometric designs, steplike tableta or crest on each side of head, 15 inches high; Hopi; from important Vorhees Collection; c. 1900–1910; $6,000–7,500.

Angwusnasomtaka or Crow Mother, carved cottonwood with polychrome caped body and flaring crest protruding vertically from each side of head, sash at waist, 10 inches high; Hopi; c. 1960–1970; $450–650.

Kwikwilyaka or Mocking, carved cottonwood with conelike head on which is balanced bundle of sticks, protruding eyes and mouth are striped, carries can in one hand, 8 inches high; Hopi; c. 1955–1960; $225–300.

Aholi, carved cottonwood with polychrome-painted body, similarly decorated cloth cape, conelike head surmounted by feathers; carries basket with grain of corn and feathered staff, 19 inches high; Hopi; c. 1955–1965; $750–1,000.

Heheya, carved cottonwood with polychrome-painted human form body (rare with Kachinas) clad in short tunic; cut tin earrings on protruding ears; carries a twine lariat, 10 inches high; Hopi; c. 1920–1930; $300–450.

Chakwaina Mana or Warrior, carved cottonwood with polychrome body clad in cloth skirt, tunic, and cape; feather headdress; carries swordlike shaft, 11 inches high; Hopi; c. 1900–1910; $1,400–1,900.

Contemporary carvings in the Kachina tradition, both of polychrome-painted carved cottonwood and from San Juan Pueblo, New Mexico; c. 1970–1975. Left: Warrior, 6.5 inches high; $125–175. Right: So-called "water maiden," 8 inches high; $150–200.

Kokopelli or Erotic, carved cottonwood with polychrome body; hump back, helmet form head with pointed stylus-like nose and large feather in hair; may carry a flute, 13 inches high; Hopi; c. 1895–1900; $1,200–1,600.

Siky A'Hote or Yellow, carved cottonwood with body primarily yellow in hue and having headdress with long train of feathers; carries swordlike shaft, 12 inches high; Hopi; c. 1930–1935; $700–950.

Sivu-I-Quil Taka or Pot-Carrying Man, carved cottonwood with polychrome body; long cloth coat, flaring ears with tasseled danglers; carries black cooking pot on back, 11 inches high; Hopi; c. 1890–1910; $1,800–2,500.

Nuvak'Chin Mana or Snow, carved cottonwood with polychrome body; figure kneels before gourd resonator while drawing animal bone across notched stick, 8 inches high; Hopi; c. 1940–1945; $275–350.

Masau'u or God of Underworld, carved conical cottonwood body with checkerboard-pattern skirt and vest decorated in geometric patterns; cookie-cutter eyes and mouth, 14 inches high; Hopi; c. 1965–1970; $200–250.

Tawa or Sun God, carved cottonwood with polychrome body, elaborately dressed and painted; head completely surrounded by circle of eagle feathers, 13 inches high; Hopi; c. 1960–1970; $400–550.

Aholi or Germination God, carved cottonwood with polychrome body; thimblelike hood surmounted by eagle feather headdress; carries symbolic leaves and seeds, 10 inches high; Hopi; c. 1940–1945; $600–850.

Northwest Coast Carving

The tribes of the Northwest coastal area from Washington to Alaska have produced a wide range of remarkable sculpture. Best known, perhaps, are the gigantic totem poles carved from cedar trees and painted in various colors. But many other forms have been made including dance masks, so-called crest hats, rattles, pipes, various utensils for cooking, hunting, and fighting; and for the tourist trade, such items as chess pieces and Western-style spoons, forks, and jewelry.

Most of these, especially the larger examples, are carved from wood, the preferred material being native cedar. However, many smaller and lovely items have been made from argillite, a shiny black slatelike stone mined and utilized only by the Haida of the Queen Charlotte Islands, off the coast of British Columbia. Other groups, whose work in wood, horn, and silver is highly prized, include the Tlingit, Kwakiutl, Salish, and Makah.

Though examples from the eighteenth century have survived, most work available to collectors dates to after 1880, when an influx of white traders, miners, and missionaries created a new and expanding market for local carvers. This industry continues today, and the work of well-known contemporary Northwest Coast artists may command prices in the thousands.

Northwest coastal carving is based on the incorporation into the piece of highly stylized representations of birds, fish, and animals regarded as totems or clan and

Pipe bowl, carved argillite or black slate, 4.5 inches long; Haida or Tlingit; Northwest coastal area; c. 1860–1870; $5,500–7,000.

individual protectors. These are often painted in brilliant colors—reds, blues, blacks, and greens being particularly favored. Though some tribes preferred certain images and styles, the exchange of motifs over the years often makes positive attribution difficult.

As is true in many other areas, separating recent work from that made before 1940 can be a problem. As always, one must look for signs of appropriate wear and use. Also, as mentioned, Japanese-made reproductions of at least one classic type, the frog form food bowl, are known. Though these employ the same style of carving and decorative inlays in abalone and operculum shells as the originals, they may be distinguished by a thinnish paint layer, lighter wood, and total lack of authentic wear.

Price Listings—Northwest Coast Carvings

Totem pole, carved polychrome-painted cedar featuring images of eagle and other birds, bear, and man, 6 inches high; Haida; Queen Charlotte Islands; c. 1880–1910; $9,000–12,000.

Totem pole, carved polychrome-painted cedar with hawk,

eagle, and human motifs, 3 inches high; Northwest Coast; c. 1910–1930; from Andy Warhol Collection; $5,000–6,500.

Totem pole, carved argillite with various animal and bird totemic figures, 30 inches high; Haida, Queen Charlotte Island; attributed to Charles Edenshaw; c. 1900–1910; $8,000–9,000.

Totem pole, carved argillite with totemic figures including bear and raven, 8 inches high; Northwest Coast; c. 1960–1970; $150–225.

Totem pole, crudely carved and polychrome-painted with bear, eagle, and other totemic figures, 5 inches high; Northwest Coast; c. 1960–1980; $30–55.

Dance mask, carved cedar stained brown and white, in the form of stylized human face with tongue lolling out, 9 inches high; Northwest Coast; c. 1900–1920; $2,000–2,800.

Dance mask, carved and polychrome-painted cedar in the form of a bear or raccoon with long nose, 11 inches long; Kwakiutl; British Columbia; c. 1890–1910; $3,400–3,900.

Dance mask, carved and polychrome-painted cedar in the form of a mosquito, 30 inches long; Northwest Coast; by Francio Home; 1979; $1,000–1,400.

Dance mask, carved and polychrome-painted cedar in the form of an eagle, 26 inches long; Kwakiutl; British Columbia; by Peter Moon; c. 1970–1980; $1,300–1,800.

Portrait mask, wood, carved and painted in red, white, blue, and black with leather thongs, 7.5 inches high; Bella Coola; western Canada; c. 1900–1910; $2,500–3,000.

Speaker's staff or "Talking Stick," carved and polychrome-painted cedar, 38 inches long, Nootka; British Columbia; by Joe David; c. 1980–1985; $600–750.

Club for ceremonial use, carved and polychrome-painted cedar root, knob in form of man's head, shaft decorated with stylized frog, 16 inches long; Northwest Coast; c. 1970–1980; $350–500.

Club for ceremonial use, carved from whalebone in form of killer whale with abalone shell eyes, 14 inches long; Salish; British Columbia; c. 1890–1910; $800–950.

Fisherman's club, argillite, carved in the shape of a fish, 13 inches long; Northwest Coast; c. 1910–1920; $1,000–1,500.

Fishhook, wood, carved to represent a halibut, wrapped in twine, 5 inches long; Tlingit; Alaska; c. 1880–1900; $750–1,000.

Fishhook, wood and horn, abstract totemic carving, wrapped in twine, 6 inches long; Haida; Queen Charlotte Islands; c. 1870–1890; $650–950.

Shaman's rattle, carved cedar in the form of a wolf, remnants of red and black paint, 9 inches long; Northwest Coast; c. 1880–1910; $4,500–6,000.

Shaman's rattle, carved and polychrome cedar in the form of a duck, 11 inches long; Nootka; British Columbia; c. 1900–1920; $1,800–2,600.

Shaman's rattle, carved and polychrome-painted cedar in the form of a raven, 10 inches long; Haida; Queen Charlotte Island, c. 1970–1980; $600–850.

Shaman's rattle, carved and polychrome-painted cedar; two-faced, one side is human, the other that of the sacred sparrow hawk; 12 inches long; Northwest Coast; c. 1950–1970; $900–1,300.

Shaman's wand, overall carving with polychrome paint; totemic figures include octopus, kingfisher, and raven, 22 inches long; Northwest Coast; c. 1890–1910; $5,500–7,000.

Souvenir spoon, engraved silver with stylized loon handle, 5.5 inches long; Tlingit; Alaska; c. 1920–1930; $80–100.

Souvenir spoon, engraved silver with stylized sea turtle handle, 5 inches long; Haida; Queen Charlotte Islands; c. 1930–1940; $70–90.

Souvenir spoon, engraved silver with stylized eagle and bear

Atlatl or spear thrower, carved argillite or black slate, 7.5 inches long; Northwest coastal area; c. 1870–1890; $3,000–4,000.

handle, 6 inches long; Tlingit, Alaska; c. 1920–1930; $90–110.

Souvenir spoon, engraved silver with stylized animal designs on handle, 5 inches long; Tlingit; Alaska; c. 1920–1930; $70–90.

Spoon, mountain goat horn, curving handle carved with totemic figures, 9 inches long; Haida; Queen Charlotte Islands; c. 1880–1900; $3,800–4,500.

Spoon, mountain goat horn, curving handle inlaid with bits of abalone shell, 8.5 inches long; Northwest Coast; c. 1900–1920; $300–450.

Spoon for berries, cedar, in a paddle form, with flat bowl decorated with totemic carving, 12 inches long; Tsimshian; British Columbia; c. 1900–1910; $700–950.

Comb, carved cedar with effigy figures of bird atop frog, polychrome-painted, 6.5 inches high; Northwest Coast; c. 1870–1900; $3,000–3,500.

Comb, carved horn with abalone shell inlay and incised totemic design filled in red, 5 inches high; Northwest Coast; c. 1860–1880; $800–1,300.

Chest, carved polychrome-painted cedar with highly abstract animal and bird images, rare kerfed construction; Tlingit; Alaska; c. 1890–1900; $18,000–22,000.

Chest, carved polychrome-painted cedar with highly abstract animal and bird images, six board construction, Kwakiutl; British Columbia; c. 1880–1890; $12,000–15,000.

Chest, carved and painted argillite, body incised with totemic figures including bear, mounted on frog form feet and top with bear form finial; Haida; attributed to Charles Edenshaw; c. 1900–1920; $16,000–20,000.

Bowl, carved cedar, incised with complex abstract totemic animal and bird figures and inlaid with cowrie shells, 8 inches high; Tlingit or Haida; Alaska; c. 1870–1890; $27,000–32,000.

Bowl, carved cedar incised with stylized totemic figures, 5 inches high; Haida; Queen Charlotte Islands; c. 1940–1960; $275–375.

Platter, carved argillite, inlaid border of triangular bits of ivory; two representations of the Killer Whale, oval, 14 inches long; Haida; Queen Charlotte Islands; c. 1910–1920; $3,750–4,500.

Food bowl, oval with knoblike handles at each end; carved cedar with stylized bear motif, inset with abalone and cowrie shells, 16 inches long; Tlingit; Alaska; c. 1900–1920; $3,000–4,000.

Food bowl, oblong box form, kerfed construction; carved cedar with stylized totemic figures, rim inset with cowrie shells, 17 inches long; Kwakiutl; British Columbia; c. 1880–1900; $7,500–9,000.

Food bowl, carved and painted cedar in the form of a puffin with head, beak, and tail; body hollowed out as receptacle, 18 inches long; Northwest Coast; c. 1920–1930; $1,800–2,600.

Food bowl, carved and painted cedar in the form of a bear with head and feet; body hollowed out as receptacle, 13 inches long; Northwest Coast; c. 1920–1940; $1,500–2,200.

Blunderbuss gun, iron and wood of English make, handle carved in complex totemic designs (rare form), 30 inches long; Northwest Coast; c. 1830–1860; $35,000–40,000.

Canoe paddle, carved and polished cedar, lower blade covered with abstract totemic figures, 55 inches long; Haida; Queen Charlotte Islands; c. 1890–1910; $4,500–6,000.

Pendant, cedar, carved in the form of a stylized whale, unpainted, 3 inches long; Northwest Coast; c. 1850–1870; $400–650.

Pendant, carved whalebone totemic figure, incised lines filled with red pigment, 4 inches long; Northwest Coast; c. 1840–1860; $750–950.

Pipe, carved cedar in the form of a bear, painted black and inlaid with bits of abalone shell, 4.5 inches long; Tlingit; Alaska; c. 1890–1910; $2,500–3,000.

Dagger or dirk, handle of carved bone with stylized totemic figures, blade of copper, 10.5 inches long; Tlingit; Alaska; c. 1900–1910; $3,000–4,000.

Figure of female shaman, carved brown argillite, finely sculpted and detailed, 10 inches high; Haida; Queen Charlotte Islands; attributed to Charles Edenshaw; c. 1880–1900; $15,000–19,000.

Figure of white ship's officer, carved argillite, finely carved and detailed, 16 inches high; Haida; Queen Charlotte Islands; c. 1850–1870; $30,000–35,000.

Puppet, carved and painted wooden head, hands, and feet; cloth body, 20 inches high; Kwakiutl Tokwit; c. 1865–1875: extremely rare ceremonial piece; $23,000–27,000.

Other Western Carving

Best known among the limited sculptural forms produced by other Western groups are the items associated with California and the Plains area. From the latter came the carved catlinite pipes, popularly termed "peace pipes," which are seen in many nineteenth century portraits of Indian notables. Catlinite, or red slate, an attractive and easily carved material, was mined in Minnesota and traded

among Native Americans throughout the West. The traditional T-shaped pipe bowl, sometimes inlaid in pewter, was
and still is made both for tribal use and for sale to tourists.
Finer examples with carved figures bring the highest
prices. Few pipe bowls can be identified, even as to tribe, so
universal was the style. It should also be noted that pipe
stems, when present, are almost always replacements. An
early or original stem embellished with feathers or beadwork substantially enhances the value of a pipe bowl.

There are relatively few other examples of Plains or
Southwestern carving: a few household utensils, tools,
weapons, and the like.

Indians of northern California also produced some
interesting work, primarily in bone and stone. Best known
are the animal form effigy figures termed "Slave Killers,"
which were made by several tribal groups in the area.

Price Listings—Other Western
Carvings

Pipe bowl, elbow form of carved catlinite, inlaid with pewter
in geometric patterns, 4.5 inches long; Northern Plains;
c. 1860–1875; $300–450.

Pipe bowl, elbow form of carved catlinite, bowl in form of sitting female figure with trade bead eyes and silver bracelet
on arm (very rare form), 3.75 inches long; Eastern Plains;
c. 1850–1870; $15,000–18,000.

Pipe bowl, elbow form of carved catlinite with carved
cottonwood stem, 4 inches long, Southern Plains;
c. 1880–1900; $140–190.

Pipe bowl, T form of carved catlinite with old rope-carved
cottonwood stem, 5.5 inches long; Northern Plains;
c. 1880–1910; $400–550.

Pipe bowl, T form of carved catlinite with two incised bands

Plains Indians carvings, top to bottom: War club of shaped and polished stone with beadwork-decorated handle, 19 inches long; c. 1880–1910; $550–750. Pipe tomahawk, carved catlinite or red sandstone with pewter bands, 12 inches long; c. 1890–1900; $400–550. Pipe, carved catlinite with replacement carved wooden stem, 21 inches long; c. 1880–1900; $275–350.

and replaced hardwood stem, 4.5 inches long; Northern Plains; c. 1900–1920; $125–175.

Pipe bowl, T form of carved catlinite, 4 inches long; Northern Plains, c. 1900–1920; $100–150.

Pipe bowl, T form of carved catlinite; early stem wrapped in beadwork and adorned with feathers, 6 inches long; Northern Plains; c. 1870–1890; $350–500.

Fan, carved pine, round with hourglass-shaped handle, back covered with painted representations of dancing Indians and drum, 8 inches in diameter; Northern Plains; c. 1890–1900; $2,800–3,600.

Dance board, oblong leather disk surmounted by carved pine representation of horse head with horsehair mane, entire piece studded with brass tacks, 9 inches high; Sioux, Nebraska; c. 1870–1880; $3,000–4,500.

War club, hardwood carved in the shape of human head with long handle; eyes and mouth highlighted in red, eagle feather attached by leather band, 13 inches long; Sioux; Dakota Territory; c. 1860–1880; $2,800–3,600.

Rattle, gourd covered with hide embellished with simple diamond pattern, shaped wooden handle, 9 inches long; Central Plains; c. 1880–1900; $250–325.

Rattle, gourd painted in abstract geometric design and

mounted on shaped stick, attached eagle feather, 9.5 inches long; Pueblo Indians; Arizona or New Mexico; c. 1900–1910; $300–400.

Fetish in the form of a bear carved from alabaster, 4.5 inches long; Pueblo Indians; New Mexico; c. 1930–1940; $60–85.

Fetish in the form of a bear carved from brown slate with fragment of turquoise attached by rawhide thong to back, 3 inches long; Pueblo Indians; New Mexico; c. 1920–1940; $120–160.

Mask, pine carved in the form of human face crowned by coiled rattlesnake, so-called booger type, 10 inches high; Cherokee; Oklahoma; c. 1890–1910; $6,000–7,500.

Mask, pine carved in the form of human face with horsehair and deerskin wig, incised teeth painted white, booger type, 9 inches high; Cherokee; Oklahoma; c. 1900–1910; $4,500–6,000.

Slave Killer stone, carved black slate in the form of an animal with long tail, 14 inches long; northwestern California; c. 1860–1880; $550–700.

Slave Killer stone, carved dark brown slate in the form of an animal with long tail, 12 inches long; northwestern California; c. 1860–1880; $400–600.

Slave Killer stone, miniature, carved black slate in the form of an animal with long tail, 3.5 inches long; northwestern California; c. 1880–1900; $250–400.

Spoon, carved elk horn, oblong bowl, with handle having openwork and pyramidal type carving, 9 inches long; Yurok-Hupa; California; c. 1870–1890; $275–350.

Spoon, carved elk horn, oval bowl, shaped handle with edges decorated with incised V shapes, 8.5 inches long; Yurok-Hupa; California; c. 1870–1890; $250–325.

Spoon, carved pine, oval bowl, handle terminating in round ball, 7 inches long; Yurok-Hupa; California; c. 1880–1910; $150–225.

Mush paddle, carved pine in paddle form with spool-like collar at midpoint, 40 inches long; northwestern California; c. 1870–1890; $300–450.

Mush paddle, carved pine in paddle form with handle in shape of elongated stepped triangles, 32 inches long; northwestern California; c. 1860–1880; $350–500.

Bow, shaped yew wood with glued-on sinew backing, front covered with overall polychrome geometric decoration consisting of diamonds, triangles, etc., 51 inches long; Yurok-Hupa; California; c. 1860–1880; $2,200–2,800.

Bow, shaped yew wood with glued-on sinew backing, front decorated with diagonal striping in red on black, 40 inches long; Yurok-Hupa type; California; c. 1880–1890; $700–900.

Southwestern Indian Weavings

>———<

Among the highest priced of all Native American collectibles are the woolen blankets, rugs, and other pieces woven by the Navajo of New Mexico. The variety of forms and, particularly, of patterns among these, and the effect of these factors on price, can be confusing to the collector. The subject is too complex to be dealt with here, and anyone interested in the field should refer to one of the several excellent books on the subject.

Generally, however, the most costly textiles are the wearing blankets from the so-called Classic Period, c. 1800–1880. These include the famous Chief's blankets (not made for Chiefs but costly enough so only they could probably afford them!). These were made in three designs referred to as "phases." First Phase blankets had broad horizontal bands (unlike prior and later Navajo blankets, these were broader than they were long) in black and white alternating with narrower ones patterned in red, brown, or blue. In Second Phase textiles, bars or ribbon-like decorations were added within the patterned bands, and in the Third Phase the entire banded surface was overlaid with large terraced diamond or triangle patterns in groups of three.

Another important category includes the so-called "Eye Dazzlers" of the 1880–1920 period: blankets which were more brightly colored (thanks to the availability of commercial aniline dyes, referred to as "Germantown" because that community was a major dye-making center) and characterized by various diamond patterns. The best of these have the quality of Op Art, and they often bring high prices at auction.

Also popular are pictorial Yei rugs, which were introduced at the turn of the century in response to white's demand and may feature anything from Navajo ritual figures (Yeis) based on sacred sand paintings to locomotives and even motor cars. There are also rugs and blankets which incorporate completely non-Indian motifs such as those found in Near Eastern textiles and Art Deco fabrics from the 1930s. All have a market, as do the more authentic, c. 1920–1970 period examples woven in traditional patterns and colors. Among the latter are Ganado, Two Gray Hills, and Tees Nos Pos fabrics.

Collectors should bear in mind that while wearing blankets are the traditional Navajo form, many other types have been produced, including rugs, serapes and women's dresses (rare and early), saddle blankets, pillow and table covers, stair runners, and even pocketbooks. Many of these forms continue to be produced, and Navajo textiles by respected contemporary weavers may bring prices in the thousands.

Navajo blanket, serape type, red, white, gray, tan, and black wool, 28 x 50 inches; Arizona; c. 1900–1910; $2,000–2,800.

There is danger of confusion with similar Spanish-American weavings (discussed elsewhere) and with the numerous Mexican rugs and blankets on the market. The latter can usually be distinguished by the fact that they have tufted ends rather than simply a tassel at each corner. Early Spanish-American fabrics are usually woven in two pieces rather than one, as is the case with the Navajo.

Less often seen are Zuni, Hopi, and other Pueblo fabrics. These groups predated Navajo weavers, but because they have always confined themselves to ceremonial belts, other garments, the complex manta or woman's cloak, and have not woven for sale to whites, their work is relatively unknown among collectors.

Price Listings—Southwestern Indian Weavings

Germantown type blanket, broad bands of white and tan upon which are superimposed stepped crosses in reds, blacks, and browns; Navajo; c. 1880–1900; 62 x 29 inches; $2,500–3,000.

Germantown type child's blanket, alternating horizontal bands of diamonds, waves, and blocks in red, green, blue, brown, black, gray, and white; Navajo; c. 1860–1870; 38 x 25 inches; $23,000–27,000.

Germantown type child's blanket, overall horizontal bands of blue and white overlaid by three bands of red and white

Navajo rug, red and gray wool, 19 x 31 inches; Arizona; c. 1940–1950; $200–250.

crosses; Navajo; c. 1870–1885; 40 x 27 inches; $11,000–12,000.

Germantown type child's blanket, overall field of terraced diamonds with tiny arrows and birds, all in red, black, gray, brown, and white; Navajo; c. 1900–1920; 41 x 26 inches; $4,400–5,000.

Germantown type serape, central belt of diamonds with bordering zigzag pattern, all in red, white, green, and purple; Navajo; c. 1880–1890; 59 x 46 inches; $38,000–43,000.

Germantown type rug, square panels incorporating geometric motifs such as swastika, cross, zigzag, and Xs, all in red, white, green, blue, black, gray, and brown; Navajo; c. 1900–1910; 95 x 70 inches; $24,000–29,000.

Germantown type rug, large white central cross surrounded by stepped diamond and V-shaped devices, all in red, white, black, and gray; Navajo; c. 1890–1900, 66 inches square; $22,000–26,000.

Germantown type rug, overall pattern of stepped diamonds in red, white, blue, gray, and black; borders at top and bottom; Navajo; c. 1880–1900; 63 x 40 inches; $6,000–7,000.

Chief's blanket, First Phase, alternating bands in brown and white, wide blue central band; Navajo; c. 1840–1860; formerly a part of the Fred Harvey and Lorimer Collections, 55 x 40 inches; $275,000–300,000.

Chief's blanket, Second Phase, bands of black and white alternate with similar ones having parallel lines and zigzag

patterning; Navajo, c. 1850–1860; 56 x 42 inches;
$55,000–65,000.

Chief's blanket, Second Phase, horizontal black and white
bands against ground of two broad pillarlike bands in
same hues and red ground dotted in white lines; Navajo;
c. 1865–1875; 59 x 46 inches; $20,000–24,000.

Chief's blanket, Third Phase, in nine-spot pattern, bands of
black and white overlaid with nine concentric diamond
devices in red and tan; Navajo; c. 1900–1910; 63 x 50
inches; $7,000–8,000.

Chief's blanket, Third Phase, broad bands of black and white
overlaid with three rows of three diamonds in red and
black; Navajo; from Lorimer Collection; c. 1870–1880;
$38,000–42,000.

Chief's blanket, Third Phase, broad bands of black and
white interspersed with narrower ones overlaid with three
rows of hexagons in red and gray; Navajo; c. 1865–1875;
65 x 54 inches; $45,000–50,000.

Navajo rug, red, black,
gray, and white wool,
30 x 58 inches; Red
Mesa area, Arizona;
c. 1920–1930;
$1,600–2,200.

Navajo rug, Eye Dazzler
type, red, blue, brown,
gray, and tan wool,
43 x 47 inches; Arizona;
c. 1890–1900;
$5,500–6,500.

Chief's blanket, Third Phase, broad bands of black and white overlaid by three vertical rows of concentric squares in red and gray; Navajo; c. 1860–1880; 62 x 50 inches; $42,000–48,000.

Woman's wearing blanket, narrow black and white bands against a red ground overlaid with terraced diamonds in red on gray ground; Navajo; c. 1885–1895; 49 x 38 inches; $2,300–2,800.

Woman's wearing blanket, border of narrow red and blue bands, wide black central portion; Navajo; c. 1850–1870; 51 x 40 inches; $6,000–7,000.

Serape, narrow bands in tan and white overlaid with three rows of three terraced diamonds in red, gold, mauve, and white, Navajo; c. 1870–1890; 57 x 47 inches; $25,000–30,000.

Serape, Saltillo type with vertical zigzag rows and central bands of diamonds, all in blue, red, brown, and white; Navajo, c. 1860–1880; 60 x 25 inches; $70,000–80,000.

Two Gray Hills rug, broad double border within which are various geometric patterns including triangles and

Navajo rug, red, tan, brown, and white wool, 42 x 71 inches; Tees Nos Pos area, Arizona; c. 1900–1910; $4,000–5,500.

Navajo rug, orange, gray, black, and tan wool, 50 x 34 inches; Arizona; c. 1920–1930; $600–950.

stepped pyramids; predominant colors are tan, brown, gray, and white; Navajo, c. 1925–1935; 72 x 48 inches; $1,800–2,300.

Two Gray Hills rug, broad border of x-shaped devices within which are various geometric motifs set in and around double diamond pattern, all in brown, white, gray, and black; Navajo, c. 1925–1930; 75 x 55 inches; $1,500–2,000.

Two Gray Hills rug, black and white border within which is central cross surrounded by various geometric forms, all in gray, brown, black, and white; Navajo; c. 1960–1970; 60 x 41 inches; $700–950.

Transitional blanket, large white central diamond banded in brown against a gray ground with small crosses at the corners; Navajo; c. 1880–1890; 55 x 44 inches; $4,000–4,800.

Transitional Eye Dazzler blanket, large central X in red, black, and gray against figured red and white ground; Navajo, c. 1900–1920; 59 x 43 inches; $2,500–3,000.

Eye Dazzler type blanket, serrated stripes and expanding diamond design in red, cream, and gray; Navajo; c. 1900–1910; 62 x 47 inches; $3,700–4,200.

Chinle pattern rug, alternating bands of stripes and stepped diamonds in red, white, gray, and black; Navajo, c. 1940–1960; 48 x 32 inches; $1,500–2,000.

Tees Nos Pos pattern rug with characteristic wide border of T-shaped motifs, interior design of geometric devices including feathers, arrows, and triangles, all in orange, blue, green, brown, white, and purple; Navajo; c. 1950–1960; 62 x 40 inches; $900–1,300.

Moki type blanket, three rows of three stepped diamonds in red and white against blue ground interspersed with small red crosses; Navajo; c. 1870–1880; 51 x 40 inches; $7,200–8,000.

Crystal Trading Post blanket, stylized arrowhead border centering two large terraced diamonds, all in red, white, and black on violet; Navajo; c. 1900–1920; $3,900–4,500.

Navajo rug, red, brown, black, and white wool, 41 x 68 inches; Arizona; c. 1925–1935; $3,000–3,700.

Navajo rug, red, black, tan, and white wool, 50 x 31 inches; Ganado type; Arizona; c. 1920–1930; $1,200–1,700.

Yei rug with five dancing figures in red, gray, brown, and blue against tan ground; Navajo; c. 1940–1960; 60 x 40 inches; $1,800–2,200.

Yei rug with four dancing figures and central corn plant motif, in white, green, yellow, red, black, and pink on gray ground; Navajo; c. 1955–1960; 64 x 45 inches; $1,200–1,700.

Yei rug with three dancing figures, one black, two white; Rainbow Guardian border, in black, white, blue, orange, green, and red; Navajo; c. 1930–1950; 50 x 32 inches; $1,500–2,000.

Hall runner, zigzag border, central area with various geometric motifs, all in red, black, gray, and white; Navajo; c. 1920–1930, 106 x 19 inches; $700–950.

Pillow top, triangular decoration in red and black on white ground; Navajo; c. 1940–1960; 17 x 18 inches; $125–175.

Pillow top, central stepped diamond pattern in black, white, brown, and yellow on beige ground; Navajo; c. 1960–1970; 19 x 21 inches; $165–245.

Pillow top, Eye Dazzler type with central radiating stepped diamond in red, orange, purple, green, yellow, pink, and white; Navajo; c. 1890–1910; 18 x 20 inches; $300–450.

Saddle blanket, diagonally striped in orange, red, white, and black; Navajo; c. 1950–1960; 26 x 35 inches; $200–300.

Saddle blanket, triple diamond pattern in red, white, and brown on beige ground; Navajo; c. 1920–1940; 25 x 32 inches; $250–325.

Saddle blanket, large central cross surrounded by four smaller crosses, all in dark brown on beige and white ground; Navajo; c. 1900–1920; 30 x 37 inches; $450–600.

Saddle blanket, white ground with small red and brown square at each corner; Navajo; c. 1900–1920; 28 x 34 inches; $300–400.

Handbag with shoulder strap, decorated with large stepped diamonds in red, white, orange, and gold on white ground; Navajo; c. 1960–1970; 11 x 9 inches; $90–120.

Navajo child's blanket, orange, red, gray, and black wool, 30 x 34 inches; Arizona; c. 1920–1930; $350–500.

Navajo saddle blanket, orange, black, and gray wool, 30 x 34 inches; Chinle type; Arizona; c. 1935–1945; $400–600.

Jacket, pullover type, arms and body decorated with arrow motifs in red and green on gray ground, large head of bobcat on chest in yellow, orange, and black; Navajo; c. 1960–1970; 49 x 18 inches; $150–225.

Manta or shawl, oblong, blue and black with embroidered borders; Zuni; c. 1880–1900; 55 x 45 inches; $2,000–2,800.

Manta or shawl, oblong, central white portion bordered by red-and-blue borders; Hopi; c. 1950–1960; 51 x 43 inches; $450–600.

Manta or wedding shawl, oblong, all white, embroidered in orange on corners; Hopi; c. 1960–1970; 53 x 45 inches; $600–850.

Skirt, turquoise with embroidered geometric border in pink and yellow; Jemez; c. 1940–1945; 32 inches long; $225–275.

Blouse, sleeveless, white ground with geometric decoration including "Iron Cross" in red and blue; Jemez; c. 1940–1945; 25 inches long; $300–375.

Kilt, oblong, white ground with embroidered geometric decoration in red, green, and black extending two-thirds of way down each side; Hopi; c. 1950–1960; 35 x 17 inches; $250–350.

Navajo pictorial rug in red, gray, tan, and brown wool, 78 x 37 inches; Arizona; c. 1925–1935; $15,000–20,000.

Kilt, oblong, white ground with embroidered geometric decoration in red, green, and black extending two-thirds of way down each side; Hopi; c. 1905–1915; 33 x 16 inches; $600–850.

Kilt, boy's, oblong, white; Hopi, c. 1920–1950, 24 x 10 inches; $70–95.

Sash, white with each end fringed and embroidered geometrically in red, green, black, and purple; Hopi; c. 1900–1920; 30 x 8 inches; $475–600.

Sash, white with each end fringed and embroidered geometrically in yellow, red, black, green, and purple; Hopi, c. 1950–1960; 32 x 8.5 inches; $200–300.

Sash, white with each end fringed and embroidered geometrically in red, black, blue, and green; Hopi; c. 1880–1900; 30 x 8 inches; $1,000–1,500.

Sash, so-called "rain sash," braided white cotton with long knotted tassels; Hopi; c. 1920–1960; 37 x 5 inches; $150–200.

Belt, woven geometric diamond pattern in red, white, and green; Taos; c. 1925–1935; 29 x 3 inches; $175–250.

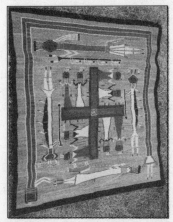

Navajo sand painting type rug, blue, white, tan, and brown wool, 66 x 70 inches; Four Corners area, Arizona; c. 1920–1930; $30,000–45,000.

Belt, woven geometric pattern, abstract butterfly and squash flower in red, green, and black; Hopi; c. 1900–1920; 30 x 3.5 inches; $300–450.

Belt, woven geometric pattern, stepped triangles in red, green, and white; Hopi; c. 1950–1960; 28 x 3 inches; $130–170.

Beadwork

Almost all of us, collectors or not, have seen and been impressed by the marvelous beadwork-decorated moccasins and belts made by Western tribes. Their intricate detail and bright colors seem so "Indian." Yet the glass beads sewn to leather or fabric in these creations were introduced by whites, as were many of the motifs associated with the craft. The initial inspiration, however, was purely Native American.

At least two thousand years ago Western peoples were embroidering fabric with porcupine quills that were stained with natural dyes, softened and flattened before being sewn to a cloth or leather base. By the early 1800s this craft was so well regarded that its female practitioners were organized into highly selective quill workers' societies, or Moneneheo.

It was also around this time that French traders began to offer the Western tribes large oval blue or white glass beads known as "pony beads." Native craftsmen quickly adapted their techniques to utilize these, and by 1850 much smaller beads in a variety of colors became available at trading posts. These "seed beads" became the standard decorative element among bead workers, largely replacing porcupine quill, though the latter has continued to be employed to a limited extent.

Composition also changed over time. The earliest designs are purely geometric, but under white influence, curvilinear floral forms appeared. By the late 1800s, when beadwork had become a staple of the tourist trade, distinctly Anglo motifs such as the American flag, marching soldiers, and even presidential portraits became popular.

Today collectors can hope to find a variety of bead-work-decorated objects dating from the mid-1800s to the present time. All are desirable, but earlier or elaborate examples such as cradle boards, tipi covers, and vests can command prices in the five-figure range. More reasonably priced are belts, moccasins, tobacco and fetish bags, neck-laces, finger rings, horse trappings, mirrors, and knife and gun cases. Many of the finer pieces were gathered by early collectors, and proven association with an important collection will always increase the value of an item.

Most of the Plains tribes produced beadwork. Among those whose craft is best known are the Cheyenne, Blackfeet, Sioux, and Crow. All had certain individual characteristics (the Blackfeet, for example, favored check-ered patterns, while the Crow employed heavy blocks of diamonds and triangles), but they also exchanged motifs, so it is often difficult to ascertain the origin of a particular

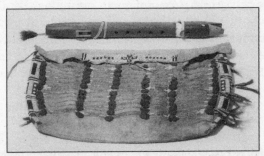

Dance flute of painted wood in storage pouch of buckskin decorated with beading and quillwork, 12 x 5 inches; Mandan or Hidatsa; c. 1900–1915; flute, $250–350; pouch, $900–1,300.

Pipe, carved black catlinite inlaid in pewter, 13 inches long; Northern Plains; c. 1870–1880; $350–500. Buckskin pipe bag decorated with geometric quillwork and beading, 16 inches long; Sioux; c. 1890–1900; $800–1,200.

piece, particularly since such work was rarely ever signed. As a result, most pieces are simply designated "Plains" or "Northern Plains."

Indians of the Northwest Coast, primarily the Tlingit and Kwakiutl, also created beadwork. Such ritual items as dance aprons, hats, and neck ornaments were decorated with beads and pearl trade buttons. Flamboyant designs included birds, animals, and flowers.

The major problem for collectors in this area is confusion with foreign, especially African, examples. Identical beads were traded to African tribesmen and utilized in similar work. African examples can sometimes be distinguished by the fact that they are sewn on local fabric or animal skin, rather than on the red trade cloth or buckskin employed on the plains. Also, many African-made forms such as skirts and headdresses were not produced here.

Price Listings—Beadwork

Assinboin war shirt, Northern Plains; c. 1880–1900; red, white, and blue geometric beadwork featuring stars and diamonds; adorned with human hair; $15,000–17,500.

Horse trappings, buckskin covered with pictorial beadwork in red, green, yellow, and white, total length 56 inches; Central Plains; c. 1900–1910; $550–750.

Assinboin leggings, Northern Plains; c. 1885–1895; blue stroud fabric decorated with bands of beading in yellow, rose, and blue featuring tipi motifs; $1,800–2,200.

Assinboin vest or mantle, Northern Plains; c. 1890–1910; buckskin with beaded hourglass designs in pink, red, and black against a white ground; $5,300–6,100.

Mandan cape, northern Missouri River area; c. 1890–1910; cylindrical green and white trade beads on a flaring buckskin cape edged with cowrie shell danglers; $2,000–3,000.

Mandan finger ring, northern Missouri River area; c. 1880–1890; bands of red, blue, and pink beading sewn on a buckskin ground; $100–150.

Ojibwa vest; Manitoba, Canada; c. 1890–1910; large floral

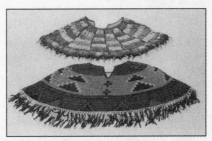

Capes, both Northern Plains. Upper: Beadwork in blue, green, yellow, and white over buckskin, 21 inches across; $1,000–1,500. Lower: Quillwork with danglers terminating in glass beads and rings, 27 inches across; $2,800–3,700.

decorations in red, yellow, and blue on a fully beaded white ground over buckskin; $2,700–3,200.

Ojibwa pipe bag; Manitoba, Canada; c. 1900–1910; fringed buckskin bag with complex floral beading in green, yellow, red, and black on white featuring Canadian maple leaf; $1,300–1,800.

Ojibwa miniature cradle; Manitoba,, Canada; c. 1830–1835; buckskin decorated with quillwork in red and black and cut tin crosses; rarity from important Hooper Collection; $20,000–24,000.

Oto-Missouria breechclout, Kansas-Missouri area; c. 1900–1910; black dyed wool decorated with abstract floral motifs in red, white, blue, and black beading; $1,700–2,000.

Oto child's moccasins, Kansas-Missouri area; c. 1890–1900; buckskin with abstract floral beading in red, blue, pink, black, and white; $3,500–4,000.

Sioux pipe bag, Dakota Territory; c. 1880–1890; beadwork animals (wolves?) in blue and white on a green ground, on fringed buckskin; $750–1,000.

Cradle board, buckskin decorated with red, yellow, blue, black, and green beadwork over a willow frame, 35 inches long; Ute; c. 1915–1930; $8,000–9,500.

Man's war shirt, buckskin decorated with ermine danglers and geometric beadwork in red, white, and blue, 26 inches long; Plains area; c. 1895–1905; $9,000–12,000.

Sioux pipe bag, Dakota Territory; c. 1870–1890; sparse geometric decoration, triangles and blocks in red and black on fringed suede with tassels terminating in tin danglers; $600–850.

Sioux moccasins, Dakota Territory; c. 1900–1920; buckskin ceremonial footwear fully covered with geometric beadwork in red, yellow, green, and black patterns; $2,500–3,000.

Sioux moccasins, Dakota Territory; c. 1880–1910; buckskin covered with geometric beading in red, white, and black with tin cone dangles; $900–1,100.

Sioux woman's leggings, Dakota Territory; c. 1890–1910; tubular buckskin leggings decorated with blocks of red and white beading in sawtooth and triangular patterns; $1,000–1,400.

Sioux vest, Dakota Territory; c. 1910–1930; overall beaded decoration on buckskin includes rows of American flags; from the famous Jack Adamson Collection; $7,200–8,000.

Sioux pictorial vest, Dakota Territory; c. 1910–1920; rare fringed buckskin vest with representation in black, brown, green, and red of Indians afoot and on horseback, all on a beaded white ground; $40,000–50,000.

Sioux child's jacket, Dakota Territory; c. 1910–1930; pictorial designs of Indians on horseback in red, yellow, green, and black beads on buckskin; $4,000–5,000.

Sioux girl's dress, Dakota Territory; c. 1900–1920; buckskin with fringed bottom and shoulder yoke beaded in green, yellow, and black with crosses, stars, and rectangles; $7,000–8,500.

Sioux knife sheath, Dakota Territory; c. 1900–1910; cowhide completely covered with beading including diamonds and rectangles in blue and black on white; tasseled bead danglers; $2,000–2,700.

Sioux knife sheath, Dakota Territory; c. 1930–1940; buckskin with simple beaded border in pink, blue, and white; reverse painted orange and yellow; $250–325.

Sioux traveling bag or valise, Northern Plains; c. 1907; cowhide bag with handle and brass fittings completely decorated with spectacular polychrome beadwork including two Indians on horseback, names, and date 1907; $45,000–55,000.

Sioux saddle blanket, Dakota Territory; c. 1880–1900; buffalo hide blanket banded in fringed beaded panels; red, yellow, and green on a white ground; $2,200–2,800.

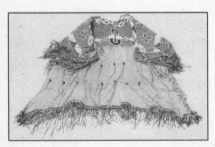

Child's dress, fringed buckskin decorated with quill and bead work in red, blue, green, yellow, and white, 23 inches long; Sioux; c. 1910–1920; $5,500–6,500.

Child's dress, red stroud fabric with quillwork collar and decorated with large shells, 20 inches long; California or Northwest Coast; c. 1900–1920; $2,000–2,700.

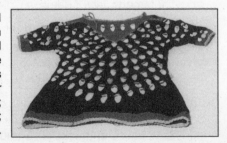

"Cowboy Songs" with vocals by Bing Crosby, 33 mono; *cover*: lithographed cardboard, 12 inches square, Decca Records, c. 1950-1960; $15-25.

Bookstore promotional board advertisement for cowboy pulp magazine, lithographed paper on cardboard, 12 x 8 inches, c. 1900-1910; $25-40.

Song book, cowboy songs with Lulu Belle and Skyland Scotty, lithographed and printed paper, 12 x 9 inches, M.M. Cole Publishing Company, Chicago, c. 1930-1940; $20-30.

Group of promotional giveaway cards advertising early cowboy film stars, printed cardboard, 3½ x 5 inches, c. 1920-1930; $25-35 each.

Native American basketry, all c. 1900-1910. *Left to right:* bowl, 3 inches high, Tulare, California, $100-135; basket, 15 inches in diameter, Tulare, California, $300-400; basket, 10 inches in diameter, Panamint, California, $225-325.

Native American pottery, all baked earthenware, c. 1930-1950. *Left to right:* wedding vase, 6 inches high, Santa Clara Pueblo, New Mexico, $40-60; handled bowl, 4 inches in diameter, Picuris, New Mexico, $35-50; jar or olla, 8 inches high, San Ildefonso, New Mexico, $100-150; pitcher, 6 inches high, Picuris, New Mexico, $65-85.

Native American baked earthenware, c. 1920-1930. *Left:* bowl, 8 inches in diameter, San Juan, New Mexico, $75-110; *right:* jar, 5½ inches in diam-eter, Maricopa, Arizona, $60-90.

Group of totem figures, carved and polychrome-painted cedar, 4½ to 10½ inches high, Northwest Coast, c. 1900-1950. *Left to right:* $150-200; $20-30; $350-500; $50-75.

Frog form food dish, carved and stained alder, inlaid with mother-of-pearl, operculum shells, and trade beads, 11½ inches long, Northwest Coast, c. 1930-1940; $1,300-1,800.

Navajo rug, woven wool,
25 x 40 inches, Two Gray
Hills style, c. 1950-1970;
$400-600.

Navajo saddle blanket, woven wool,
30 x 23 inches, c. 1920-1930;
$165-235.

Beadwork. *Left:* knife sheath, bead-
decorated buckskin, 7 inches long,
Sioux, c. 1930-1945, $225-300;
right: belt, beaded buckskin,
Southern Plains, c. 1940-1960,
$125-175.

Southwestern silver; Navajo, Zuni,
and Hopi, some pieces with
turquoise settings, New Mexico and
Arizona, c. 1930-1970: bracelets,
$135-335; ring, $125-175; brooch,
$90-120.

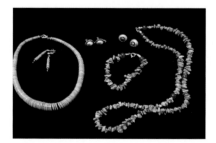

Southwestern turquoise jewelry,
some pieces in silver, Zuni, and Hopi,
New Mexico and Arizona, c. 1940-
1970: pendant earrings, $110-140;
stud earrings, $80-100; necklaces,
$175-250; bracelet, $70-95.

Souvenir booklet or program for Indian show at the New York Hippodrome, lithographed paper, 8½ x 10 inches, c. 1906-1907; $25-40.

Postcard, Indians selling pottery to passengers at train station, lithographed cardboard, 4 x 6 inches, c. 1910-1920; $10-15.

Left: still bank in the form of an Indian, painted cast iron, 5½ inches high, c. 1900-1910, $70-95; *right:* pocket match holder, brass and electroplated silver with embossed representation of cowboy roping Longhorns, 3 inches high, c. 1890-1910; $155-215.

Torso, carved fossilized ivory, 6 inches high, Alaskan Eskimo, Old Bering Sea Culture, c. 350 B.C.-300 A.D.; $8,000-9,500.

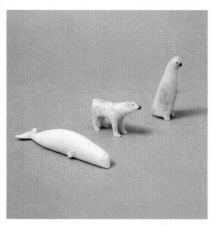

Toys or game counters, carved ivory, 2–3½ inches long, Alaskan, c. 1920-1940; $50-90 each.

Doll's head, carved wood with trade bead eyes, 4½ inches high, Diomede Island, Alaska, c. 1850-1870, $10,000-15,000.

Shaman's or wizard's hat, carved and painted wood with feathers, 18 inches across, Nunivak Island, Alaska, c. 1915-1925; $9,000-11,000.

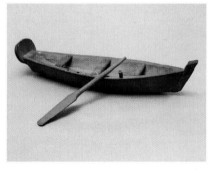

Model of open boat or Umiak, carved cedar, 7½ inches long, Alaska, c. 1925-1935; $175-225.

Bulto, Our Lady of the Immaculate Conception, carved and painted cotton wood, 9 inches high, workshop of Jose Aragon, New Mexico, c. 1820-1835; $9,000-11,500.

Retablo, Our Lady of Talpa, polychrome painted cottonwood, 8 x 11 inches, school of Jose Aragon, New Mexico, c. 1820-1840; $4,500-6,000.

Retablo, *The Flight Into Egypt*, polychrome painted cottonwood, 6½ x 12 inches, Rafael Aragon, New Mexico, c. 1840-1860; $7,000-8,500.

Ore cars, cast and sheet steel; Colorado. *Two at left:* c. 1930-1940, $400-600 each; *far right,* c. 1910-1930, $750-900.

Northwest Bay trade gun, flint lock muzzle loader, steel and hardwood with brass details, 49 inches long; typical of those used by early trappers and hunters, dated 1866; $800-950.

Station sign, lithographed sheet steel, 30 x 20 inches, Colorado and Southern Railway, c. 1950-1960; $140-190.

Railway timetable, lithographed and printed paper, 5 x 9 inches, Missouri Pacific Lines, c. 1950-1960; $10-15.

Railway line map, lithographed paper, 8½ x 13 inches, Missouri Pacific Lines, c. 1950-1960; $20-30.

Miniature chuck-a-luck cage with layout and cardboard box; chrome steel, fabric and bakelite dice; 7-inch high cage, c. 1925-1935; $50-75.

Detail of casino roulette wheel, burl walnut, satinwood and chrome, 30 inches in diameter, Colorado, c. 1890-1910; with built-in table, $8,000-10,000.

Santee Sioux moccasins, Minnesota; c. 1870–1880; beadwork stars and abstract floral patterns in red and black embellished with red silk; $700–950.

Santee Sioux vest, Minnesota; c. 1880–1910; buckskin and trade fabric covered with quillwork dyed red, yellow, black, and green; $900–1,200.

Santee Sioux woman's bonnet, Minnesota; c. 1885–1895; plaid fabric-lined buckskin bonnet decorated with red, yellow, brown, and green quillwork in abstract floral patterns; $4,400–5,200.

Cheyenne dress, Central Plains; c. 1890–1910; hide dress covered with red, green, black, and white beading in various geometric and floral patterns; $5,000–7,000.

Cheyenne cuffs, Central Plains; c. 1910–1920; floral beadwork in red and green on buckskin; $175–250.

Cheyenne gauntlets or riding gloves, Central Plains; c. 1900–1910; beaded flowers in red, white, and green on fringed buckskin; $250–350.

Cheyenne miniature cradle board, Central Plains; c. 1910–1920; carved wood covered with buckskin beaded in red, white, and blue geometric patterns including diamonds; $4,500–5,500.

Woman's dress, fringed buckskin sparsely decorated with red and blue beadwork including butterflies, 35 inches long; Northern Plains; c. 1900–1920; $2,500–3,300.

Man's jacket, fringed buckskin decorated with floral beadwork patterns in red, yellow, blue, green, and white, 30 inches long; Central Plains; c. 1900–1930; $3,800–4,500.

Blackfoot belt, Montana; c. 1890–1910; swirling geometric devices in red and blue and vertical black bands, all on a white ground over buckskin; $550–750.

Blackfoot pipe bag, Montana; c. 1880–1900; geometric patterns including rectangles, crosses, and triangles in red, white, yellow, and black on buckskin; $900–1,400.

Blackfoot war shirt, Montana; c. 1880–1900; buckskin decorated with red and white geometric beadwork and hand-painted representations of the tadpole motif; $18,000–21,000.

Blackfoot shirt, Montana; c. 1915–1925; fringed buckskin, shoulders heavily beaded in geometric forms including Xs and Vs in blue, black, and white; $11,000–14,000.

Cree saddle cover; Red River area, Canada; c. 1890–1910; cowhide partially covered with overall floral beading in red, yellow, orange, blue, green, black, and brown on white; red wool yarn tassels with large blue beads; $16,000–20,000.

Cree pipe bag; Red River area, Canada; c. 1860–1870; red trade cloth on buckskin with floral beadwork in red and green on white; from early collection with full documentation; $14,000–17,000.

Cree coverlet; Red River area, Canada; c. 1910–1915; beaded velvet coverlet with motifs resembling those in an album quilt: eagles, stars, flags, etc.; in red, white, blue, green, yellow, and pink beads; $23,000–30,000.

Cree moccasins; Red River area, Canada; c. 1840–1860; buckskin moccasins with simple quillwork border in blue and green; $900–1,200.

Cree knife sheath and belt; Red River area, Canada; c. 1850–1870; fringed buffalo hide decorated with yellow and black quillwork and complex geometric beading in red, green, yellow, and black; $1,400–2,000.

Comanche or Kiowa high-top woman's moccasins, Southern Plains; c. 1880–1890; buckskin dyed orange-brown and covered with red, green, and black beads as well as buttons shaped from nineteenth-century silver dimes; $3,200–3,800.

Comanche or Kiowa woman's dress, Southern Plains; c. 1880–1900; fringed buckskin dress dyed yellow with blue and green seed bead decoration, cowrie shell pendants, brass bells, and metal sequins; $25,000–29,000.

Man's leggings or pants, elk skin decorated with red, green, and yellow beadwork including flowers, 31 inches long; Northern Plains; c. 1870–1890; $2,300–3,000. Hat, suede, of the type worn by both cavalrymen and Native Americans; c. 1880–1900; $300–450.

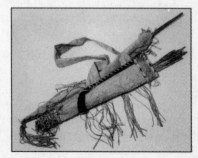

Quiver and bow case, elk skin, decorated with red stroud and a band of black and white beadwork, 33 inches long; Jicarilla Apache; c. 1915–1925; $1,800–2,300.

Comanche high-top moccasins, Southern Plains; c. 1870–1880; buckskin boots with fringed tops and green and yellow beaded strips accompanied by silver concho buttons; $4,500–5,500.

Crow rifle cover or sheath, Montana; c. 1880–1895; buckskin covered with overall black, green, and yellow beading in elaborate geometric patterns; $9,500–11,000.

Crow knife sheath, Montana; c. 1880–1900; buckskin painted in red and blue and decorated with thick lines of white trade beads; $1,000–1,500.

Crow mirror bag, Montana; c. 1890–1910; buckskin fringed and covered with overall red and black beadwork in hourglass patterns; $4,900–5,600.

Crow puberty robe, Montana; c. 1910–1930; calfskin with simple geometric beading in pink and white; $1,500–2,000.

Crow cradle board, Montana; c. 1890–1900; buckskin and canvas on shaped board; beaded decoration in blue and green featuring hourglass forms, crosses, and banding; $12,000–15,000.

Crow martingale or horse collar, Montana; c. 1880–1900; H-shaped buckskin horse trapping completely beaded in red, blue, orange, white, and yellow, in various geometric devices including hourglass, square, and rectangle; $1,800–2,600.

Crow decorated bridle, Montana; c. 1885–1895; metal bit and cowhide bridle decorated with sawtooth and checkerboard patterns in pink, red, black, white, and yellow beading; horsehair tassels; $8,500–9,500.

Kiowa miniature cradle board, Kansas; c. 1880–1890; carved wood covered with beadwork on fringed buckskin in red, white, blue, and green geometric patterns; $10,000–13,000.

Kiowa cradle board, Kansas; c. 1880–1890; lattice form board covered with buckskin beaded in a diamond pattern in red, yellow, white, blue, and black, all on a green ground; wooden portions embellished with brass tacks; a remarkable piece; $40,000–50,000.

Kiowa high boots, Kansas; c. 1910–1930; buckskin with fringed tops and vertical beading in blue and black as well as brass buttons; $2,500–3,000.

Kiowa moccasins, Kansas; c. 1900–1910; buckskin painted blue in part and decorated with fringing, dangling copper cones, and beadwork in blue and white; $2,100–2,600.

Kiowa-Apache jacket, Arizona; c. 1860–1880; tasseled buckskin jacket decorated with patches of red, white, and yellow beads including star and triangle motifs; $4,500–5,000.

Apache boots, Arizona; c. 1880–1910; high buckskin boots, tops and edges of feet decorated with sawtooth decoration in blue-and-white beading; $1,300–1,800.

Oto leggings, Oklahoma; c. 1890–1900; buckskin leggings with beaded edges and cuffs; geometric and floral patterns in red, white, blue, and yellow; $13,000–15,000.

Oto coat, Oklahoma; c. 1880–1890; black woolen coat, back decorated in red, blue, pink, and white with horse head and fleur-de-lis designs; $9,000–12,000.

Plains area shirt, Iowa-Kansas; c. 1890–1900; buckskin shirt with fringed shoulders across which run bands of red, black, blue, and white beading; $1,700–2,500.

Plains area skirt, Kansas-Nebraska; c. 1900–1910; rough-cut buckskin skirt with areas of simple geometric beading in red and blue; $500–650.

Plains area long leggings (like overalls), Kansas-Nebraska; c. 1880–1900; buckskin, lower portions decorated with vase and hourglass designs in red and blue on white; $1,500–2,000.

Plains area trouser type leggings, Kansas-Iowa; c. 1880–1900; fringed buckskin decorated with blocks of diamond, cross, and rectangle geometric beading in red, blue, pink, and yellow; $4,500–6,000.

Plains area apron, Kansas-Nebraska; c. 1870–1800; buffalo hide covered with horizontal bands of quillwork in red, blue, black, and brown; feather attachments; $3,500–5,000.

Plains area knife sheath; c. 1870–1880; buffalo hide decorated with simple geometric beading in red, blue, and black; $400–650.

Plains area knife sheath; c. 1880–1900; tasseled buckskin sheath with tin danglers; overall geometric beading in red, black, and yellow featuring crosses, hourglasses, and bands of triangles; $3,500–4,300.

Plains area pipe bag, Kansas-Nebraska; c. 1900–1910; very large fringed buckskin bag with elaborate beaded decoration including squares, triangles, and banding, all in red, green, black, and white; $9,000–10,500.

Plains area pipe bag, Montana; c. 1860–1880; fringed buffalo hide bag with quillwork bands in red, blue, and yellow; $3,000–3,500.

Plains area paint bag, Montana; c. 1890–1900; fringed buckskin pouch with vertical quillwork in red and yellow and beaded hourglass figure in red against white ground; $2,400–3,200.

Plains area awl case, Kansas; c. 1870–1890; tubular buffalo hide case covered with bands of black and yellow beading and having copper cone danglers; $700–950.

Plains area hairbrush, Iowa-Kansas; c. 1900–1910; tubular brush, the handle of which is wrapped in red and black geometric beadwork; $275–350.

Plains area saddlebags, Montana; c. 1880–1900; buckskin, front covered with geometric beading in red, green, black, and white including crosses, rectangles, and hourglass; $2,200–2,900.

Plateau area toy cradle board; c. 1900–1920; carved and painted wood covered with red, white, and yellow beads in floral and geometric patterns; $1,200–1,700.

Plateau area sash; c. 1910–1930; beltlike sash decorated with birds and crosses in green, yellow, and black beads; $500–650.

Plateau area gauntlets or riding gloves; c. 1910–1930; fringed buckskin gloves, upper portion of which is decorated with beaded floral motifs in red, yellow, pink, and green on white; $600–750.

Plateau area gauntlets or riding gloves; c. 1920–1930; fringed buckskin gloves; upper portion decorated in red, yellow, pink, and blue abstract beading including stars and arrowheads; $800–950.

Plateau area pipe bag; c. 1900–1920; fringed buckskin bag with beaded decoration in red, green, and black on white including bird on branch and berries; $900–1,300.

Plateau area martingale or horse collar; c. 1860–1880; overall geometric decoration of circles, squares, and rectangles in red, black, yellow, and pink pony beads on buckskin; $3,800–4,400.

Ptateau area Klickitat bag; c. 1920–1930; trade cloth bag with beaded representation of man on horseback in red, black, brown, and green on white; $1,200–1,500.

Shoshone moccasins, Idaho; c. 1880–1900; elaborate abstract floral beadwork decoration in red, white, yellow, and green on buckskin; $4,400–5,200.

Ute bandolier bag, Colorado; c. 1880–1900; buffalo hide with diamond, hourglass, and rectangular motifs in red and black on beaded white ground; $22,000–26,000.

Ute tobacco bag and pipe holder, Colorado; c. 1890–1900; fringed buckskin with beaded decoration in form of central stepped diamond in red on white ground surrounded by checked border in red and black (rare form); $5,500–6,500.

Ute cradle board, Colorado; c. 1880–1890; holster-shaped wooden board covered with buckskin, upper portion of which is decorated with bands of geometric beading in red, black, white, and green; $6,000–7,500.

Tlingit pouch, Alaska; c. 1905–1915; red wool with pink, green, blue, and white beadwork in form of eagle surrounded by floral pattern; $4,500–6,000.

Tlingit neck ornament, Alaska; c. 1920–1930; red wool decorated with pearl buttons and abstract floral patterns in blue, black, and white beads; $3,000–4,200.

Tlingit leggings, Alaska; c. 1880–1890; buckskin-fringed blue wool with complex totemic figural design in red, white, green, blue, pink, and tan beads; $14,000–18,000.

Kwakiutl dance apron, British Columbia; c. 1910–1925; red wool apron decorated with brass bells and stylized bird figure outlined in yellow, black, green, and orange beads; $7,000–9,000.

Kwakiutl dance apron, British Columbia; c. 1920–1930; red and black wool with brass thimble, puffin beak danglers, and overall beadwork composition featuring birds and floral devices; $6,000–8,000.

Umatilla wing dress; Columbia River area, Northwest Coast; c. 1865–1890; red trade cloth embellished across shoul-

Miscellaneous Plains Indian artifacts including knife sheath, fringed buckskin decorated with red, black, and white beadwork, 8 inches long; Mandan; c. 1890–1900; $300–450. Left to right, all c. 1870–1880: Carved wooden bowl, 4.5 inches in diameter; $165–235; Hide scraper, elk horn and steel, 7.5 inches long; $120–160. Trade knife, wood and steel, 9.5 inches long; $60–85. Dipper, shaped buffalo horn, 13 inches long; $200–275.

ders with bands of trade beads, cowrie shells, satin ribbon, and metal sequins; $4,500–6,000.

Athabaskan dress, British Columbia; c. 1870–1880; two-piece fringed buckskin dress with heavy abstract floral beading in red, white, blue, black, and pink; from the Elmore Collection; $19,000–24,000.

Athabaskan shirt, British Columbia; c. 1890–1910; fringed buckskin shirt with zigzag beading in white on red at cuffs, collar, and shoulders; $6,800–7,700.

White River knife sheath; Yukon Territory, Canada c. 1890–1900; buckskin sheath with beaded "snake" design in black against a white and green ground; $3,000–3,750.

Southwestern Silver

Though various groups of Native Americans have produced jewelry from such diverse materials as shells, animal bones, shark teeth, various rocks, minerals, and metals, collector interest focuses on the silver and turquoise creations from the Southwest.

Three groups—the Navajo, Zuni, and Hopi—work in silver. First in the field was a Navajo, Atsidi Sani, who learned silversmithing from Mexican artisans around 1850. Others of his tribe refined the art during the 1860–1880 period by introducing native turquoise, which largely replaced previously employed jet and garnet. Today, for many collectors, Navajo silver is the most desirable.

However, Zuni silversmiths, who had previously worked in brass and copper, entered the field in the 1880s, and within a decade the Hopi were also active. Today all three groups offer the buyer a wide range of traditional and contemporary forms.

While it is often hard to distinguish the work of one tribe from another (and few earlier pieces are signed), certain guidelines will prove helpful. Navajo jewelry is often cast and shaped in massive forms with minimal use of turquoise. Hopi craftsmen use even less turquoise, preferring to sculpt their silver in overlay and cutwork techniques similar to those employed in their ceramic designs. The Zuni, on the other hand, favor this mineral, the blue of which reminds them of the sky, while the greener variations represent grass. As a consequence, Zuni silver often serves primarily as a setting for inlay of large pieces of turquoise or of jet and shell, which they also utilize.

All else being equal, most collectors prefer earlier silver in traditional forms, which they may refer to as "pawn," reflecting the fact that Southwestern silver jewelry was often pawned by its Indian owners at local trading posts, to be redeemed when crops came in or economic conditions improved. Pieces that were never redeemed are termed "dead pawn." However, whether a piece was pawned or not has little to do with its artistic merit, and collectors are better advised to buy on the basis of style and quality than on some dubious claim that a particular piece came from a certain trading post.

Certain Mexican-made silver and turquoise jewelry has been made to resemble American Indian wares. Be sure to look for Mexican silver marks; also, keep an eye out for plastic and pot metal look-alikes produced recently in Asia. These may even be sold by Indian traders!

As a whole, prices in this field are moderate, with a large number of interesting pieces such as earrings, bracelets, rings, and belts available in the $100–1,000 range. Some of the most expensive examples are those produced and signed by well-known contemporary craftsmen like Charles Loloma, Fred Kabotie, and Leekya

Desyee. One may also encounter pieces bearing the logos or hallmarks of shops, such as the thunderbird motif of the Thunderbird Shop or the stamp of a small hogan (house) and number "3," used by the Three Hogans Trading Post.

Price Listings—Southwestern Silver

Bracelet, oval disks of turquoise set vertically in silver filigree mounts linked by silver beads; Navajo; c. 1920–1930; 1.5 inches wide; $400–475.

Bracelet, large oblong blocks of turquoise set vertically, joined by bands of silver ropework to turquoise ovals set horizontally in groups of three; Navajo; c. 1920–1930; 2.5 inches wide; $750–850.

Bracelet, silver openwork in ropelike design with three oval turquoise medallions, a large one in center, smaller one at each side; Navajo; c. 1970–1980; 1.75 inches wide; $90–135.

Bracelet, silver engraved with three wavelike decorative bands; Navajo; c. 1960–1980; 2 inches wide; $150–200.

Bracelet, silver frame set with massive chunks of turquoise and red coral, placed vertically; Zuni; c. 1950–1970; 2.5 inches wide; $350–450.

Bracelet, silver links each of which consists of cluster of oval turquoise stones; Zuni; c. 1960–1970; 1.5 inches wide; $225–275.

Bracelet, silver overlay with geometric design featuring diamonds and triangles; Hopi; c. 1970–1980, 2 inches wide; $200–250.

Concha belt, stamped silver conchos alternate with oblong devices, all with turquoise bead centers; Navajo; by the artisan Crossed Arrows; c. 1935–1945; 2.5 inches wide; $1,600–1,900.

Concha belt, large, finely worked and stamped silver conchos on a leather belt; Navajo; c. 1900–1905; 3.5 inches wide; $5,000–6,000.

Concha belt, large oval stamped conchos alternating with vertically mounted butterfly forms, all on original leather backing; Navajo; c. 1925–1935; 3 inches wide; $2,750–3,250.

Concha belt, large brass and German silver conchos with brass links; New Mexico; by contemporary artist Max Anderson; c. 1980–1990; 4 inches wide; $850–950.

Concha belt, silver conchos inlaid with geometric pattern in turquoise; Zuni; by contemporary artist Betty Etsatie; c. 1970–1975; 2.5 inches wide; $1,200–1,600.

Necklace, squash blossom type; large silver beads and squash blossom devices with central crescent-shaped pendant, or Naja; Navajo; c. 1920–1930; 19 inches long; $2,200–2,600.

Necklace, squash blossom type; large silver beads, squash blossom devices, and Naja which is set with turquoise; Navajo; c. 1940–1960; 17 inches long; $1,200–1,600.

Necklace, brass and coral beads with suspensions of stylized silver crosses; Navajo; c. 1910–1930; 18 inches long; $650–900.

Necklace, chunks of turquoise alternating with large, faceted silver beads; Zuni; c. 1920–1930; 15 inches long; $300–450.

Necklace or choker, flexible oblong silver bars with a central suspension of turquoise, coral, and mother-of-pearl beads; Navajo; c. 1940–1960; 14 inches long; $350–550.

Necklace, squash blossom type; massive silver setting, including Naja, covered with chunks of turquoise and red coral; Zuni; c. 1950–1960; 16 inches long; $1,000–1,500.

Ring, silver overlay work with Greek Key motif; Hopi; c. 1940–1960; approx. 1 inch in diameter; $125–175.

Ring, silver overlay work with figures of men carrying staffs and bags on their backs; Hopi; c. 1940–1950; approx. 1 inch in diameter; $150–200.

Ring, silver overlay work with abstract geometric design; Hopi; c. 1960–1980; approx. 1 inch in diameter; $75–100.

Ring, silver with overall turquoise mosaic work; Zuni; c. 1940–1950; approx. 1 inch in diameter; $175–225.

Ring, silver inlaid with many rows of tiny turquoise beads; Zuni; c. 1940–1960; $200–275.

Ring, silver cut in openwork geometric design; Navajo; c. 1920–1940; approx. 1 inch in diameter; $100–150.

Ring, silver with sunburst pattern and three oval turquoise beads; Navajo; c. 1930–1950; approx. 1 inch in diameter; $200–300.

Ring, silver with openwork and central oblong piece of turquoise flanked by two diamond-shaped pieces; Navajo; c. 1935–1955, approx. 1 inch in diameter; $175–250.

Pendant, oblong, silver overlay design of two Kachinas, silver link chain; Hopi; c. 1960–1980; 14 inches long; $125–175.

Pin, silver sunburst design; Navajo; c. 1950–1970; 2 inches in diameter; $65–85.

Pin, silver in form of double squash blossoms with central turquoise bead; Navajo; c. 1940–1960; 2.5 inches wide; $75–100.

Pin, silver in form of Kachina, inlaid in turquoise, mother-of-pearl, and jet; Zuni; c. 1950–1970; 2 inches high; $125–175.

Pin, silver filigree set with tiny turquoise beads in sunburst pattern; Zuni; c. 1940–1960; $160–210.

Pin, silver in form of butterfly, inlaid in turquoise and jet; Zuni; c. 1955–1975; 1.5 inches high; $90–130.

Pin, silver overlay with abstract sunburst design; Hopi; c. 1960–1980; 1 inch in diameter; $35–55.

Pin, silver overlay design, central Kachina figure flanked by abstract patterns; Hopi; c. 1950–1970; 1.5 inches high; $70–95.

Earrings, oblong silver, inlaid with many tiny turquoise beads; Zuni; c. 1950–1970; 1 inch high; $75–125.

Earrings, oblong silver, inlaid with abstract geometric design in turquoise and jet; Zuni; c. 1950–1970; 1 inch high; $120–175.

Earrings, oblong silver with beaded border and containing large, rough turquoise stones; Zuni; c. 1970–1980; 3 inches high; $200–300.

Earrings, silver set with large chunk of turquoise on each side of which is smaller piece of red coral; Zuni; c. 1950–1960; 1.5 inches high; $175–225.

Earrings, oblong silver with relief design of squash blossom; Navajo; c. 1940–1965; 1 inch high; $70–95.

Belt buckle, oblong silver with geometric engraving; Navajo; c. 1960–1980; 2 x 3 inches; $60–75.

Belt buckle, oblong silver filigree work with double Naja design; Navajo; c. 1960–1980; 1.75 x 2.5 inches; $80–120.

Belt buckle, oblong silver engraved and inset with four large pieces of turquoise; Zuni; c. 1950–1970; 2.5 x 3.75 inches; $175–225.

Belt buckle, oblong engraved silver in the butterfly design; Hopi; c. 1940–1960; 2.5 x 3.5 inches; $150–225.

Indian Dolls

Like every other ethnic group, Native Americans made dolls for their children, both as playthings and as instructional devices through which to teach little girls the responsibilities of motherhood. Eighteenth-century travelers in the West described Indian dolls. However, these were extremely simple creations, often no more than a bone or a roughly shaped stick wrapped in buffalo hide.

Such dolls are both rare and of little interest to collectors who seek out the more elaborate examples created primarily during the past century in response to the demands of tourists. By far the most popular dolls are those made by Plains Indian tribes such as the Sioux and Cheyenne. The earliest and most desirable have soft buckskin bodies, hand-painted features, and horsehair wigs, and are meticulously dressed to resemble men and women of the tribe. Fringed buckskin leggings or dresses decorated with beadwork as well as miniature bows, knives, and baskets add to the realistic portrayals. Early and fine examples of this sort have brought over $30,000 at auction.

Collectors should be aware, however, that there are many lesser, later dolls which are neither as desirable nor as costly. Though Indian-dressed dolls, which have factory-made composition or celluloid bodies usually date from after 1930, there are also very recent low-grade, plastic-body reproductions made in Hong Kong and Taiwan. While they are now sometimes sold by Western tribes, these are not authentic Indian dolls.

A second and very different type of collectible doll is that made by the Navajo and other Southwestern tribal groups. These dolls date from the 1870s on and reflect contact with whites. The dolls, which may have either buckskin or, later, stuffed cotton bodies, are dressed in calico skirts, velveteen blouses, and Navajo-woven wool blankets. They too have painted features, but their hair is of thread or raveled wool, and their most distinguishing feature is the miniaturized silver and turquoise jewelry with which they are adorned. More recent versions will have plastic bodies, pot metal, and paste jewelry.

Occasionally seen are polychrome pottery dolls produced by the Mohave. These are usually pre-1900 and rare enough that they do not appear in most collections.

The third important category in the world of Native American dolls encompasses the relatively uncommon, carved wooden examples produced by the Northwest coastal tribes. Earliest examples date to the mid-nineteenth century and show their connection to the traditional carving of the same area in their strong sculptural quality. Unlike the case with Plains and Navajo dolls, there is minimal concern for details of dress, and bodies are often simply roughed out, then covered with a trade cloth gown. Hair is human or animal and jewelry is minimal, no more than a shell or bead necklace.

It is the carving and the painting that make these pieces so desirable (early examples often bring five-figure sums). Never cute or charming, they are works of art and usually sought by collectors of other forms of totemic art from the same area.

Price Listings—Indian Dolls

Buckskin, painted face, horsehair wig, buckskin dress with simple beading, 14 inches high; Plateau area; c. 1860–1880; $4,500–6,000.

Buckskin, pair, male and female, painted faces, horsehair wigs, beaded trade cloth clothing and buckskin boots, 12 to 13 inches high; Crow; c. 1890–1910; $2,500–3,000 the pair.

Buckskin, painted face, horsehair wig, buckskin poncho and skirt decorated with beadwork and tin cone suspensions, 12 inches high; Apache; c. 1900–1920; $3,000–3,600.

Buckskin, painted face, horsehair wig, buckskin poncho and skirt decorated with tin cone suspensions and tinted red and orange, 12.5 inches high; Apache; c. 1900–1910; $4,500–5,200.

Buckskin, painted face, horsehair wig, beaded buckskin dress and moccasins, 10.5 inches high; Flathead; Northern Plains; c. 1925–1935; $600–700.

Buckskin, painted face, horsehair wig, beaded red wool dress and buckskin moccasins, 9 inches high; Cheyenne; c. 1920–1940; $1,000–1,300.

Buckskin, painted and bead-defined face, brown horsehair wig, buckskin dress with blue and white beading and belt, beaded earrings, 14 inches high; Cheyenne; c. 1930–1940; $750–900.

Buckskin, painted face, human hair wig, beaded buckskin shirt and leggings, red trade cloth breechclout, 11 inches high; Southern Plains; c. 1900–1920; $2,800–3,100.

Buckskin, painted face, horsehair wig, beaded buckskin dress, 10 inches high; Southern Plains; c. 1900–1920; $1,700–2,000.

Buckskin, painted face, woolen hair, red cotton dress with buckskin belt decorated with tin disks and buckskin leggings beaded in blue and white; carries beaded leather awl case; 13.5 inches high; Sioux; from Rosebud Reservation, South Dakota; c. 1885–1890; $800–1,200.

Buckskin, painted face, horsehair wig, buckskin shirt and leggings with beaded banding, 18 inches high; Central Plains; c. 1880–1900; $750–950.

Buckskin, crudely painted face, human hair wig, buckskin dress and moccasins with sparse beading; unusual bead nose ring; 14 inches high; Northern Plains; c. 1870–1890; $550–700.

Buckskin, painted face, human hair wig, buckskin shirt and leggings, red trade cloth breechclout, 9 inches high; Central Plains; c. 1900–1910; $200–300.

Buckskin and muslin, painted face, braided silk wig, printed cotton blouse, skirt, and apron; trade bead earrings; 20 inches high; Navajo; c. 1890–1900; $750–950.

Cloth, painted face, thread wig, velveteen shirt, buckskin pants and moccasins, striped woven blanket or serape, and silver concho belt, 13 inches high; Navajo; c. 1935–1945; $200–275.

Cloth, painted face, thread wig, velveteen blouse and cotton skirt, buckskin boots, concho belt, bead necklace and earrings, turquoise bracelet, 12 inches high; Navajo; c. 1935–1945; $175–250.

Pottery, polychrome-painted face, in bark cradle board decorated with blue and white trade beads, woven fabric and feathers, silver necklace, 14 inches high; Mohave-Yuma; c. 1890–1900; $8,500–10,000.

Pottery, polychrome-painted, horsehair wig bound with rawhide band, 8 inches high; Mohave; c. 1880–1900; $450–650.

Pottery, polychrome-painted, horsehair wig, cotton print skirt, beaded earrings and necklace, 10 inches high; Mohave; by Annie Fields; c. 1960–1970; $300–450.

Wooden, carved cedar, face colored red, black, and blue on white; swollen lower lip with decorative labret, human hair wig, simply carved hands and feet, trade cloth dress, shell necklace, 17 inches high; Northwest Coast; c. 1850–1870; $20,000–25,000.

Wooden, carved cedar, traces of old red and black pigment, swollen lower lip with decorative labret, remnants of human hair wig, simply carved hands and feet, trade cloth gown, 16 inches high; Northwest Coast; c. 1840–1860; $18,000–22,000.

Wooden, carved cedar with polychrome decoration, human hair wig; hands, feet, and body fully carved, red trade cloth gown with fur trim, 12 inches high; Northwest Coast; c. 1910–1930; $600–900.

Wooden, carved cedar with face decorated in red and black, human hair wig; hands, feet, and body carved, unclothed, 11 inches high; Northwest Coast; c. 1920–1940; $400–700.

Indian Kitsch

While authenticity is extremely important in the area of Native American collectibles, especially in light of the increasing number of fakes and reproductions entering the field, there is one category in which collectors can buy almost without concern. Frequently referred to as "kitsch," these objects were and are made by non-Indians to capitalize on the general fascination with Native American objects.

The field is incredibly broad, bringing to mind such diverse objects as cigar store Indians, patent medicines allegedly based on native recipes, advertising materials which employ Indians and Indian themes to sell a wide variety of products, "Indian" souvenirs made in Hong Kong or Japan, and countless objects—from lamps to ash-trays—made in the shape of Indians or in some way related to Indian themes.

The vast majority of this material is generic—that is, it depicts or relates to Indians, but not necessarily those of the Western states. Few collectors see this as a detriment. What they want is the look or the atmosphere, and the knowledge that what they seek is available in great quantity at often very modest prices. Anyone who has attended a high-end auction of Native American crafts and watched baskets, pottery, and blankets sell for prices in the $1,000–100,000 range realizes that not all of us can play that game. For those of more modest means, Indian kitsch provides the look without the cost.

Moreover, much that is collectible in this field is available not through auctions or an expensive specialist deal-

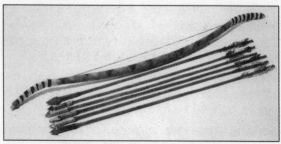

Bow and arrows, polychrome-painted hardwood; bow, 45 inches long; arrows, 32 to 36 inches; Blackfoot; c. 1860–1880; $1,800–2,500 the set.

er, but at your friendly local yard sale, swap meet, second-hand store, or even in your own attic. It's "do-it-yourself" collecting, the way things were before antiques and collectibles became big business.

So broad is this field that the items, categories, and prices set forth in this section should be read only as guidelines. There are many collectible objects that may not be covered here, and the fact that what you are interested in is not mentioned should not be seen as indicating its lack of importance. It just means that you are a pioneer!

Price Listings—Indian Kitsch

Skookum doll, male doll with composition head, cloth body, and wearing flannel Pendleton blanket; marked "Skookum"; made by H. H. Tannen Co.; Los Angeles; c. 1920–1930, 12 inches high; $90–120.

Skookum doll, female doll with plastic body, carrying baby of similar make in her flannel blanket; marked "Skookum"; made by H. H. Tannen Co.; Los Angeles; c. 1940–1950; 9 inches high; $60–75.

Indian doll, brave with bisque head, felt and fur clothing and mohair wig, jointed arms and legs; c. 1910–1920; 8.5 inches high; $75–100.

Indian doll, squaw holding baby in arms, molded colored celluloid; Japanese; c. 1930–1940; 4 inches high; $20–30.

Indian Head bank, polychromed cast aluminum penny bank in form of bust of Chief in feathered headdress; c. 1900–1910; 5 inches high; $100–150.

Indian Head bank, bust of Indian with headband and feather, polychrome-glazed molded earthenware; c. 1910–1920; 4.5 inches high; $80–120.

Bank, standing Indian with hand shading eyes, bronzed cast iron; c. 1915–1925; 6.5 inches high; $65–95.

Bank, mechanical, polychromed cast iron figures of kneeling Indian shooting rifle at standing bear; coin inserted in rifle

Patent medicine almanac, lithographed and printed paper with depiction of Western Indian squaw, 5 x 7.5 inches; c. 1910–1920; $8–12.

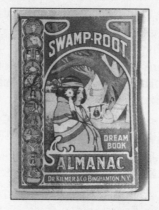

is discharged into bear; c. 1880–1900; 8 inches long; $800–1,200.

Bank, mechanical, Chief Big Moon, Indian sitting in front of tipi, polychrome cast iron; c. 1900–1910; 9 inches long; $1,200–1,800.

Salt and pepper shakers in form of Indian Chief and brave, polychromed white earthenware; c. 1940–1960; 3 inches high; $6–9.

Salt and pepper shakers in form of Indian drums, polychromed white earthenware; c. 1940–1950; 2.5 inches high; $5–7.

Shaving mug, hand-painted representation of Indian brave and letters TOTE (fraternal); c. 1880–1910; 4 inches high; $150–200.

Souvenir spoon, handle in form of Indian brave, electroplated silver; Casper, Wyoming; c. 1900–1920; 6 inches long; $55–75.

Souvenir spoon, handle in form of totem pole, electroplated silver; Seattle, Washington; c. 1910–1930; 6 inches long; $35–50.

Souvenir spoon, handle in form of crouching Indian brave, electroplated silver; Omaha, Nebraska; c. 1900–1920; 5.5 inches long; $40–55.

Souvenir spoon, handle in form of Indian head, electroplated silver; Park City, Utah; c. 1930–1940; 6 inches long; $25–40.

Souvenir spoon, handle in form of Indian and buffalo, electroplated silver; St. Louis, Missouri; dated 1904; 5.5 inches long; $50–65.

Medicine bottle, Wright's Indian Cough Balsam, aqua glass; c. 1880–1900; 7 inches high; $8–12.

Medicine bottle, Indian Root Beer extract, aqua glass; c. 1890–1910; 4 inches high; $2–4.

Medicine bottle, Healey & Bigelow's Kickapoo Indian Tape Worm Secret, green glass; c. 1900–1910; 6 inches high; $5–8.

Medicine bottle, Healey & Bigelow's Indian Sagwa, embossed picture of Indian, aqua glass; c. 1890–1900; 8 inches high; $10–15.

Medicine bottle, Dr. Josephus' Great Shoshonee Remedy, aqua glass; c. 1870–1880; 9 inches high; $55–75.

Medicine bottle. Dr. Kilmer's Indian Cough Cure, aqua glass; c. 1890–1910; 8 inches high; $12–16.

Medicine bottle, Brant's Indian Pulmonary Balsam, octagonal, aqua glass; c. 1870–1890; 7 inches high; $25–35.

Advertising sign, Colorado Midland Railway, lithographed paper in wooden frame, 20 x 16 inches; North American Indian Council; Denver, Colorado; 1915; $2,000–2,500.

Medicine bottle, Old Dr. Solomon's Great Indian Bitters, amber glass; c. 1880–1900; 9 inches high; $50–65.

Whiskey bottle, in form of cigar store Indian, colored pottery; by Ezra Brooks Distillery; 1968; 9 inches high; $10–15.

Whiskey bottle, in form of Mudhead Kachina, colored pottery; by Ezra Brooks Distillery; 1978; 10.5 inches high; $35–50.

Whiskey bottle, in form of Rattlesnake Kachina, colored pottery; by Ezra Brooks Distillery; 1980; 11 inches high; $30–40.

Whiskey bottle, in form of Indian Chief, colored porcelain; by James Beam Distillery; 1979; 12 inches high; $20–40.

Whiskey bottle, in form of Indian brave, colored glass; by Garnier; France; 1958; 12 inches high; $15–20.

Whiskey bottle, in form of sitting Indian with pipe and headdress, polychrome porcelain; by Lionstone; 1973; 7 inches high; $35–45.

Whiskey bottle, Indian in canoe, polychrome porcelain; by Potters; 1979; 11 inches long; $40–55.

Cosmetics bottle, in form of Indian tipi, colored glass; by Avon Products; 1974; 4 inches high; $2–3.

Cosmetics bottle, in form of Indian Chief with headdress, colored glass; by Avon Products; 1972; 3.5 inches high; $1–2.

Tonto and Scout, plastic figures of Indian and horse with accessories including anvil, branding irons, etc.; made by the Pressman Co.; Brooklyn, New York; c. 1965–1970; $50–75.

Windup toy, Indian on horse; when wound, horse rears up and turns in circle; polychrome composition and tin; German; c. 1950–1955; 4.5 inches high; $30–40.

Boy's Indian costume, khaki jacket and trousers in red and yellow, feathered war bonnet; c. 1910–1920; $45–75.

Indian Chief badge; premium for Post Raisin Bran; tin; c. 1950–1960; 2.5 inches high; $2–4.

Ring in form of Chief's head; premium for Indian Gum; silvered pot metal; c. 1930–1940; 1 inch high; $3-5.

Drum or tom-tom, National Biscuit Co. premium for Straight Arrow program; lithographed tin and cardboard; c. 1950–1960; $15–25.

Advertising sign, Plains Indian brave on horseback; painted wood; Ithaca Sign Co., c. 1910–1930; 40 inches high; $500–750.

Advertising sign for Colorado Midland Railroad, Plains Indian brave with lance, bow, and shield; lithographed cardboard; c. 1895–1900; 37 x 24 inches; $300–450.

Advertising display for Sure Shot Chewing Tobacco, kneeling Indian shooting arrow from bow, slogan "SURE SHOT/IT TOUCHES THE SPOT"; lithographed tin; c. 1900–1920; 28 x 20 inches; $350–500.

Advertising sign for None Such Mince Meat, well-done head of Indian Chief, a rare piece, lithographed tin; c. 1880–1890; 20 x 29 inches; $13,500–15,000.

Advertising sign for Dr. Pierce's Golden Medical Discovery, two Indians on watch from hilltop, lithographed paper; c. 1910–1915; 39 x 26 inches; $750–900.

Advertising panel for Chief Two Moon Bitter Oil, lithographed cardboard, 24 x 40 inches; c. 1910–1930; $125–175.

Advertising sign for Prince Albert Smoking Tobacco, Indian Chief in full headdress, lithographed cardboard; c. 1920–1930; 21 x 15 inches; $250–350.

Advertising handbill for Sitting Bull Durham Tobacco, Indian with rifle on horse, lithographed paper; c. 1890–1900; 7 x 10 inches; $500–650.

Advertising handbill for Dr. Morse's Indian Root Pills, Plains Indian on horse spearing bear, color lithographed paper; c. 1890–1910; 3 x 5 inches; $60–90.

Andirons, cast iron in form of standing Indians; c. 1920–1940; 13 inches high; $250–350.

Cookie box, color lithographed tin with picture of actress Gloria Swanson as an Indian maiden; design by Henry Clive; c. 1930–1935; 9 inches in diameter; $100–175.

Cigar tin, Apache Trail Cigars, oval lithographed tin container with image of warrior on horse, rare; c. 1915–1925; 7 inches high; $900–1,200.

Bar tray, "Iroquois Beer," lithographed sheet metal, 11.5 inches in diameter; c. 1940–1950. Though the Iroquois were an Eastern tribe, the Indian depicted wears a Western headdress, a typical characteristic of early twentieth century advertising; $80–110.

Cookie box, lithographed tin; design by illustrator Henry Clive depicting the actress Gloria Swanson as a Western Indian, 9 inches in diameter; c. 1930–1935; $100–175.

Sign for resort, Indian climbing pine tree, polychrome-painted sheet iron; c. 1900–1930; 23 x 31 inches; $350–500.

Mug, turned hardwood with root handle, decal of Plains Indian in headdress; c. 1920–1940; 8 inches high; $25–35.

Miniature sled, pine and iron wire with decal of Plains Indian brave with feathered headband; c. 1910–1930; 9.5 inches long; $50–70.

Souvenir tipi, birch bark with painted decoration; c. 1930–1940, 6 inches high; $20–30.

Souvenir canoe, birch bark, bottom stamped "Nevada"; c. 1930–1940; 7.5 inches long; $25–35.

Souvenir drum, rawhide and wood with painted decoration, Indian head, and stars; c. 1930–1940; 8 inches in diameter; $30–45.

Painted cast chalk figure of Plains Indian chieftain with long headdress, carnival art; c. 1920–1940; 12 inches high; $20–30.

Painted cast chalk figure of Plains Indian on horseback, carnival art; c. 1930–1950; 11 inches high; $30–45.

Painted cast chalk figure of squatting Indian, carnival art; c. 1920–1940; 8.5 inches high; $20–30.

Whirligig, Indian paddling canoe, cut and painted wood; c. 1930–1950; 10.5 inches long; $80–110.

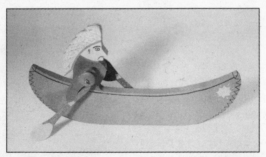

Whirligig, Indian paddling canoe, saw cut and painted wood, 8 inches long; c. 1940–1960; $65–85.

Weathervane, Indian shooting arrow from bow, rusted sheet iron; c. 1900–1920; 20 inches high; $700–950.

Weathervane, Indian shooting arrow from bow, artificially rusted sheet iron with orange tinge; made on island of Jamaica; c. 1985–1990; 27 inches high; $75–125.

Weathervane, crouching Indian shooting arrow from bow, painted plywood; c. 1940–1960; 18 inches high; $165–235.

Decorative corner bracket, head of Indian, wrought and sheet iron; c. 1910–1930; 21 x 22 inches; $550–700.

Photograph, Navajo Indian in village background; c. 1900–1910; 4.5 x 3 inches; $135–185.

Photograph, carte de visite of Northwest Coast Indian in blanket aboard ship; c. 1870–1880; 5 x 4 inches; $200–300.

Photograph, group of Western Indians with horses; c. 1910–1920; 4 x 5 inches; $60–85.

Clock, head of Indian with clock face, bronzed pot metal; c. 1930–1950; 7 inches high; $40–55.

Cigar store Indian, polychrome-painted pine, 5 feet tall; c. 1890–1910; typical of advertising pieces in Western garb used throughout the country; $12,000–16,000.

Diorama, of Western Indian scene, carved and painted wood and canvas, 2 x 3 feet; c. 1930–1940; $150–200.

Wall plaque, Indian shading eyes with hand, painted plastic wood; c. 1930–1945; 8 x 11 inches; $30–40.

Ashtray, embossed representations of Indian heads, drums, and hatchets, silvered pot metal; c. 1940–1950; 5.5 inches in diameter; $20–35.

Ashtray, floor-standing pedestal in form of Indian woman who holds ashtray in her hands, bronzed pot metal and glass; c. 1935–1945; 24 inches high; $90–120.

Set of plastic coasters used for drinking glasses, each with representation of different Indian bust; c. 1950–1970; each 4 inches in diameter; $15–20, set of six.

Bookends, Indian on horseback, bronzed pot metal; c. 1930–1940; 5.5 inches high; $40–55, set of two.

Eskimo
Collectibles

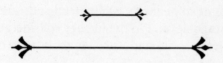

Scattered across the Arctic and subarctic regions of North America, the ancient Eskimo or Inuit culture reflects a remarkable adaptation to an extremely hostile environment. The 100,000 or so Inuit living in Alaska, northern Canada, and Greenland are the inheritors of a rich but extremely limited artistic tradition.

Due both to their living conditions and to a lack of raw materials, they became minimalists, producing a far smaller range of collectible objects than Indians. Partially for this reason and partially because the Inuit were not, like the Native Americans, a vibrant part of our own history, their artifacts were slower to attract wide collector attention.

During the past two decades, however, interest in this field has increased and prices have risen sharply. This is particularly true in the area of sculpture and scrimshaw, a field where the Inuit have excelled since prehistoric times. Early Eskimo ivory carvings and nineteenth-century wooden masks bring high prices, while recent and reasonably priced soapstone sculpture has found an important audience. The latter work is primarily of Greenland or northern Canadian origin but is included here to provide a complete picture of Eskimo crafts.

Though certainly collectible, household objects, tools, basketry, clothing, and articles of personal adornment are less often seen on the market. This is due both to the fact that the Inuit were quick to adopt useful white replacements (there was little reason to continue the laborious manufacture of stone bowls when metal and, later, plastic ones were available) and to the further consideration that, unlike the case with sculpture, there was little white tourist demand for these items.

Inuit Carving and Scrimshaw

Eskimo sculpture came to the attention of Russian, English, and American explorers in the early nineteenth century, and though greatly changed through white influence, it remains a vital art form as well as an important source of tribal income.

The earliest-known Inuit sculpture may be traced to Alaska's ancient Okvik culture. Small but highly realistic human and animal forms were carved from ivory, often the so-called "old ivory" acquired from the remains of whales and walrus found along the coast or even from the tusks of prehistoric mammoths exposed by thawing of the earth. Such objects are still being found at ancient village sites and burial grounds, but collectors should be advised that not all are legally acquired. Get a written warranty, not only of authenticity, but also of legal acquisition.

While it is often difficult to determine the purpose of these early pieces, some were certainly religious amulets or talismen worn or carried to ensure good hunting or good health. Others were gambling pieces, and some

Scrimshaw decorated pipe, curving walrus ivory barrel is engraved with scenes of Eskimos and deer or elk, turret form bowl, 11 inches long; Alaska or western Canada; c. 1900–1920; $1,800–2,300.

might have been dolls. By the 1800s such things were being shaped primarily from walrus ivory.

It was at this point that English and American sailors introduced scrimshaw, the carving and etching of bone with the images highlighted by filling them in with ink or lampblack. Inuit artists quickly took to this technique, and by 1900 they were masters of it, producing a wide variety of objects for their white customers. Many of these, such as cribbage boards and pipes, were not native forms.

Unlike the case with sailor scrimshaw, where fakes and reproductions in both ivory and plastic abound, there is usually little problem with nonauthentic Eskimo scrimshaw. However, it is often difficult to determine the age of a piece, since style and pictorial content have changed little over the years. As a general rule, the older the ivory is, the more yellow or even brown, and this serves as some guide to age, though a piece can be stained to create the illusion of antiquity.

Eskimos have carved stone fat lamps and cooking pots for hundreds of years. In the late 1940s, as the supply of ivory dwindled, and with the encouragement of white sponsors, some craftsmen turned to local soapstone. This soft green, gray, or black mineral proved ideal for the shaping of human and animal figures and even complete village scenes. Early examples were highly naturalistic, but later carvers turned to more abstract forms.

Scrimshaw decorated
snuff box with wooden
cover, engraved with
scenes of hunting,
whaling, and travel,
3.5 inches high; Alaska;
c. 1890–1910;
$1,500–1,900.

Soapstone sculpture has proved extremely popular with white buyers. Recent pieces can be obtained for $100 or even less, and early examples (pre-1960) or those by respected carvers may fetch prices in the low thousands. For many new collectors, soapstone is Eskimo art.

Sculpture in wood, on the other hand, is generally uncommon. For the most part, it was confined to the Pacific coast and Aleutian Islands, where the material was readily available. Though decorated boxes, fishing floats, and other items were made, by far the most desirable artifacts in this medium are the ritual masks made to reflect the visions of shamans, or healers. Carved in distorted, asymmetrical forms, these subtly painted masks are related to those produced by Northwest Coast Indians and, like that work, bring high prices. Mask making appears to have developed relatively late, in the mid-nineteenth century, and some of the finest examples date to around 1900.

Inuit masks are fragile, and those offered for sale have often been restored, particularly the halo of feathers which may surround the face. Though I have not heard of fakes, the rarity and high price of these items would justify their production. Buyers should choose with care.

Price Listings—Inuit Carvings and Scrimshaw

Scrimshaw decorated pipe, curved walrus ivory barrel engraved with scenes of birds, fish, felines, and a fish-drying rack, turret-shaped bowl, 12 inches long; Alaska or western Canada; c. 1890–1900; $2,200–2,800.

Scrimshaw decorated pipe, curved walrus ivory barrel with overall lampblack-filled engraving of various birds and animals and complex village scene, turret-shaped bowl; 9 inches long; Alaska; c. 1890–1900; $3,500–4,300.

Scrimshaw decorated pipe, curved walrus ivory barrel engraved with whaling and walrus hunting scenes, no bowl, 8 inches long; Alaska; c. 1910–1920; $600–850.

Scrimshaw decorated bow drill, curved piece of whale ivory engraved with scenes of Eskimos in boats pursuing whales, 16 inches long; Alaska; c. 1900–1910; $1,800–2,600.

Scrimshaw decorated cribbage board, oblong ivory board engraved with map of Alaska, hunting scene, and inscription "Nome City Alaska/1913," 20 inches long; Alaska; 1913; $1,300–1,800.

Scrimshaw decorated cribbage board, whole walrus tusk with inset board and engraved representations of Eskimo village, a whale, and hunters, 21 inches long; Alaska; c. 1910–1920; $1,000–1,400.

Scrimshaw decorated cribbage board, whole walrus tusk with inset board and engraved figures of whales, bears, fish, and a hunter, 15 inches long; Alaska; c. 1920–1930; $500–750.

Scrimshaw decorated cribbage board, whole walrus tusk with inset board and engraved scenes of whale and Inuit hunting seal, 14.5 inches long; Alaska; c. 1910–1920; $650–900.

Scrimshaw decorated tusk, rectangular piece of walrus ivory engraved with scene of Eskimos dancing, 7.5 inches long; Alaska; c. 1890–1910; $250–350.

Scrimshaw decorated busk, rectangular piece of walrus ivory engraved with scene of Eskimos in kayaks, 6 inches long; Alaska; c. 1890–1900; $300–400.

Scrimshaw decorated busk, rectangular piece of walrus ivory engraved with scene of Eskimos hunting walrus or seal, 6.5 inches long; Alaska; c. 1880–1900; $350–450.

Scrimshaw decorated harpoon head, whale ivory in spear form with incised circle-and-dot decoration filled with red pigment, 6 inches long; Bering Strait; c. 1870–1890; $900–1,300.

Carved brown ivory human figure, elongated oval head, small, finlike hands, cylindrical torso, legs missing, 5 inches high; Okvik culture; Alaska; c. 100 B.C.–A.D. 300; $7,500–9,500.

Carved brown ivory human figure, tapering oval body with crosshatch decoration, diamond-shaped head with deeply incised eyebrows, eyes, and mouth, narrow nose in relief, all highly stylized, 5.5 inches high; Okvik culture; Alaska; c. 200 B.C.–A.D. 200; $9,000–13,000.

Carved fossilized brown ivory head, lozenge-shaped with large, elongated nose and deeply incised eyes, eyebrows, and mouth, finely carved, 3.5 inches high; Okvik culture; Alaska; c. 200 B.C.–A.D. 200; $18,000–26,000.

Carved whalebone mask, stylized features with broad triangle-shape nose, deep-set eyes, and straight-line mouth, 7.5 inches high; northern Alaska; c. 1400–1700; $9,000–12,000.

Carved mask of fossilized ivory, stylized features with elongated protruding nose, almond-shaped eyes, and open, curving mouth, traces of red and black pigment, 8 inches high; Alaska; c. 1300–1600; $11,000–14,000.

Carved ivory figure, simple cylindrical body with ovoid head; crudely incised eyes, nose, and mouth; 4 inches high; Alaska; c. 1400–1700; $300–450.

Carved ivory figure, probably a hunting amulet, simple cylindrical body pierced for thong and having crudely shaped

Sculptural head, fossilized ivory, 4 inches high; Okvik culture; Alaska; c. 500–100 B.C. Though usually small, prehistoric Inuit carvings can bring very high prices; $15,000–20,000.

head and platformlike feet; incised eyes, nose, and mouth; 4.5 inches high; Thule culture; St. Edward's Island, Alaska; c. 1200–1600; $450–600.

Carved ivory miniature or "finger mask," round plaque with sunlike face and loop for finger at base; replacement feathers inserted in rim; 5 inches high; Alaska; c. 1850–1870; $2,300–2,800.

Carved fossilized brown ivory crouching bear figurine, 5 inches long; Alaska; c. 1100–1400; $900–1,200.

Two carved figures, fossilized ivory: left, 4 inches high; right, 3 inches high; both Okvik culture; Alaska; c. 300 B.C.–A.D. 100. Left, $600–800; right, $450–600.

Carved figurine in the form of a bear, fossilized ivory, 4.5 inches long; St. Lawrence Island area, Alaska; c. 1100–1300; $900–1,300.

Carved ivory game counter in form of a recumbent seal, body decorated with cross-hatching, 3 inches long; Thule culture; Alaska; c. 1100–1300; $325–475.

Carved ivory game counter in form of upright seal's head and shoulders, 2 inches high, Thule culture; Alaska; c. 1100–1300; $190–230.

Carved ivory game counter in form of seal, incised, lamp-black-filled eyes and head decoration, 3.5 inches long; Alaska; c. 1890–1920; $95–135.

Carved ivory toy or game counter in form of duck, body covered with red-pigment-filled incised dots, 2.5 inches long; Alaska; c. 1900–1920; $70–95.

Carved ivory toy or game counter in form of duck or similar bird, 2 inches long; Alaska; c. 1910–1930; $45–65.

Carved ivory toy or game counter in form of polar bear, 2.5 inches long; Alaska; c. 1900–1930; $75–100.

Carved walrus ivory toy in form of two dogs pulling sled, all carved from single piece of bone, 5 inches long; Alaska; c. 1890–1910; $450–650.

Carved ivory toy in form of man in kayak, 3.5 inches long; Alaska; c. 1910–1930; $80–120.

Carved ivory toy in form of miniature open boat (umiak), 4 inches long; Alaska; c. 1910–1930; $70–95.

Carved whale ivory toy spinning top, 3 inches in diameter; Alaska; c. 1880–1900; $100–130.

Carved hunting
amulet in the form of
a walrus head,
fossilized ivory,
3 x 3.5 inches; Alaska
c. A.D. 500–1000;
$1,700–2,500.

Carved ivory toy spinning top with incised geometric decoration, 3.5 inches in diameter; Alaska; c. 1880–1900;
$150–200.

Carved ivory hunting amulet in form of standing fox, 3.5 inches long; Fort Barrow; Alaska; c. 1870–1890; $200–275.

Carved ivory hunting amulet in form of walrus with hole
through body for leather thong, 2.5 inches long; Alaska;
c. 1850–1880; $175–235.

Carved ivory hunting amulet in form of whale with hole for
leather thong through body, 3 inches long; Alaska; c.
1850–1880; $225–300.

Carved whale ivory club with abstract bird's head handle
originally inset with shells and beads, 16.5 inches long;
Unimak Island, Alaska; c. 1200–1600; $3,500–4,500.

Carved whale ivory effigy wand, abstract openwork representation of fish with incised eyes and gills, 20 inches
long; Alaska; c. 1880–1900; $2,750–3,500.

Carved walrus ivory effigy wand, carved in abstract curvilinear
form, 17.5 inches long; Alaska; c. 1900–1910; $1,000–1,400.

Decorative plaque, flattened oblong piece of walrus ivory
engraved with representations of Eskimos hunting and
fighting, 9 inches long; Alaska; c. 1900–1920; $1,200–1,700.

Decorative plaque, flattened oblong piece of walrus ivory engraved with scene of Eskimo herding deer or elk, 11 inches long; Alaska; c. 1900–1920; $900–1,300.

Carved walrus ivory "seal scratcher," curved piece of bone with incised decoration and inset seal claws (used to scratch on ice to attract seals), 15 inches long; Alaska; c. 1870–1900; $450–600.

Carved walrus ivory "seal scratcher," curved piece of bone with simple incising and inset seal claws, 10 inches long; Alaska; c. 1880–1910; $250–400.

Carved walrus ivory wound plug (used to seal wounds in slain game), tapering tubular shape with finial in form of walrus head with inset trade bead eyes, 4.5 inches long; Alaska; c. 1900–1920; $450–650.

Carved walrus ivory comb, circular comb with two sets of teeth cut from walrus tusk, faint incised decorative patterns, 5 inches long; Alaska; c. 1900–1930; $150–200.

Carved walrus ivory comb, flattened hourglass-shaped form terminating in incised teeth, 5.5 inches long; Alaska or northern Canada; c. 1900–1910; $75–125.

Carved walrus ivory comb, flattened whale's tail form with engraved Vs, terminating in incised teeth; Alaska; c. 1880–1900; $150–225.

Miniature geese, fossilized ivory, 2 to 4.5 inches in length; Thule culture; Alaska; c. 1100–1300; $250–400 depending on size and quality of carving.

Miniature animals, fossilized ivory, 2 to 2.5 inches high; Thule culture; Alaska; c. 1200–1400. Left, walrus, $400–550; right, geese or seabirds, $200–300.

Carved walrus ivory decorative button, embossed representation of walrus head, 1.5 inches in diameter; Alaska; c. 1910–1930; $65–85.

Carved walrus ivory decorative button, simple embossed representation of recumbent seal, 1 inch in diameter; Alaska; c. 1910–1930; $40–60.

Carved walrus ivory decorative button, representation of hunter with spear, 1.5 inches in diameter; Alaska; c. 1910–1930; $75–100.

Carved walrus ivory hide scraper, piece of tusk with shaped indentations for fingers, 5.5 inches long; Alaska; c. 1880–1890; $350–500.

Carved walrus ivory hide scraper, half round piece of tusk with back cut to represent stylized human face, 4 inches long; Alaska; c. 1860–1880; $550–700.

Carved walrus ivory needle case, tubular form covered with engraved, red- and black-pigment-filled circles, 6 inches long; Alaska; c. 1890–1910; $200–275.

Carved walrus ivory needle case, flattened tubular form with overall geometric engraving and fish head form finial, 8 inches long; Alaska; c. 1880–1900; $500–750.

Carved walrus ivory bag handle, flattened curved piece of ivory decorated with incised diamonds and arrows, 17 inches long; Alaska; c. 1890–1910; $150–225.

Carved walrus ivory bag handle, flattened straight piece of

Carving of hunters in umiak with seal, ivory, 8.5 inches long; Alaska; c. 1850–1900; $3,000–4,500. An example of the earliest tourist carving.

ivory decorated with incised, red-pigment-filled circles, 13 inches long; Alaska; c. 1880–1900; $225–300.

Carved walrus ivory snow-beater (used to remove snow from garments before entering igloo), paddle-shaped piece of ivory with faint incised decoration, 18 inches long; Alaska or northern Canada; c. 1860–1880; $275–350.

Carved walrus ivory snow-beater, curving blade shape with engraved representations of whales and hunters, 23 inches long; Alaska; c. 1880–1900; $450–650.

Carved walrus ivory snow knife (used to cut blocks to build igloos), in form of knife with shaped handle and incised line around edge, 17 inches long; Alaska; c. 1880–1900; $550–725.

Carved walrus ivory snow knife, knife form with handle dec-

Miniature seal carvings, ivory with punchwork and lampblack highlights, 1.5 to 3.5 inches long; Alaska; c. 1910–1930; $80–120. Miniatures of this sort are relatively common and very popular with collectors.

Two miniature carvings of foxes, old ivory, 3 to 4.5 inches long; Alaska; c. 1850–1900; $150–250.

Miniatures or game counters in the form of ducks, old ivory, 2 to 2.5 inches high; Fort Barrow area, Alaska; c. 1920–1940; $200–300.

orated by three carved teardrop forms, blade engraved with bands of chevrons, 18.5 inches long; Alaska; c. 1870–1890; $700–900.

Carved walrus ivory snow knife, blade-shaped piece of bone with handle terminating in seal form head, incised geometric decoration, 14.5 inches long; Alaska; c. 1890–1900; $850–1,150.

Carved whale ivory musical instrument, paddle-shaped bone with two embossed stylized human heads surrounded by engraved geometric patterns; playing strings run vertically; 11.5 inches long; Alaska; c. 1870–1890; $4,000–4,800.

Soapstone carving of parka-clad Eskimo dancing on one foot, 5 inches high; northern Canada; c. 1950–1960; $300–450.

Soapstone carving of Eskimo with spear or lance, 4 inches high; northern Canada; c. 1970–1980; $100–150.

Soapstone carving of Eskimo in kayak, 6.5 inches long; northern Canada; c. 1970–1980; $175–235.

Soapstone carving of Inuit hunter with dead walrus, 7.5 inches long; northern Canada; c. 1960–1970; $350–500.

Arrow straightener, prehistoric mastadon ivory with simple incised decoration, 8.5 inches long; Alaska; c. 1800–1850; $400–550.

Soapstone carving of Inuit woman scraping sealskin, 4.5 inches high; northern Canada; c. 1960–1980; $325–400.

Soapstone carving of reclining seal, 4.5 inches long; Greenland or northern Canada; c. 1970–1980; $150–200.

Soapstone carving of two seals, one crouching, one lying down, northern Canada; c. 1965–1975; $225–275.

Soapstone carving of polar bear standing on hind legs, 5 inches high; northern Canada; c. 1970–1980; $200–250.

Soapstone carving of polar bear standing on all four feet with neck extended, 7 inches long; northern Canada or Greenland; c. 1950–1960; $250–350.

Soapstone carving of whale, 6 inches long; northern Canada; c. 1970–1980; $175–225.

Soapstone carving of unidentified seabird, 3.5 inches high; northern Canada; c. 1970–1990; $75–125.

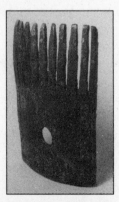

Comb, old ivory, 4.5 inches high; Alaska; c. 1750–1800; $300–450..Pieces like this often are not recognized by dealers.

Eskimo mask, carved and painted wood, teardrop form with broad triangular nose, round mouth, and demilune eye slits; represents driftwood spirit, 12 inches high; southern Alaska; c. 1880–1900; $8,500–11,500.

Eskimo mask, carved wood painted white, oval with concentric circle form terminating in large round mouth hole, angled eye slits; represents a hunting spirit, or Tunghak, 10 inches high; Yukon area, Alaska; c. 1865–1875; $9,000–11,000.

Eskimo mask, carved oval wooden mask with pronounced eyebrows over round eye holes and triangular nose, shaped chin with oval mouth, traces of red pigment, 11 inches high; Kuskokwim area, Alaska; c. 1870–1890; $7,000–9,500.

Eskimo mask, carved wood in form of piglike animal with snout and protruding teeth, oval eye holes, 9.5 inches long, 7 inches high; Kuskokwim area, Alaska; c. 1890–1910; $5,500–7,000.

Eskimo mask, carved and painted wooden mask of rounded oval shape with surrounding bentwood frame to hold feathers, broad demilune mouth, round eye and nose holes beneath triangular brow, 11.5 inches high; Kuskokwim area, Alaska; c. 1890–1900; $10,000–12,000.

Eskimo mask, carved unpainted wood, oblong with owl-like features including beak-shaped nose between deep-set almond form eye slits, triangular mouth, 9 inches high; Kuskokwim area, Alaska; c. 1870–1890; $5,000–6,500.

Pair of harpoon shafts in ivory, 8 to 10 inches long; Alaska; c. 1850–1875; $350–500.

Woman's knife or Ulo in steel with ivory handle carved to represent seal, 6.5 inches high; Nunivak area, Alaska; c. 1920–1930; $1,200–1,800. Excellent form brings a high price here.

Eskimo mask, carved wood painted white, distorted features with twisted, gaping mouth, oval eyes, and snub nose; a so-called "death mask," replacement feathers surround head, 12 inches high; Hooper Bay, Alaska; c. 1875–1895; $7,000–8,500.

Eskimo mask, carved and painted wood representing a shaman, distorted features with tiny shell "eyes," large nose holes through which wearer sees, and gaping mouth with shell teeth and protruding tongue, 12.5 inches high; Alaska; c. 1900–1910; $15,000–18,000.

Miniature or finger mask, puppetlike figures used in dances, carved and painted wood, circular form with two finger rings below; round smiling face on one side, frowning face on other; 5 inches high; Kuskokwim area, Alaska; c. 1880–1890; $2,000–3,000.

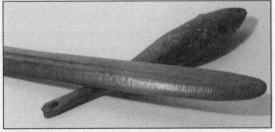

Above: marlin spike, carved ivory, 11 inches long; below: net or fishing weight, whalebone, 7 inches; both Alaska; c. 1880–1910. Above, $150–200; below, $135–185.

Shaman's hat, carved and painted wood in form of sun figure with applied hands and legs resting upon a well-detailed seal; halo of feathers surrounds figure, 16 inches across; Nunivak Island, Alaska; c. 1920–1925; $8,000–9,500.

Eskimo grave post or marker, unpainted wood carved in clothespinlike human form with oval head, round eye sockets, and downturned mouth; approx. 3 feet high; Kuskokwim area, Alaska; c. 1860–1880; $4,000–6,000.

Household Objects

Certain objects made in the Eskimo community either for use or for sale to tourists have attracted widespread collector interest. Among these are the popular miniature kayak models and rare baleen (a type of flexible whalebone) baskets. However, the great majority of other wood and stone items in this category are seldom seen on the market and may often pass unnoticed even among dealers. Prices are unstable and difficult to determine due to the few examples that change hands.

Collectors are advised to examine the photos in this book and those in other publications dealing with Eskimo arts in order to familiarize themselves with unrecognized pieces which they may encounter at flea markets or garage sales, often at extremely low prices.

Price Listings—Household Objects

Model kayak, carved wood with figure of passenger, 20.5 inches long; Alaska; c. 1880–1900 (rare, as most models are of skin); $1,500–2,000.

Model kayak, walrus skin over wooden frame, carved wooden passenger wearing fur costume, floats and carved seal on bow and stern, 26 inches long; Alaska; c. 1910–1930; $600–850.

Model kayak, walrus skin over wooden frame, carved wooden figure of passenger holding oar, carved walrus on stern, 14 inches long; Alaska; c. 1900–1920; $250–350.

Model kayak, walrus skin over wooden frame, 8 inches long; Alaska; c. 1920–1940; $75–100.

Model umiak, walrus skin over wooden frame, three carved figures mounted on seats, 13 inches long; Alaska; c. 1910–1930; $300–450.

Model umiak, walrus skin over wooden frame, 7.5 inches long; Alaska; c. 1920–1940; $125–175.

Fishing reel, carved wood with bone inlay, 4 inches in diameter; Alaska or northern Canada; c. 1900–1920; $450–550.

Fishing tackle box, oblong box carved from single piece of wood, board top and leather wrappings, 15 x 7 inches; Alaska; c. 1900–1920; $275–375.

Fishhook, bone or ivory with simple engraving, 4 inches long; Alaska; c. 1700–1800; $150–225.

Fishhook, carved wood with inset bone barb, 5.5 inches long; Alaska; c. 1870–1900; $80–120.

Ice scoop, used to remove ice from fishing hole, shaped wooden handle, round frame of whalebone and baleen netting, 19 inches long; Alaska; c. 1850–1900; $400–600.

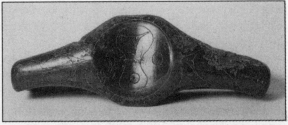

Ornament for fishing hat, whalebone with incised decoration, 4 inches long; Alaska; c. 1800–1850; $500–750.

Net-making bobbin, walrus ivory, flat spatulalike form with curving open ends, 6.5 inches long; Alaska; c. 1900–1920; $80–110.

Net-making bobbin, wood, flat spatulalike form with curving open ends, 8 inches long; Alaska; c. 1890–1910; $45–65.

Scraper, dark stone blade with attached bone handle decorated with crude geometric engraving, 5 inches long; Alaska; c. 1200–1400; $550–750.

Scraper, oblong tapering soapstone blade with shaped finger holds, 4 x 3 inches; northern Canada; c. 1900–1930; $100–150.

Gouge, shaped wooden handle with beaver tooth inset at each end, 7 inches long; Alaska; c. 1890–1910; $75–100.

Gouge, shaped wooden handle with beaver tooth inset at end, 5 inches long; Alaska; c. 1880–1910; $60–85.

Drill bit, shaped wooden shaft, inset flint bit, 10 inches long; Alaska; c. 1890–1910; $75–100.

Drill, pump type with flywheel made from whalebone, socket from soapstone, hide fittings, 12.5 inches high; Alaska or northern Canada; c. 1880–1910; $300–450.

Meat hook, hook-shaped piece of wood with triangular piece of bone set at 30 degree angle to shaft and secured by baleen strips used to handle and hang meat, 11 inches long; Alaska; c. 1900–1920; $450–650.

Woman's knife, oval piece of stone with sharpened edge and carved hand grip, 5.5 inches long; Alaska or northern Canada; c. 1880–1900; $275–375.

Knife, steel-bladed skinning knife with walrus ivory handle decorated with geometric engraving, 8.5 inches long; Alaska or northern Canada; c. 1920–1940; $250–350.

Knife sheath, bone decorated with engravings of human figure and running moose, leather-bound, 10 inches long; Alaska; c. 1920–1940; $300–450.

Knife, stabbing dirk made from sharpened piece of bone with inset grip covered with hide, crude geometric engraving on blade, 9 inches long; Alaska; c. 1870–1900; $350–500.

Pick for digging roots, L-shaped, crudely carved wooden handle secured by leather binding to sharpened bone bit, handle 17 inches long; Alaska; c. 1870–1890; $235–295.

Boots, long sealskin boots decorated in appliquê with vertical bands of light and dark skin, 23 inches high; Alaska; c. 1920–1940; $850–1,250.

Boots, sealskin in natural shades of brown and white decorated with geometric banding stained red and black, 16.5 inches high; Alaska; c. 1920–1940; $700–950.

Boots, undecorated sealskin, 16 inches high; Alaska; c. 1900–1920; $275–350.

Boots, short mukluk type boots made of sealskin and polar bear fur, 10 inches high; Alaska; c. 1920–1940; $450–600.

Moccasins, sealskin decorated with beadwork motif of bird on flower in red, yellow, blue, and black, 10.5 inches long; Alaska or northern Canada; c. 1930–1950; $700–950.

Socks, woven grass, 9.5 inches high; Alaska; c. 1890–1910; $60–90.

Hat, cone-shaped, made of thin sheet of bentwood painted white, 11 inches in diameter; Alaska; c. 1910–1930; $175–250.

Hat, cone-shaped, made of thin sheet of natural bentwood decorated with band of geometric appliquê in red- and yellow-stained grass, 12 inches in diameter; Alaska; c. 1930–1950; $325–400.

Hat ornament, flattened spatula form piece of bone with incised geometric decoration filled in lampblack, 5 inches long, Alaska; c. 1880–1900; $200–275.

Snow goggles, carved wooden eyeglass form with narrow eye slits, 5.5 inches across; Alaska; c. 1870–1890; $175–275.

Eyeshade, carved wooden sunshade in demilune shape with leather thong fastener; Alaska; c. 1880–1910; $150–225.

Pair of snow or sun goggles in carved whalebone, 6.5 inches long; Alaska; c. 1860–1890; $450–600.

Belt, sealskin decorated with geometric beading in red, black, blue, and white and having buckle in shape of walrus head, 37 inches long; Alaska; c. 1910–1940; $275–400.

Mittens, woven grass, 8 inches long; northern Canada; c. 1900–1920; $65–95.

Mittens, sealskin, 9.5 inches long; Alaska; c. 1910–1930; $100–150.

Parka, triangular shape, made of animal intestines sewn together with gut, 28 inches long; Alaska; c. 1870–1890; $300–450.

Necklace, seal teeth strung on leather thong, 22 inches long; Alaska; c. 1880–1920; $135–185.

Pendant, in form of whale, carved and painted wood, 3 inches long; Alaska; c. 1900–1920; $175–255.

Hunting amulet in the form of a miniature mask, carved wood, 3.5 inches high; Brevig Mission area, Alaska; c. 1780–1810; $1,700–2,300. Inuit items in wood are relatively uncommon.

Food bowl, finely carved rectangular wooden bowl with flaring sides and overhung rim, 8 x 5.5 inches; Alaska; c. 1880–1900 (from important private collection); $1,300–1,700.

Food bowl, oblong with flaring sides, carved from a single piece of wood, 11 x 7.5 inches; Alaska; c. 1890–1910; $650–850.

Food bowl, oblong bentwood bowl with pegged-on base, interior decorated with well-painted representation of deer or elk, 12 x 8.5 inches; Alaska; c. 1870–1890; $2,500–3,500.

Cooking pot, rectangular with incurving sides, carved soapstone, 10 x 7 inches; northern Canada or Greenland; c. 1890–1910; $75–125.

Cooking pot, oval with shallow sides, carved soapstone, 12 x 9 inches; Alaska; c. 1900–1920; $90–140.

Paint or storage box in form of seal holding a smaller seal on its belly, carved and painted wood, 8.5 inches long; Alaska; c. 1910–1930; $3,500–4,500.

Fat lamp, shallow triangular piece of carved soapstone, 8 x 6 inches; northern Canada; c. 1870–1900; $90–130.

Fat lamp, shallow round piece of carved soapstone, 4.5 inches in diameter; northern Canada; c. 1890–1910; $50–75.

Fat lamp, shallow oval carved piece of soapstone with indentation for wick, 7.5 x 5.5 inches; northern Canada; c. 1870–1890; $120–160.

Fat lamp, shallow round piece of carved soapstone decorated with incised bands and central sunlike motif, 8 inches in diameter; northern Canada; c. 1910–1930; $200–300.

Fat heater, shallow triangular piece of carved soapstone, 30 x 20 inches; Alaska; c. 1870–1900; $250–400.

Spoon, carved walrus ivory, flat handle decorated with incised images of men in kayaks, 7 inches long; Alaska; c. 1900–1920; $225–300.

Storage box, wood decorated with incised designs, fitted top, 7 inches long; Alaska; c. 1850–1900; $500–700.

Food bowl, oblong, carved from a single piece of wood, 13 x 8 inches; Alaska; c. 1880–1900; $800–1,000.

Spoon, carved ivory decorated with three incised human stick figures, 6 inches long; Alaska; c. 1880–1900; $175–250.

Spoon, carved walrus ivory decorated with bands of incising, 5.5 inches long; Alaska; c. 1890–1910; $90–125.

Spoon, carved wood, bowl decorated with incised and pigment-filled animal figure, 6 inches long; Alaska or northern Canada; c. 1900–1920; $200–275.

Spoon, carved wood decorated with protruding knobs just above bowl, 6.5 inches long; Alaska; c. 1890–1910; $125–165.

Spoon, carved and shaped horn, 7.5 inches long; northern Canada; c. 1890–1920; $65–95.

Dipper, round bowl and handle formed from piece of baleen which has been curved in on itself at one end and secured with leather thongs, walrus ivory bottom, 11 inches long; Alaska; c. 1910–1930; $250–350.

Bucket, oblong, thin sheets of wood overlapped and secured with hide laces, 9 inches high; Alaska; c. 1900–1920; $300–450.

Storage pot for fats, oblong, thin sheets of wood overlapped and secured with hide laces, 12 x 7.5 inches; Alaska; c. 1880–1900; $250–350.

Pestle, rounded mushroom-shaped piece of wood used to grind food, 5.5 inches high; Alaska; c. 1900–1920; $90–120.

Bottle neck, horn-shaped piece of walrus ivory which is tied to bladder-skin bottle, 3.5 inches long; Alaska; c. 1900–1920; $65–85.

Basket, cylindrical, lidded, woven of baleen with light striped square motifs on darker ground, faceted ivory knob on lid, 4 inches high; Alaska; c. 1910–1930; $700–1,000.

Basket, round, lidded, woven of baleen with bands of lighter material against darker ground on both sides and lid, lid knob in form of two seal heads, 5.5 inches in diameter; Alaska; c. 1910–1930; $900–1,300.

Basket, bag form woven of light-colored grass; Alaska; c. 1910–1930; $125–175.

Basket, cylindrical storage basket of grass and rush with narrow mouth, bands of darker dots against light ground, 8 inches high; Alaska; c. 1890–1920; $275–400.

Dipper or ladle, oblong bowl with handle, all carved from single piece of wood, 9.5 inches long; Alaska; c. 1870–1890; $550–750.

Sewing bag, cut and sewn animal fur and sealskin, 7 x 5 inches; Alaska or northern Canada; c. 1900–1920; $200–285.

Needle case, carved tubular piece of wood with stopper in form of fish head, 3.5 inches long; Alaska; c. 1880–1900; $150–225.

Drum, circular piece of baleen over which is stretched piece of hide decorated with polychrome representations of hunters and animals, 9 inches in diameter; Alaska; c. 1870–1900; $1,400–1,900.

Toy jumping jack, articulated carved wood with skeleton painted on in black, leather thong stringing, 7 inches long; Alaska; c. 1900–1920; $300–450.

Toy root pick, L-shaped toy composed of shaped wooden handle secured by leather thong to bone pick, 9 inches long; Alaska or northern Canada; c. 1900–1920; $125–175.

Doll head, flat piece of wood with carved features and two holes for joining it to cloth body, 4 inches high; Alaska; c. 1890–1910; $200–300.

Doll, carved rounded wood body with legs but no arms, shallow carved features, wrapped in piece of fur, 6 inches long; Alaska; c. 1900–1920; $250–350.

Ball, large stuffed leather ball decorated with painted geometric designs and fur tassels, 9 inches in diameter; northern Canada; c. 1900–1930; $500–650.

Mortar, carved and hollowed-out wooden bowl with short handle, used in grinding tundra moss "snuff," 8.5 inches long; Alaska or northern Canada; c. 1870–1900; $325–425.

Pestle, short tubular wooden stick with applied knoblike ivory finial, 6 inches long; Alaska or northern Canada; c. 1870–1900; $125–150.

Snuff box, round lidded wooden box decorated with incised lines around top and bottom, 3 inches in diameter; Alaska or northern Canada; c. 1870–1900; $150–225.

Wound plug, wood carved in the form of a walrus, leather binding, 10.5 inches long; Alaska; c. 1850–1870; $1,200–1,600.

Snuff box, tubular container carved from piece of animal bone and decorated with incised lines top and bottom, carved wooden top, 3.5 inches long; Alaska or northern Canada; c. 1880–1910; $135–175.

Spanish-American Art and Antiques

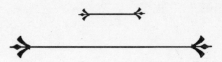

Collectible material associated with the Spanish-speaking population of the Southwest falls into three main categories: folk art, household furnishings, and woven textiles. None of these are particularly plentiful.

Though Spanish colonists were established in New Mexico, Colorado, and California by 1700, their communities were isolated, and the population always remained small and of modest means. Much of what was produced has been destroyed over the years. As a consequence, collectible material is relatively uncommon. Moreover, since the settlers were closely linked with Mexico, many of the things they made resemble similar items produced in that country. As a result, collectors need to be particularly knowledgeable in this area.

It was not, however, until well into this century that more than a handful of museum professionals and collectors appreciated the field of Hispano arts, and interest in the area remains predominantly local. Unlike the case with Native American and Inuit crafts, tourists to Santa Fe or Albuquerque did not customarily bring back Latino souvenirs.

This was due primarily to the fact that the craft tradition had largely died out by 1900, not to be revived until after World War II. Today, though, there is growing demand for Spanish-American crafts, particularly carvings and textiles. Earlier, pre-1900 items are scarce and command high prices.

Folk Art

Until very recently, Hispano folk art was religious art. Craftsmen, known as santeros, produced carvings (bultos) and paintings (retablos) for use in local churches and home shrines. Taking their images from popular religious prints (estampitas) or illustrated broadside prayers (oraciones), they depicted favored saints as well as members of the Holy Family.

These charming images appear to have been produced from the eighteenth century to late in the nineteenth century, when they were largely superseded by commercially produced chalk figures and Currier & Ives type religious prints. Today, original examples are in great demand.

Bulto of crucified Christ and disciples, polychrome-painted cottonwood, 13 inches high; New Mexico; c. 1870–1880; $1,800–2,300.

Bulto, manger scene with San Ysidro, polychrome-painted wood, 15 inches high; New Mexico; c. 1870–1890; $1,600–2,000.

There are, however, problems. Few santeros signed their work. Moreover, bultos and retablos were also made throughout Central and South America. It is often difficult to distinguish the Southwestern products. The fact that these are usually made of piñon pine or cottonwood may serve to distinguish them from many Latin American examples shaped from exotic timber, but this is little help when trying to distinguish them from the Mexican products, since the same woods were used there. On the other hand, it should also be noted that of the 1,200 or so Catholic holy figures, Spanish-American artisans regularly depicted no more than a few dozen. That a figure, such as St. Anthony or St. John, was popular in the area may be some evidence of its having originated there.

A new and exciting category of Spanish-American folk art is that of animal carving. Bird and animal figures frequently appear in bultos (St. Francis and the birds being a good example), and small animals were traditionally made both as toys and crèche figures. However, beginning in the late 1960s, a group of New Mexican sculptors began to turn out large, sometimes life-size representations of animals, birds, and fish. The work of men such as Felipe

Archuleta and Ben Ortega is now in museum collections and leading folk art galleries, and art agents are scouring the Southwest for the next generation of carvers.

Price Listings—Folk Art

Bulto of Christ on the cross, polychrome-painted pine, 40 inches high; Colorado; c. 1840–1860; $2,500–3,000.

Bulto of Our Lady of Sorrows, polychrome-painted cottonwood, 23 inches high; New Mexico; c. 1850–1870; $2,000–2,750.

Bulto of St. Anthony holding child, polychrome-painted cottonwood, 14 inches high; New Mexico; c. 1830–1860; $1,000–1,500.

Bulto of St. Michael with sword and scales, polychrome-painted wood, 14.5 inches high; New Mexico; c. 1850–1870; $1,700–2,500.

Bulto of St. Michael, polychrome-painted wood, 32 inches high; attributed to Rafael Aragon; New Mexico; c. 1820–1850; $10,000–13,000.

Bulto of St. Gertrude, polychrome-painted pine, 29 inches high; New Mexico; c. 1840–1870; $3,000–4,000.

Bulto a vestir, Dolores figure, torso of polychrome-painted cottonwood, lower body gesso-coated linen over stickwork frame, 22 inches high; New Mexico; c. 1880–1900; much rarer than fully carved figures; $2,500–3,000.

Bulto, life-size figure of crucified Christ, polychrome-painted cottonwood, 5 feet 6 inches high; attributed to Jose Rafael Aragon; New Mexico; c. 1840–1845; $25,000–30,000.

Bulto of Our Lady of Guadalupe, polychrome-painted pine, 18 inches high; New Mexico or Colorado; c. 1840–1860; $1,800–2,600.

Bulto of the Holy Family, polychrome-painted cottonwood, 9 inches high; by Feliz Lopez, Espanola, New Mexico; c. 1975–1980; $400–650.

Bulto of the Holy Child of Prague, polychrome-painted cottonwood, 13.5 inches high; New Mexico; c. 1830–1870; $1,300–1,800.

Bulto of Saint Rita of Cascia, polychrome-painted cottonwood, 18 inches high; New Mexico; c. 1830–1850; $3,500–4,200.

Bulto of St. Lawrence with skull, polychrome-painted pine, 23 inches high; New Mexico; c. 1800–1840; $6,000–7,500.

Bulto of St. Joseph with child, polychrome-painted cottonwood, 40 inches high; New Mexico; c. 1830–1860; $4,000–5,500.

Bulto of St. Joseph, polychrome-painted cottonwood, 14 inches high; by Frank Britto, Sr.; Santa Fe, New Mexico; 1973; $500–700.

Bulto of St. Francis of Assisi, polychrome-painted wood, 26.5 inches high; attributed to the Arroyo Hondo carver; New Mexico; c. 1840–1850; $9,000–11,500.

Bulto of St. Francis of Assisi, polychrome-painted cottonwood, 13 inches high; by Ben Ortega; Tesuque, New Mexico; 1983; $300–450.

Bulto of St. John, polychrome-painted wood, 12 inches high; New Mexico; c. 1850–1870; $650–950.

Carving of tiger, polychrome-painted cottonwood, 37 inches long; by Felipe Archuleta; Tesuque, New Mexico; 1970; $2,500–3,000.

Carving of coyote, polychrome-painted cottonwood, 55 inches long; by Felipe Archuleta; Tesuque, New Mexico; 1980; $3,000–3,750.

Carving of rabbit, polychrome-painted cottonwood, 15 inches long; by Leroy Archuleta; Tesuque, New Mexico; 1985; $600–750.

Carving of horse, polychrome-painted pine and cottonwood, 18 inches long; by Ben Ortega; Tesuque, New Mexico; 1985; $650–900.

Carving of snake, polychrome-painted wood and metal, 40 inches long; by Richard Luis Davila; El Rancho, New Mexico; 1985; $500–750.

Death cart, caretta del muerto, pine and cottonwood, painted in part, 14 inches long; New Mexico; c. 1920–1930; $600–750.

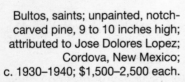

Bultos, saints; unpainted, notch-carved pine, 9 to 10 inches high; attributed to Jose Dolores Lopez; Cordova, New Mexico; c. 1930–1940; $1,500–2,500 each.

Retablo, San Juan Nomucene,
polychrome-painted pine,
10 inches high; New Mexico;
c. 1870–1890; $2,500–3,200.

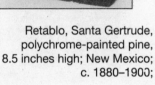

Retablo, Santa Gertrude,
polychrome-painted pine,
8.5 inches high; New Mexico;
c. 1880–1900;

Carving of wild boar, polychrome-painted cottonwood, horsehair, and plastic, 27.5 inches long; by Mike Rodriguez; Rowe Mesa, New Mexico; 1984; $750–1,000.

Carving of orangutan, polychrome-painted cottonwood and twine, 62 inches high; by Alonzo Jimenez; Chupadero, New Mexico; 1978; $1,200–1,600.

Carving of bull, polychrome-painted cottonwood, 11 inches long; by Alejandro Sandoval; Santa Fe, New Mexico; 1985; $150–250.

Carving of rooster, polychrome-painted pine, 12.5 inches high; by Frank Britto, Sr.; Santa Fe, New Mexico; 1985; $350–500.

Carving of pig, polychrome-painted cottonwood, 14.5 inches long; by David Alvarez; Santa Fe, New Mexico; 1982; $300–450.

Carving of seated coyote, polychrome-painted cottonwood, 45 inches high; by Max Alvarez; Santa Fe, New Mexico; 1985; $750–950.

Retablo, St. Vincent Ferrar, polychrome-painted wood

Retablo, face of Christ, tempera paints on tin plate, 11 inches high; New Mexico; c. 1870–1900. Retablos on tin are more typically Mexican in origin; $750–900.

Retablo, Holy Family, tempera paints on tin plate, 12.5 inches high; New Mexico; c. 1880–1900; $650–800.

panel, 11.5 x 7.5 inches; New Mexico; c. 1820–1840; $3,000–4,500.

Retablo, Saint Liberata, polychrome-painted wood panel, 12 x 8 inches; attributed to the Truchas Master; New Mexico; c. 1790–1840; $6,500–8,000.

Retablo, St. Anthony, polychrome-painted pine panel, 11 x 9 inches; New Mexico; c. 1800–1850; $4,000–4,800.

Retablo, St. Jerome, polychrome-painted wood panel, 8 x 6 inches; New Mexico; c. 1840–1860; $1,800–2,500.

Retablo, Our Lady of Sorrows, polychrome-painted wood panel, 12 x 7 inches; New Mexico; c. 1835–1865; $1,500–2,000.

Retablo, St. Michael, polychrome-painted wood panel, 12 x 9 inches; attributed to the Santo Niño santera, New Mexico; c. 1840–1860; $7,500–10,000.

Retablo, St. Christopher, polychrome-painted wood panel, 11 x 8.5 inches; New Mexico; c. 1850–1870; $1,500–2,000.

Retablo, the Holy Child of Atocha, polychrome-painted pine

Retablo, Niño de Atocha, polychrome-painted pine, 9.5 inches high; New Mexico; c. 1870–1890; $2,200–2,800.

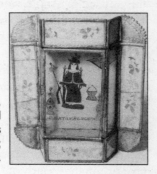

Family shrine, Niño de Atocha, polychrome-painted glass and punchwork-decorated tin, 15 inches high; New Mexico; c. 1900–1910; $900–1,200.

panel, 11.5 x 6 inches; New Mexico; c. 1840–1860; $1,800–2,200.

Retablo, St. Joseph, polychrome-painted wood panel, 11.5 x 9 inches; New Mexico; c. 1825–1855; $2,300–3,000.

Retablo, Our Lady of Mount Carmel, polychrome-painted wood panel, 12 x 8.5 inches; New Mexico; c. 1820–1840; $2,000–2,500.

Retablo, St. Ignatius with child, polychrome-painted wood panel, 10 x 8 inches; New Mexico; c. 1830–1850; $2,200–2,700.

Household Furnishings

The rancho homes of Spanish-Americans were small and the furnishings few. The most basic items of furniture were made: chairs, benches, stools, tables, chests, beds, and a type of cupboard called a trastero. Carpinteros produced these from native pine and cottonwood, usually employing dovetails, wooden pins, and leather hinges to join their pieces, rather than the nails, screws, and metal hinges used by Anglo workmen.

The style, based on sixteenth-century Iberian forms, changed little over the years. Surfaces were broad and angular with shallow decorative carving. The preferred colors were bold reds, blues, and yellows. Since much the same can be said of northern Mexican furniture, it is often hard to distinguish the two.

Recent collector interest in these pieces has resulted in the appearance on the market of much so-called "New Mexican" furniture. However, some of this is known to have originated south of the border, and there are rumors that other examples have even been brought in from Europe. Collectors must be cautious.

Household furnishings and utensils were made of wood, metal, or leather. The first consisted primarily of carved or hand-turned plates and drinking vessels, mortars and pestles, and churns. Less usual were wooden boxes or other objects covered with straw work designs.

Chair, carved and decorated pine, 34 inches high; by Manuel Archuleta; Taos, New Mexico; c. 1850–1860; $900–1,400.

Table, piñon pine, with decorative turnings and wrought iron drawer lock; Taos area, New Mexico; c. 1840–1860;

Wrought iron, tin, brass, and copper were employed in the crafting of cooking pots, candle holders, and other lighting devices and even picture frames; strips of rawhide leather were woven into hammocks, trunks, or storage boxes.

As with furniture, most of these objects closely resemble similar items produced in Mexico or in old Spain, and it is important to obtain a reliable history of their manufacture and use in the Southwest.

Price Listings—Household Furnishings

Chest, piñon pine with shallow carved rosettes, painted blue, 35 inches long, dovetailed corners and leather hinges, wrought iron lock; New Mexico or Colorado; c. 1850–1900; $2,000–2,800.

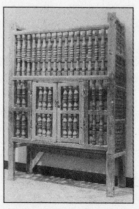

Cupboard or trastero, piñon pine with turned gallery spindles and wrought iron fixtures; New Mexico; c. 1840–1860; $6,000–7,500.

Candle holders, unpainted pine, 10.5 inches high; New Mexico; c. 1880–1910; $150–200 the pair.

Chest, cottonwood, unpainted, 31 inches long, dovetailed corners and wrought iron lock and hinges; New Mexico; c. 1860–1880; $900–1,200.

Chest, cottonwood, painted red and yellow, 22 inches long, dovetailed corners, leather hinges, no lock; New Mexico; c. 1880–1910; $550–700.

Bedstead, piñon pine, unpainted, 78 inches long, rough-hewn, joined with wooden pins; New Mexico; c. 1850–1890; $1,200–1,700.

Bedstead, piñon pine, head and foot painted green, side rails unpainted, 75.5 inches long, joined with wooden pins, simple turned legs; New Mexico; c. 1880–1910; $850–1,250.

Bench, cottonwood, unpainted, 51 inches long, through tenon construction with braced legs; New Mexico; c. 1860–1890; $650–950.

Bench, piñon pine, painted blue, 62 inches long, through tenon construction with braced legs; New Mexico; c. 1890–1910; $800–1,000.

Bench, cottonwood, unpainted, 30.5 inches long, rodlike legs mortised through seat; New Mexico; c. 1850–1900; $200–300.

Stool, piñon pine and cottonwood, unpainted, 19 inches high, turned legs mortised through seat; New Mexico; c. 1900–1920; $175–250.

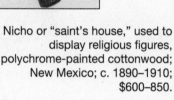

Household crosses. Above: pine with elaborate incised geometric decoration, 11 inches long; below: cottonwood covered with straw work inlay, 10 inches long; both, New Mexico; c. 1880–1910. Above, $400–550; below, $200–275.

Nicho or "saint's house," used to display religious figures, polychrome-painted cottonwood; New Mexico; c. 1890–1910; $600–850.

Stool, piñon pine, painted red, 17 inches high, rough-hewn legs mortised through seat; New Mexico; c. 1880–1910; $350–500.

Chair, piñon pine, unpainted, seat 16.5 inches high, back of turned spindles, turned legs; New Mexico; c. 1890–1910; $600–950.

Chair, piñon pine, painted blue and yellow, seat 17 inches high, solid back and square legs; New Mexico; c. 1880–1900; $800–950.

Table, piñon pine and cottonwood, unpainted, 27 inches high, rectangular top attached with wooden pins to rough-hewn base joined with through tenons; New Mexico; c. 1850–1880; $1,800–2,500.

Table, piñon pine, unpainted top and red base, 25 inches high, square top nailed to skirt with drawer, turned legs; New Mexico; c. 1890–1910; $1,300–1,700.

Wall shelf, cottonwood, painted yellow, 17 inches long, two

wrought iron hangers; New Mexico; c. 1880–1910; $125–200.

Set of hanging shelves, piñon pine, painted red and blue, 18.5 inches high, three shelves, dovetailed construction; New Mexico; c. 1870–1900; $450–600.

Cupboard or trastero, piñon pine and cottonwood, unpainted, 59 inches high, three shelves behind galleried front and sides of turned spindles, mortise and tenon construction, square legs; New Mexico; c. 1860–1880; $4,500–6,000.

Chopping bowl, piñon pine, unpainted, 17 x 10 inches, oblong hand-hewn vessel; New Mexico; c. 1870–1900; $200–275.

Chopping bowl, piñon pine, unpainted, 15.5 inches in diameter, lathe-turned; New Mexico; c. 1890–1910; $150–225.

Chopping bowl, piñon pine, unpainted interior, exterior red, 11 inches in diameter, lathe-turned; New Mexico; c. 1900–1920; $225–300.

Eating dish, piñon pine, unpainted, 8 inches in diameter, shallow rim, lathe-turned; New Mexico; c. 1870–1890; $160–220.

Candle holder, polychrome-painted pine in unusual geometric form; New Mexico; c. 1885–1895; $275–375.

Pair of polychrome-painted pine wall brackets, 10 inches high; New Mexico; c. 1900–1910; $550–750 the pair.

Two noise makers or "clackers," unpainted hardwood, used in religious processions; left, 11 inches long; right, 7 inches long; both, New Mexico; c. 1915–1935. Left, $60–80; right, $40–60.

Mortar, cottonwood, unpainted, 21 inches high, hand-hewn; New Mexico; c. 1850–1900; $350–500.

Mortar, piñon pine, unpainted, 7.5 inches high, lathe-turned; New Mexico; c. 1890–1910; $100–150.

Churn, piñon pine, interior unpainted, exterior red, 21 inches high, cone-shaped, made of ironbound staves; New Mexico; c. 1890–1910; $300–450.

Churn, cottonwood, unpainted, 22.5 inches high, cylinder-shaped, made from hollowed-out tree trunk; New Mexico; c. 1850–1870; $700–950.

Candle holders, pair, cottonwood, painted red and blue, 6 inches high, lathe-turned; New Mexico; c. 1880–1900; $250–350.

Storage box, cottonwood, covered with geometric straw work designs, 9 x 6 inches, box joined with wooden pins, has leather hinges; New Mexico; c. 1860–1880; $600–850.

Trunk, cottonwood, covered with geometric straw work

Pair of snowshoes, hardwood and rawhide leather, 16 inches in diameter; New Mexico; c. 1870–1890; $300–400 the pair.

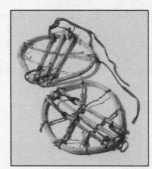

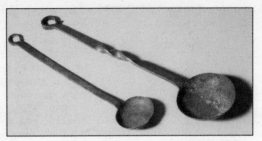

Ladles, wrought iron; New Mexico; c. 1880–1900. Above, with decorative twisted handle, $135–185; below, $80–100.

designs, 16 inches long, dovetailed box with dome top having iron wire hinges; New Mexico; c. 1850–1880; $1,000–1,300.

Picture frame, cottonwood, covered with geometric straw work designs, 7 x 9 inches; New Mexico; c. 1880–1900; $300–475.

Cross, piñon pine, covered with geometric straw work designs, 9.5 inches high; New Mexico; c. 1860–1890; $275–350.

Spatula, wrought iron with rope twist handle, 11 inches long; New Mexico; c. 1860–1890; $90–130.

Cooking fork, wrought iron with hanging hook, 13.5 inches long, three tines; New Mexico; c. 1880–1900; $80–120.

Chandelier, cut and punch-decorated sheet tin with wrought iron chain, 22 inches in diameter; Honda Mora, New Mexico; c. 1890–1910; $2,000–2,600.

Cooking spoon, wrought iron with hanging hook, 12 inches long; New Mexico; c. 1890–1910; $70–95.

Frying pan, wrought iron, 14.5 inches long; New Mexico; c. 1880–1900; $120–160.

Kettle, cast iron, 8 inches in diameter, three stub legs; New Mexico; c. 1870–1900; $110–140.

Fat lamp, wrought iron, 6 inches long, so-called Betty lamp with rope-twist iron wire hanging hook; New Mexico; c. 1880–1910; $200–275.

Candle holder, sheet iron, 7.5 inches high, cylindrical holder with disk base; New Mexico; c. 1860–1880; $150–225.

Candle lantern, tin with geometric punchwork decoration, 10.5 inches high, dome top and hinged door for candle removal; New Mexico; c. 1860–1890; $175–250.

Cross, tin inlaid with colored glass, 9 inches high; New Mexico; c. 1880–1910; $135–185.

Mirror, tin and glass, 10 x 7.5 inches, sheet tin decorated with stamped geometric devices; New Mexico; c. 1880–1910; $200–300.

Sauce pan, sheet copper with wrought iron handle, 6.5 inch-

Household shrine, glass with polychrome-painted punchwork-decorated tin, 13.5 inches high; New Mexico; c. 1910–1920; $350–500.

Candle lantern, punchwork-decorated tin with unusual handle; New Mexico; c.1880–1900; $200–275.

Household crosses, colored glass inset in punchwork-decorated tin. Left, 5 inches high; right, 16 inches high; both New Mexico; c. 1890–1920. Left, $75–100; right, $225–300.

es high, gourd-shaped with matching cover; New Mexico; c. 1870–1900; $80–120.

Eating pan or dish, sheet copper, 7.5 inches in diameter; low rim and wrought iron hanging hook; New Mexico; c. 1870–1900; $100–150.

Boiling pot, copper with wrought iron handles and rim reinforcement, 15.5 inches in diameter; New Mexico; c. 1870–1900; $275–350.

Hammock, rawhide strips woven into netlike form, 3 x 6 inches; New Mexico; c. 1860–1890; $250–400.

Canteen, rawhide with carved wood stopper, 8 inches high,

Box, rawhide with decoration of interwoven rawhide strips and red flannel, 10 x 7 x 4 inches; New Mexico; c. 1870–1885; $325–425.

Powder or shot flask, leather with embossed stitchwork decoration, carved wooden stopper; New Mexico; c. 1880–1900; $225–285.

teardrop-shaped with embossed floral pattern; New Mexico; c. 1880–1910; $200–300.

Box, made from woven rawhide strips in geometric pattern, 8 x 6 inches with matching slip over cover; New Mexico; c. 1860–1880; $275–400.

Box, made from woven rawhide strips in geometric pattern and red flannel cloth, 5 inches in diameter with matching slip over cover; New Mexico; c. 1870–1890; $350–500.

Textiles

Spanish-American-made textiles are uncommon compared with those produced by neighboring Native American and Mexican weavers. Moreover, the field remains largely unstudied, and many confuse Hispano weavings with those produced in the Saltillo area of northern Mexico or even with Navajo rugs.

It was, however, Spanish settlers who first introduced sheep and the weaving of wool into the Southwest. Customarily, their weavings consist of narrow strips sewn together, unlike Mexican and American Indian fabrics, which were made on wider looms and lack the center binding. Also, though sometimes worn as garments, these fabrics lack the medial head slit associated with Saltillo serapes, as well, in most cases, as the typical Mexican fringe.

Now known as Rio Grande weavings, the textiles produced in New Mexico and Colorado up until the late nineteenth century consisted primarily of woolen blankets, termed mantas; jerga, which was a loosely woven floor covering; and embroidered woolen bed coverings or coverlets, called colchas.

Early mantas were woven in alternating narrow and wide bands, while those made during the second half of the nineteenth century incorporated Mexican Saltillo decorative devices such as central star and hourglass designs. Jerga was normally made in simple checkerboard plaid or narrow overall stripes. Colchas, which are extremely rare (they took many hours to make), consisted of a natural white cotton weave, called sabanilla, upon which elaborate colored floral patterns were embroidered.

By the late nineteenth century few craftsmen were producing these textiles, as their customers had turned to popular and inexpensive factory-made Anglo fabrics. However, in the 1880s, traders encouraged weavers in the Chimayo region of New Mexico to produce blankets which combined popular Native American symbolism with traditional Hispano motifs. During the early twentieth century this trade was expanded to include such things as table coverings, purses, and even coats. The Chimayo tradition remains vital today.

Manta or blanket, woven wool, 54 x 80 inches, Rio Grande style; Chimayo, New Mexico; c. 1880–1900; $850–1,250.

Manta or blanket, woven wool, 48 x 74 inches; Chimayo region, New Mexico; c. 1930–1950; $400–550.

Price Listings—Textiles

Manta or blanket in Rio Grande style, woven wool broadly banded in brown, white, yellow, black and blue, 53 x 80 inches; New Mexico or Colorado; c. 1850–1870; $6,000–8,000.

Manta or blanket in Rio Grande style, woven wool, alternating wide and narrow bands in white, brown, black, green, and blue, 55 x 82 inches; New Mexico or Colorado; c. 1850–1870; $4,500–6,500.

Manta or blanket, Saltillo style, woven wool, vertical bands of geometric figures and large central diamond within diamond motif, in white, black, brown, and blue, 51 x 99 inches; New Mexico or Colorado; c. 1850–1870; $7,000–9,000.

Manta or blanket, Saltillo style, woven wool, elaborate vertical bands in abstract star pattern and large central stylized diamond, in black, white, brown, and blue, 53 x 78 inches; New Mexico or Colorado; c. 1850–1870; $15,000–18,000.

Detail of blanket, woven wool; Chimayo region, New Mexico; c. 1940–1960;

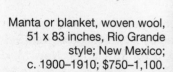

Manta or blanket, woven wool, 51 x 83 inches, Rio Grande style; New Mexico; c. 1900–1910; $750–1,100.

Manta or blanket, woven wool, 49 x 76 inches, Rio Grande style; Chimayo, New Mexico; c. 1870–1890; $1,500–2,000.

Shawl, woven wool, 31 x 16 inches; Chimayo, New Mexico; c. 1930–1950; $200–300.

Manta or blanket, Saltillo style, woven wool, vertical bands of abstract stars bordered by diagonal twill-like pattern, large central stylized diamond, in white, brown, black, blue, green, and red, 55 x 80 inches; New Mexico or Colorado; c. 1850–1860; $17,000–20,000.

Manta or blanket, Vallero style, woven wool, diamond pattern border with eight pointed stars at corners and large central stylized diamond framed by four smaller diamonds, in red, yellow, pink, white, blue, and brown, 45 x 88 inches; New Mexico; c. 1880–1890; $4,500–5,500.

Manta or blanket, Vallero style, woven wool, six rows of vertical zigzag patterning set within diamond pattern border, in blue, black, and white, 98 x 53 inches; New Mexico or Colorado; c. 1880–1900; $4,000–5,000.

Manta or blanket, Chimayo style, woven wool, broad bands of color against which are set geometric patterns and abstract human and animal figures, red, brown, white, blue, and green, 84 x 49 inches; New Mexico; c. 1900–1920; $1,500–2,000.

Manta or blanket, Chimayo style, woven wool, central diamond pattern surrounded by abstract figures, red, yellow, blue, brown, and gray, 55 x 33 inches; New Mexico; c. 1920–1940; $600–950.

Colcha or embroidered bedcover, wool, 65 x 78 inches; New Mexico; c. 1870–1880; $2,500–3,500.

Colcha or embroidered bedcover, wool on cotton, 63 x 80 inches; New Mexico; c. 1870–1890; $4,000–5,500.

Woman's handbag, Chimayo style, shoulder bag of woven wool with engraved silver clasp and abstract human and animal figures in blue, orange, yellow, and green on red, 9 x 7 inches; New Mexico; c. 1920–1940; $175–250.

Woman's clutch bag, Chimayo style, handbag of woven wool with engraved silver clasp, abstract figures in red, yellow, and green on blue, 7.5 x 4.5 inches; New Mexico; c. 1930–1950; $150–225.

Woman's short coat or jacket, Chimayo style, woven wool, bold geometric patterns front and back, silver buttons, red, green, orange, and brown on white, 32 inches long; New Mexico; c. 1930–1940; $300–450.

Colcha or embroidered bedcover, wool, 66 x 82 inches; New Mexico; c. 1880–1900; $3,500–4,500.

Western
Railroadiana

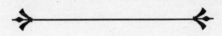

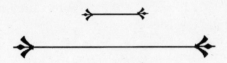

If the hallmarks of a popular hobby are availability of much and diverse material and reasonably low prices, then it is not hard to understand why railway collectibles in general and those associated with the West in particular are so sought after.

While a few seek out the original locomotives and cars, most enthusiasts settle for equipment such as engine bells, whistles, and headlights. Others acquire the railwayman's working gear: everything from uniform buttons and badges to switchmen's lanterns, signal flags, and tools. The range of paper goods is extensive: time tables, tickets, advertising posters, and all sorts of promotional material. A very special area is that of dining car memorabilia. Everything from menus to silver and porcelain bore the logos of the Western lines. It is all of interest to railroad buffs. Like much Western railroad material, it is both available from dealers and auctioneers, and affordable.

Now, of course, memorabilia associated with the Western lines form only a portion of all railroad collectibles, but they are an important portion. Names like the Union Pacific and the Atchison, Topeka and Santa Fe are a part of the Western legend, and the laying of the golden spike at Promontory Point, Utah, in 1869 marked the linking of the nation by rail. Moreover, the West, particularly the Rocky Mountains, was home to the unique narrow-gauge lines, the "baby railways" which continued until the 1950s to service the remote valley towns of Colorado and New Mexico.

Railwaymen's Clothing and Equipment

Those who worked the Western rails were specialists in their craft, and their clothing and equipment reflected not only what they did but which line they did it for. Equipment such as lanterns and switch locks was usually marked with a company logo to prevent its being "borrowed," while uniforms, hats, buttons, and badges proclaimed a worker's affiliation with a proud and prosperous line.

The fact that so many railway collectibles are marked is one of the reasons collectors are drawn to the field. One not only can collect railroadiana, but it is possible to build a large collection while focusing on one state's railways or even a single line. Moreover, many of the smaller items like railway spikes, uniform buttons, and caps are relatively inexpensive as well as easy to store and display.

Collectors particularly seek out items bearing the logos or marks of railways that operated for just a few years or in unusual circumstances, such as the narrow-gauge lines.

Though a few popular cap badges (usually those of well-known companies like the Union Pacific) have been reproduced, fakes and reproductions are not much of a problem in this field. Collectors should, however, be wary of new switch locks and keys being made in the Far East. These are brass and usually quite crude in construction.

Price Listings—Railwaymen's Clothing and Equipment

Cap, khaki with leatherette bill, embroidered C.P.R. (Canadian Pacific Railways); c. 1920–1940; $20–35.

Cap, blue felt with leatherette bill, embroidered BAGGAGE CHECKER/CANADIAN PACIFIC; c. 1940–1960; $15–20.

Cap, blue felt with leatherette bill, embroidered PORTER; c. 1930–1950; $20–30.

Cap, blue felt with leatherette bill, embroidered BURLING-TON ROUTE; c. 1930–1940; $35–50.

Railway employees' caps. Left: blue felt with leatherette bill, embroidered CHIEF; right: khaki felt with leatherette bill, embroidered "Boulder"; both Colorado; c. 1910–1930; $30–45.

A group of railway collectibles. Caps, blue felt with leatherette bills, CONDUCTOR, $35–50; Burlington Route TRAINMAN, $40–60. Lower: cap and uniform badges, brass, $35–65; center: uniform buttons, $5–15; right: cap badges, brass, $45–65.

Railway employees' uniform buttons, stamped brass, .5 to 1 inch in diameter; c. 1920–1940; $5–15 each. Smaller buttons and those from short-lived or obscure lines bring higher prices.

Railroadman's jacket and vest, blue wool with brass buttons, Denver & Rio Grande Railroad; c. 1900–1920; $225–300.

Cap, blue felt with leatherette bill, embroidered NORTHERN PACIFIC RAILWAY; c. 1920–1935; $60–85.

Cap, blue felt with leatherette bill, embroidered S. P. CO.; c. 1910–1930; $70–95.

Cap, blue felt with leatherette bill, embroidered SANTA FE; c. 1930–1950; $35–50.

Cap badge, nickel-plated brass, stamped BRAKEMAN/ NORTHERN PACIFIC RAILWAY, 3 inches long; c. 1925–1935; $45–65.

Cap badge, nickel-plated brass, stamped GREAT NORTH-ERN RY./AGENT, 2.5 inches long; c. 1910–1920; $60–75.

Railway locks, keys, and baggage checks, all brass and dating c. 1900–1920. Locks, 2 to 3 inches long, $35–50; keys, 1.5 to 3.5 inches long, $25–40; baggage checks, 1 inch long, $25–35.

Railway machinist's toolbox, polychrome-painted pine with representation of early steam locomotive, 30 x 14 x 10 inches; Union Pacific, Denver & Gulf Railroad, c. 1890–1900, $350–500.

Cap badge, nickel-plated brass, stamped S. P. CO./LOCOMOTIVE FIREMAN, 3 inches long; c. 1930–1940; $50–70.

Cap badge, nickel-plated brass with white enamel, stamped TRAIN CALLER, 2.5 inches long; c. 1900–1920; $40–60.

Cap badge, brass, stamped in black, DENVER & RIO GRANDE/BRAKEMAN, 3 inches long; c. 1920–1940; $65–85.

Cap badge, brass, stamped UNION PACIFIC, 3 inches long; c. 1940–1960; $30–45.

Uniform button, brass, embossed UNION/PACIFIC, 1 inch in diameter; c. 1930–1950; $3–5.

Uniform button, brass, embossed PORTLAND RAILROAD, 1 inch in diameter; c. 1910–1920; $12–16.

Uniform button, nickel-plated brass, embossed MISSOURI/PACIFIC/LINES, 1 inch in diameter; c. 1920–1940; $6–9.

Drinking water can, aluminum, 14 inches high; Colorado; c. 1930–1940; $40–55.

Water pail, sheet tin and wrought iron, 14.5 inches high; California; c. 1900–1910. The cone-shaped bottom was useful along the dirt right-of-way and discouraged theft for home use; $75–105.

A variety of railway oil cans, left to right: Cone type, sheet tin, 13 inches high, $15–25; aluminum, 15 inches high, $35–55; barrel type, 10 inches high, $20–30; all c. 1920–1940.

Uniform button, nickel-plated brass, embossed CANADIAN PACIFIC with representation of beaver, 1 inch in diameter; c. 1930–1945; $5–8.

Uniform button, brass, embossed BR (Burlington Route), 1 inch in diameter; c. 1930–1950; $3–5.

Uniform button, nickel-plated brass, embossed S. P. CO., 1 inch in diameter; c. 1930–1950; $4–7.

Uniform button, brass, embossed D/&/R/G (Denver & Rio Grande Railroad), .5 inch in diameter; c. 1910–1930; $15–20.

Railway first aid kit in stenciled sheet tin box, 10 x 7.5 x 3.5 inches; Chicago, Burlington & Quincy Railroad; c. 1915–1925; $100–150.

Wrecking car first-aid kit in stenciled walnut case, 12 inches square by 7 inches high, from Colorado narrow-gauge railway line; c. 1900–1920; $225–300.

Service pin, enameled nickel-plated brass, marked BOOST-ER CLUB/MISSOURI/PACIFIC/LINES, 1.5 inches in diameter; c. 1920–1930; $25–35.

Service pin, enameled brass, marked SAFETY/FIRST/BURLINGTON/ROUTE, 1 inch in diameter; c. 1930–1945; $20–30.

Uniform patch, wool embroidered in gold, INFORMATION, 3 inches long; c. 1930–1950; $8–12.

Uniform patch, wool embroidered in gold, BAGGAGE MAN, 3 inches long; c. 1930–1950; $10–15.

Uniform patch, wool embroidered in gold, SOUTHERN PACIFIC, 3.5 inches long; c. 1940–1960; $12–17.

Uniform jacket, blue wool with brass buttons, Union Pacific; c. 1930–1945; $150–200.

Uniform: jacket, vest, and pants; blue wool with brass button

Fire extinguisher, molded glass, cast iron wall mountings, 16 inches long, Colorado and Northwestern Railway; c. 1900–1910; $175–250.

Stencils used to number railroad cars, sheet brass and tin, 5 to 12 inches long; c. 1920–1940; $10–20.

Railway lanterns, sheet steel, glass, and iron wire with brass kerosene burners, 11 to 12 inches high; c. 1910–1930. Left: marked "Union Pacific," $75–100; right: with orange-tinted glass and marked "Denver & Southern," $125–175.

marked S.P.CO. (Southern Pacific); c. 1930–1940; $375–450.

Conductor's hand ticket punch, chrome-plated steel, used on the MKT (Missouri, Kansas, Texas Line), 6 inches long; c. 1920–1935; $60–85.

Desk stamp, cast iron and brass, Northern Pacific Express Co., 4 x 8 inches; c. 1910–1920; $50–75.

Ticket hand stamp, brass and wood, Rio Grande Railroad, 1.5 inches in diameter; c. 1920–1940; $20–30.

Ticket hand stamp, brass and wood, Missouri Pacific Lines, 1.7 inches in diameter; c. 1935–1945; $15–20.

Railway hand lamps, sheet steel and glass, 9 to 13 inches long. Left: carbide lamp; c. 1915–1935; $50–75. Right: battery-powered electric torch; c. 1930–1950; $35–50.

Railroad switch-stand lamp, sheet steel and cast iron with red and green glass lenses, 22 inches high; c. 1910–1920; $200–300.

Railroad switch-stand lamp, combined with red/white semaphore; sheet steel, cast iron, and glass, 49 inches high; by Deitz; c. 1920–1930; $750–1,000.

Baggage check, brass, stamped C.R. & N.R. (Copper River & Northwestern Railway, Alaska), 2 inches in diameter; c. 1900–1920; $30–45.

Baggage check, brass, stamped S.P.CO. (Southern Pacific), 1.5 inches in diameter; c. 1910–1930; $18–27.

Switch lock, iron and steel, stamped C.P.R.R. (Canadian Pacific Railways), 3.5 inches long; c. 1920–1940; $20–30.

Switch lock, iron and steel, stamped A.T. & S.F. RY. (Atchison, Topeka and Santa Fe), 3.5 inches long; c. 1915–1925; $25–35.

Switch lock, brass, embossed SO. PACIFIC CO., 3 inches long; c. 1920–1940; $30–40.

Switch lock, iron, stamped MO. P. R.R. (Missouri Pacific), 3.5 inches long; c. 1915–1930; $30–45.

Key, brass, stamped G.T.W. (Grand Trunk Western), 2.5 inches long; c. 1910–1920; $15–20.

Key, iron, stamped D & RGW RR (Denver & Rio Grande), 2.5 inches long; c. 1915–1930; $20–25.

Key, brass, stamped NP RY (Northern Pacific), 2 inches long; c. 1935–1950; $15–20.

Railroad marker light, sheet steel, cast iron, and glass, 14 inches high; c. 1900–1930; $450–600.

Switching signal generator, used to power railroad track switches, steel, 28 x 20 inches; c. 1902; $300–450.

Key, brass, stamped C. & N. P. RR. (Chicago and Northern Pacific), 2 inches long; c. 1920–1930; $20–30.

Key, steel, stamped O & W RR (Oregon and Washington Railway), 2.5 inches long; c. 1915–1925; $30–45.

Railway toolbox, wood with sheet iron reinforcement, stenciled WESTERN PACIFIC RR, 26 x 14 x 12 inches; c. 1920–1940; $135–185.

Water pail, sheet tin and iron wire, exterior painted green and

Locomotive headlamp, sheet steel, cast iron, and glass with kerosene burner, 36 inches high; Denver, South Park & Pacific Railroad; c. 1870–1880; $1,750–2,250.

Locomotive headlamp, sheet steel, cast iron, and glass with kerosene burner, 29 inches high; c. 1870–1890; $1,200–1,600.

Brake covers and brake cover handle, aluminum, 9 to 11 inches high; c. 1945–1955; $20–30

stenciled FRISCO (St. Louis & San Francisco Railroad), 13 inches high; c. 1920–1930; $90–120.

Watering can, sheet tin and iron wire with long spout, used on Southern Pacific, 15 inches high; c. 1930–1950; $35–50.

Stencil, sheet tin, D & RGW (Denver & Rio Grande), used to mark boxcars, 10 inches high; c. 1930–1940; $55–75.

Railway lantern, sheet steel, iron wire, glass, and brass kerosene burner, stamped MO PAC (Missouri Pacific), 11 inches high; c. 1920–1940; $80–110.

Railway lantern, sheet steel, iron wire, red glass, and brass kerosene burner, stamped SP CO (Southern Pacific), glass etched SAFETY FIRST, 12.5 inches high; c. 1930–1950; $125–175.

Railway lantern, sheet steel, iron wire, red glass, and brass kerosene burner, stamped STL SW (St. Louis & Southwestern Railroad), 12 inches high; c. 1915–1925; $140–180.

Railway lantern, sheet steel and brass, battery powered, stamped SPCO (Southern Pacific), 10.5 inches high; c. 1945–1955; $60–75.

Railway signal flags, wood with red, green, and white cloth, 14 to 17 inches square; c. 1900–1920; $35–55 each.

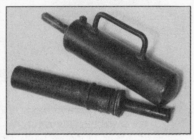

Railway locomotive signal torches, cast iron, 20 to 22 inches. Left: dated 1895; $90–115. Right: c. 1910–1925; $65–95.

Caboose lantern, sheet steel, iron wire, glass, and brass kerosene burner, stamped GTW (Grand Trunk Western Railroad), 17 inches high; c. 1910–1930; $150–200.

Caboose lantern, sheet steel painted yellow, iron wire, red and white glass, brass kerosene burner, stamped C & NW (Chicago & Northwest Railroad), 19 inches high; c. 1915–1925; $165–215.

Inspector's lantern, sheet steel, iron wire, and glass with brass kerosene burner, stamped UP RR (Union Pacific), 11 inches high; c. 1930–1940; $60–85.

Locomotive engine bell, stainless steel and cast iron, 22 inches high exclusive of framework, Denver & Rio Grande Railroad; c. 1895–1900; $1,300–1,800.

Railway chime whistle, brass and cast iron, 13 inches high, from Denver & Rio Grande narrow-gauge line; c. 1910–1920; $450–600.

Locomotive number plate, painted cast steel, 17 inches high, from a Union Pacific Challenger class locomotive; c. 1935–1940; $550–700.

Locomotive number plate, painted cast iron, 10 x 16 inches, from a Rio Grande & Southern narrow-gauge engine; c. 1920–1935; $650–900.

Switch-stand lamp, sheet steel, iron wire, green and red glass, brass kerosene burner, stamped A RR (Alaska Railroad), 23 inches high; c. 1920–1935; $425–550.

Switch-stand lamp, sheet steel, iron wire, green and red glass, electrified, embossed UP RR (Union Pacific), 24.5 inches high; c. 1940–1960; $250–350.

Railway engine headlamp, sheet steel, cast iron, and glass, electrified, used on Santa Fe Railroad, 29 inches high; c. 1930–1950; $900–1,200.

Railway engine headlamp, sheet steel, cast iron, and glass with brass kerosene burner, used on Southern Pacific Railway, 31 inches high; c. 1880–1890; $1,600–2,200.

Railway engine marker light, sheet steel, cast iron, and glass,

Reverse lever or "Johnson Bar," cast and wrought iron, 34 inches long, used on Denver & Royal Gorge Railroad; c. 1903–1915; $125–175.

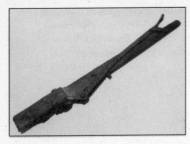

Railway telegraph keys, brass and steel, mounted on wood. Upper: 11 inches long; c. 1910–1930; $75–100. Lower: 7.5 inches long; c. 1900–1910; used on Rio Grande & Southern Railway, 17 inches high; c. 1920–1940; $400–550.

Signal flag, red and white cloth on wooden handle, used on Santa Fe Railroad, 16 inches square; c. 1920–1930; $45–65.

Locomotive torch, cast iron (used on Southern Pacific to signal disabled trains), 19 inches long; c. 1900–1910; $75–100.

Telegraph insulator, dark green glass, marked "Hemingray," 5 inches high; c. 1890–1910; $10–15.

Depot telephone, brass
and bakelite, 12 inches
high, Denver & Rio
Grande Railroad;
c. 1920–1925; $200–275.

Expandable wall
telephone, stainless
steel and bakelite,
10.5 inches high; by
Western Electric Co.;
c. 1920–1930;
$135–195.

Railroad bell, cast bronze, embossed GREAT WESTERN/
RAILWAY, 7 inches high; c. 1920–1930; $175–225.

Engine bell, stainless steel, used on Canadian Pacific
Railways, 20 inches high; c. 1930–1950; $500–650.

Engine bell, steel, used on Missouri Pacific Railroad, 18.5
inches high; c. 1910–1930; $700–900.

Train whistle, steam-powered brass and cast iron, used
on Colorado and Southern Railway, 14 inches high;
c. 1920–1935; $300–475.

Railroad telegraphy key, brass and steel, used at Denver,
Colorado, station, 7 inches long; c. 1890–1910; $70–95.

Railroad telegraphy key, brass and steel, mounted in wood-
en wall box, 7.5 inches long; c. 1900–1920; $50–75.

Railway dispatcher's telephone; steel, brass, and bakelite
with scissors type extension and wire and bakelite ear-
phone; used on California railroads; 12 inches high;
c. 1920–1935; $150–225.

Portable telephone case, steel-reinforced leather, 18 x 10 x 12 inches, with canvas carrying strap, Denver & Rio Grande Railroad; c. 1925–1935; $80–120.

Railway spikes, wrought iron, 5 to 6 inches long; c. 1900–1920; $1–2 each.

Depot telephone; steel, brass, and bakelite; candlestick type, 11.5 inches high; c. 1920–1940; $135–185.

Trackside telephone box, cast iron, embossed UNION PACIFIC, 18 x 13 inches; c. 1930–1950; $140–190.

Telegraph line insulators, green glass, 3.5 inches high; c. 1900–1920; $5–10 each.

Telegraph line insulators, brown pottery, 3 inches high; c. 1910–1930; $8–12 each.

Railway spikes, wrought iron, removed from Nevada tracks, 5 to 7 inches long; c. 1880–1900; $1–2 each.

Railway spikes, wrought iron, stamped SP (Southern Pacific), 5 to 7 inches long; c. 1900–1920; $35 each.

Chain-driven velocipede handcar used by track workers, steel and iron, 6 feet long; c. 1890–1900; $650–950.

Dining Car Memorabilia

Though it was not until around 1900 that Western railways began to provide dining cars, the lines rapidly made up for lost time by producing a great variety of china, electroplated silver, glass, and textiles as well as menus, match holders, and other ephemera. Since the great majority of these bear the mark of the sponsoring railway, they have provided a virtual treasure trove for collectors of railroadiana.

Despite the fact that much of this material is in the currently fashionable Art Deco style, prices have generally remained reasonable. Moreover, neither fakes nor reproductions present a problem in this field. However, like most railway collectibles, dining car items may be hard to obtain except through specialized dealers or auctions.

Price Listings—Dining Car Memorabilia

Ironstone china oval platter, 10 inches long, transfer-decorated feather motif and monogram WESTERN PACIFIC/FEATHER RIVER ROUTE; by Shenango China; c. 1930–1940; $35–45.

Ironstone china bouillon cup, 4 inches high, decorated and monogrammed as above; c. 1930–1940; $20–25.

Ironstone china oblong relish dish, 7.5 inches long, with Southwestern or Navajo design and monogram of Santa Fe Railroad; c. 1930–1950; $50–65.

Ironstone china cup, 4 inches high, in Mimbreno pattern with monogram of Santa Fe Railroad; by Syracuse China Co.; c. 1930–1940; $30–40.

So-called "States Plate" ironstone china, 12 inches in diameter; issued c. 1890–1900 by Missouri Pacific Lines and quite rare; $275–375.

Soup or cereal bowl, ironstone china, 10 inches in diameter; issued for the 20th Century Limited trains; c. 1930–1940; $125–165.

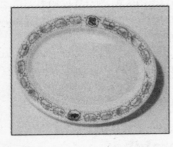

Historical platter, ironstone china, 11 inches long; issued by Union Pacific; rare scenes of the Old West; c. 1890–1900; $750–900.

Ironstone china plate, scalloped rim, 10 inches in diameter, floral transfer decoration and monogram of Union Pacific Railroad; by Shenango China Co.; c. 1910–1930; $40–55.

Ironstone china ice-cream dish, 3.5 inches high, transfer decoration of winged streamline train, monogram of Union Pacific Railroad; c. 1930–1950; $15–25.

Ironstone china plate, 10 inches in diameter, transfer decoration of train and word ROCKET, monogram of Chicago, Rock Island and Pacific Railway; c. 1920–1940; $60–80.

Ironstone china saucer, 5.5 inches in diameter, transfer decoration in Prairie Mountain Wildflower pattern, monogram of Southern Pacific Railway; by Onondaga Pottery Co.; c. 1915–1925; $25–35.

Ironstone china platters, 8 and 10 inches long, Rio Grande Railroad; c. 1935–1945; $20–30 each.

Ironstone china plate, 10.5 inches in diameter, same transfer decoration and monogram as above; c. 1915–1925; $50–75.

Ironstone china plate, 10 inches in diameter, fine scenic transfer decoration, monogram of Great Northern Railway; by Syracuse China Co.; c. 1940–1955; $60–85.

Ironstone china compote and under plate, 5.5 inches high, monogram of Denver & Rio Grande Western Railroad; by Syracuse China Co.; c. 1925–1940; $60–75.

Ironstone china oval platter, 11.5 inches long, in the Prospector pattern, monogram of Denver & Rio Granade Western Railroad; by Syracuse China; c. 1930–1950; $55–70.

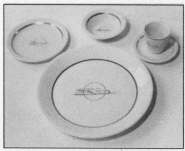

Dishware, ironstone china, all bearing logo of Union Pacific Railroad; c. 1935–1945. Left to right: bread and butter plate, 7.5 inches in diameter, $12–17; dinner plate, 10 inches in diameter, $30–45; dessert bowl, 6 inches in diameter, $15–20; demitasse cup and saucer, 5.5 inches in diameter, $25–35.

A group of ironstone railway china, c. 1930–1950. Left to right: 9-inch platter, Northern Pacific Railway, $55–75; 7-inch bread and butter plate, Union Pacific, $20–30; rare 11-inch platter, Colorado and Southern Railway; c. 1890–1895; $450–550.

Souvenir figurine, polychrome glaze earthenware figure of black cook holding large baked potato, 4 inches high, embossed NORTHERN PACIFIC/GREAT BIG BAKED POTATO; c. 1925–1935; $100–135.

Electroplated silver dinner fork, 7 inches long, Albany pattern, monogram of Santa Fe Railroad; c. 1920–1935; $7–10.

Electroplated silver dinner fork, 7 inches long, monogram of Canadian National Railways; c. 1950–1960; $4–6.

Electroplated silver butter knife, 5 inches long, Broadway pattern, monogram of Southern Pacific Railway; c. 1930–1950; $6–9.

Tableware, electroplated silver, left to right: table crumber, 10 inches long, Milwaukee Line, $35–50; serving dish, 9 inches long, Missouri Pacific, $55–75; covered sugar bowl, marked PULLMAN; c. 1925–1940; $45–60.

Electroplated silver iced-tea spoon, 7.5 inches long, Century pattern, monogram of Missouri Pacific Lines; c. 1935–1955; $15–20.

Electroplated silver teaspoon, 5 inches long, Art Nouveau style, monogram of the Frisco System; c. 1915–1925; $20–30.

Electroplated silver coffeepot with ebonized wooden handle, 8 inches high, monogram of Atchison, Topeka and Santa Fe Railroad; c. 1925–1940; $70–95.

Electroplated silver soup tureen, 10.5 inches long, marked as above; by Reed & Barton; c. 1930–1945; $55–70.

Electroplated silver finger bowl, 7.5 inches in diameter, monogram of Southern Pacific Railway; c. 1930–1950; $35–45.

Electroplated silver covered creamer, 5.5 inches high, monogram of Chicago, Milwaukee, St. Paul and Pacific Railroad; c. 1915–1925; $30–40.

Glass tumblers, 6 inches high, unmarked, used on Southern Pacific Railway; c. 1950–1960; $7–10 each.

Wineglasses, crystal, 5.5 inches high, monogram of Northern Pacific Railway; c. 1930–1940; $15–20 each.

Ashtray, hexagonal, heavy glass, decal reads FRISCO/5,000 MILES/IN NINE STATES; c. 1930–1950; $25–35.

Set of electroplated silver multipurpose serving dishes, 6 to 8 inches in diameter, Western Pacific Railway; c. 1935–1945; $135–185 the set.

Flatware, electroplated silver knives, forks, and spoons, 6 to 8.5 inches long, used on Western railroads; c. 1930–1945; $10–15 apiece.

Art Deco style crystal glass centerpiece, 11 inches long, Central Pacific Railroad; c. 1930–1940; $250–350.

Ashtray, circular, heavy glass, decal reads UNION/PACIFIC/RAILROAD; c. 1940–1960; $15–20.

Paperweight, circular, heavy glass, 3.5 inches in diameter, interior reads MISSOURI/ PACIFIC/RAILWAY between lines of track; c. 1900–1920; $30–45.

Tablecloth, white linen, 40 x 38 inches, monogram of Frisco Railway; c. 1920–1930; $30–45.

Tablecloth, white linen, 52 x 45 inches, monogram of Northern Pacific Railway; c. 1930–1950; $25–40.

Tablecloth, pink linen, 46 inches square, monogram of Union Pacific Railroad; c. 1940–1960; $20–30.

Napkin, white linen, 21 inches square, monogram of Atchison, Topeka and Santa Fe Railroad; c. 1940–1960; $10–15.

Headrest cover, cotton, 24 x 14 inches, stenciled GREAT NORTHERN; c. 1930–1940; $7–10.

Menu, lithographed cardboard, 10.5 inches high,

Thunderbird motif; Chicago, Milwaukee, St. Paul and Pacific Railroad; c. 1930–1950; $5–7.

Menu, printed cardboard, 9.5 inches high, Christmas menu; Northern Pacific Railway; 1910; $20–25.

Menu, lithographed cardboard, 9 inches high; Santa Fe Super Chief; 1970s; $3-5.

Menu, lithographed cardboard, 10 inches high, mountain scene; Chicago & Great Northwestern Railway; 1950s; $4–6.

Menu cover, lithographed cardboard, 10.5 inches high, view of Canadian government buildings; Canadian Pacific Railways; 1950s; $2-4.

Dining car worker's hat, heavy paper stock with printed monogram of Frisco Railway on each side; c. 1950–1960; $5–8.

Matchbook cover, lithographed cardboard, logo and advertising of Missouri, Kansas, Texas Railway including train; c. 1930–1940; $1-2.

Matchbook cover, lithographed cardboard, logo and advertising of Rio Grande Railroad; c. 1940–1960; $1 or less.

Matchbook cover, lithographed cardboard, logo and advertising of Missouri Pacific Lines; c. 1930–1950; $1 or less.

Matchbook cover, lithographed cardboard, logo and advertising of Santa Fe Railroad, c. 1950–1970; $1 or less.

Ashtrays, colored glass, 4 to 8 inches long. Left to right: Santa Fe Super Chief, $20–25; Chesapeake & Ohio, $15–20; Rock Island Line; c. 1930–1950; $25–35.

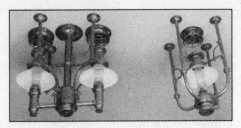

Dining room ceiling light fixtures, brass and milk glass. Left: double, 16 inches wide; c. 1900–1915; $750–900; right: single, 12 inches wide; c. 1910–1920; $550–700.

Cased deck of pinochle playing cards, lithographed cardboard, 4 x 3 inches, case with logo FRISCO/WE'RE BETTING ON YOU, cards with scenic views of Northwest; c. 1930–1940; $50–75.

Cased deck of playing cards, lithographed cardboard, 4 x 3 inches, logo of Northern Pacific Railway; c. 1940–1960; $20–25.

Spittoon, brass, 9 inches in diameter, embossed PULLMAN COMPANY; c. 1910–1930; $40–55.

Stoneware jug for cleaning fluid, 11 inches high, stenciled DEODORIZER/THE PULLMAN COMPANY; c. 1900–1920; $55–75.

Rest room sign, 7 x 3 inches, enameled tin, WOMEN; c. 1940–1960; $20–30.

Railway Ephemera

The term ephemera as applied to Western railroad collectibles covers a broad range of items from the traditional paper such as tickets, time tables, and instructional

Passenger car signs, top to bottom: Lithographed tin, MEN and WOMEN, both 10 inches long; c. 1930–1950; $30–45 each. Builder's sign for railway cars constructed by the Pullman Co. of Pullman, Illinois; c. 1940–1955; $50–65.

booklets to objects in other materials like metal right-of-way signs, lifetime free-travel passes engraved on silver, and a variety of advertising memorabilia.

While many of these are modestly priced, certain desirable advertising items, or "advertiques," as some call them, can bring prices in the thousands due in part to the fact that they are sought after not only by railroad buffs but also by the much larger fraternity of advertising collectors. Also, other things being equal, items with illustrations of trains will bring higher prices.

On the other hand, Western railroad ephemera collectors need not seek out their treasures only through swap meets, collector papers, and specialized dealers. Paper items, particularly the smaller ones, often show up among the holdings of general ephemera dealers as well as at house and tag sales.

With the exception of a few large, spectacular travel posters which have been reproduced, collectors need have little fear of fakes or reproductions in this field, Moreover, except for rarities like lifetime passes, most items are common enough that one need not buy badly damaged pieces. A better example will be along soon enough.

Price Listings—Railway Ephemera

Calendar (perpetual), lithographed tin plate with image of train, 12 x 9 inches; Missouri Pacific Lines; c. 1920–1935; $135–185.

Calendar, lithographed cardboard, 14 x 9 inches; Rock Island Line; 1892; $35–50.

Calendar, lithographed cardboard, 10 x 7 inches, image of train; Wabash Railway; 1899; $60–85.

Poster, lithographed paper, 28 x 14.5 inches, image of train, reference to "Kansas Immigrants"; Toledo, Wabash & Great Western Railway, 1858; $600–750.

Poster, lithographed paper, 12 x 8 inches, issued by striking railway engineers on the Michigan, Southern and Northern Indiana Line; c. 1870–1890; $250–350.

Poster, lithographed cardboard, 26 x 15 inches, illustration of sleeping car interior; Chicago & Alton Railroad to San Francisco; c. 1880–1890; $400–550.

Poster, lithographed cardboard, 27 x 17 inches, illustration of Indian playing flutelike instrument; California Limited; c. 1930–1940; $125–175.

Poster, lithographed cardboard, 17 x 10.5 inches, illustration of train; Great Northern Railway; c. 1940–1950; $80–120.

Station platform step box, painted pine, 10 inches high, Denver & Rio Grande Railroad; c. 1920–1930; $65–95.

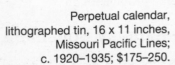

Perpetual calendar, lithographed tin, 16 x 11 inches, Missouri Pacific Lines; c. 1920–1935; $175–250.

Advertising sign, lithographed paper, 18 x 12 inches, Rio Grande Railroad; c. 1950–1960; $80–120.

Tourist brochure, lithographed paper and cardboard, 8.5 x 6 inches, Western Pacific Railway; c. 1900–1915; $65–95.

Handbill, printed paper, 8 x 6 inches, advertising Fourth of July Celebration excursion on Nevada City Railroad; 1887; $75–100.

Trade card, lithographed cardboard, 3 x 4.5 inches, prospectors and train line map; Tonopah & Tidewater Railroad; c. 1890–1900; $50–75.

Stationery, lithographed paper, 8 x 10 inches, logo of Los Angeles Limited, c. 1930–1950; $3-5.

Baggage label, lithographed paper, 2.5 inches in diameter; Santa Fe Railroad; c. 1950–1970; $3-5.

Baggage label, lithographed paper, 3.5 inches square, image of train; Burlington Route; c. 1940–1950; $5–8.

Fan, lithographed cardboard, 8 inches in diameter, with advertising material from St. Louis & St. Paul Railroad; c. 1880–1910; $40–55.

Passenger ticket, printed cardboard, 1 x 2 inches; Missouri Pacific Lines; c. 1920–1930; $5-7.

Passenger ticket, printed cardboard, 1 x 2 inches; Sierra Railway Co.; California; c. 1900–1910; $15–20.

Passenger ticket, printed paper, 3 x 6 inches, "Special

Homeseekers' Excursion Ticket"; Missouri Pacific Railway Co.; 1906; $30–45.

Annual pass, lithographed cardboard, 3.5 x 2.5 inches, image of Indian; Colorado Midland Railway, 1901; $100–140.

Annual pass, lithographed cardboard, 3.5 x 2.5 inches; Denver, Leadville & Gunnison Railway; 1898; $75–95.

Annual pass, lithographed cardboard, 3.5 x 2.5 inches; Colorado and Northwestern Railway Co.; 1904; $45–65.

Time table, lithographed paper, 7 x 3 inches, image of train in mountain country; Denver, South Park & Pacific Railroad; c. 1890–1910; $65–95.

Time table, lithographed paper, 7.5 x 3 inches, image of Indian with shield; Colorado Midland Railway; 1895; $85–110.

Time table, lithographed paper, 7 x 3.5 inches; Tonopah & Tidewater Co. (Nevada); c. 1900–1910; $40–60.

Railway sign, lithographed sheet steel, 16 inches high, Denver & Rio Grande Western Railroad; c. 1925–1935; $200–300.

Railway sign, stenciled sheet steel, 26 inches long; Biggs, New Mexico; c. 1930–1950; $150–225.

Railway speed limit sign, stenciled sheet metal, 28 inches long; c. 1930–1940; $175–250.

Time table, lithographed paper, 7 x 3 inches, image of train in mountains; White Pass & Yukon Route (Alaska); c. 1905 –1915; $70–95.

Time table, lithographed paper, 8 x 4 inches, view of San Francisco; Union & Central Pacific Railroad Line; c. 1890–1900; $75–100.

Time table, lithographed paper, 7 x 3.5 inches; Southern Pacific Railway; 1915; $25–35.

Station poster time table, lithographed paper, 10 x 14 inches, image of train; San Francisco & North Pacific Railway; c. 1880–1900; $200–275.

Station poster time table, lithographed paper, 7 x 16 inches; Denver & Rio Grande Railroad; c. 1900–1920; $80–120.

Employees' time table, lithographed paper, 6 x 2.5 inches; Copper Range Railroad Co.; 1933; $25–35.

Employees' time table, lithographed paper, 9 x 7.5 inches;

Railway Express Agency sign, lithographed sheet steel, 75 inches long; c. 1930–1950; $450–600.

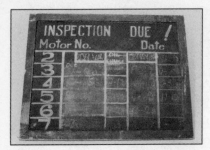

Motor Inspection Board, slate in wooden frame, 19 x 15 inches, Rio Grande & Southern Railroad; c. 1930–1940; $120–170.

Construction blueprint for railway post office car, blue tinted paper, painted wooden frame; c. 1904; $200–275.

Galveston, Harrisburg & San Antonio Railway Co.; 1914; $45–60.

Postcard time table, lithographed cardboard, 3.5 x 5.5 inches; Burlington Route, Chicago and Denver; c. 1930–1940; $10–15.

Employees' rule book, printed paper and cardboard, 5 x 7 inches; New York, Ontario & Western Railroad; 1913; $20–30.

Stock certificate, lithographed paper, 8.5 x 7 inches, small engraving of train; Denver & Rio Grande Railroad; c. 1900–1910; $20–30.

Stock certificate, lithographed paper, 9 x 7 inches, large engraving of train; Chicago, Burlington & Quincy Railroad; 1896; $25–35.

Postcard, lithographed cardboard, 3.5 x 5.5 inches; station at Sapulpa, Oklahoma; c. 1915–1925; $8–12.

Postcard, lithographed cardboard, 3.5 x 5.5 inches; Southern Pacific station at San Antonio, Texas; c. 1920–1930; $10–15.

Photograph of Western train wreck, treated paper, 8 x 5 inches; c. 1910–1930; $85–125. Wreck photographs are popular with collectors.

Presentation lantern, electroplated silver and glass, 9 inches high; given to retiring railway employees; c. 1920–1930; $350–500.

Postcard, lithographed cardboard, 3.5 x 5.5 inches; Union Station; San Bernardino, California; c. 1900–1920; $8–12.

Postcard, lithographed cardboard, 3.5 x 5.5 inches; Santa Fe Railroad station at Oklahoma City, Oklahoma; c. 1930–1940; $7–10.

Informational booklet, lithographed paper, "Plain Facts About Dakota," issued by Chicago, Milwaukee & St. Paul Railway; 1888; $125–165.

Informational booklet, lithographed paper, "Guide to the Northern Pacific Railroad Lands in Minnesota"; 1873; $140–180.

Informational booklet, lithographed paper, "California Picture Book," issued by the Atchison, Topeka and Santa Fe Railroad; c. 1930–1940; $7–12.

Informational booklet, lithographed paper, image of train, issued by Oregon & Idaho Railroad; 1907; $25–40.

Informational booklet, lithographed paper, "Idaho-Utah Outings," issued by Union Pacific Railroad; 1928; $15–25.

Model of a railway trestle, wood and iron wire, 23 inches long, Salt Lake Line; c. 1920–1925; $90–120.

Commemorative plaque, cast iron, 14 inches square; for Western narrow-gauge railways; c. 1920–1930; $300–450.

Land map of "Eastern Washington and Northern Idaho," lithographed paper, issued by Northern Pacific Railway; c. 1880–1900; $120–150.

Railway office sign, lithographed sheet metal, 18 inches square, SANTA FE; c. 1920–1940; $135–185.

Railway office sign, lithographed sheet metal, 25 x 15 inches, UNITED STATES EXPRESS CO.; c. 1900–1915; $225–285.

Railway office sign, lithographed sheet metal, 13 x 6 inches, BAGGAGE ROOM; used in Los Angeles terminal; c. 1910–1930; $55–75.

Railway office sign, lithographed sheet metal, 9 x 4 inches, AGENTS OFFICE; from Denver, Colorado; c. 1890–1910; $80–110.

Railway terminal line, lithographed sheet metal, 20 x 5 inches, WOMEN'S WAITING ROOM; from San Francisco station; c. 1910–1930; $65–85.

Mining Collectibles

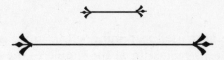

Though still little known outside the Western states, the field of mining memorabilia has a growing number of enthusiasts. The range of possible collectibles is wide, from large machines actually used in the mines to the simple accoutrements of the average sourdough, to the numerous souvenirs relating to the field. Prices, relative to other areas such as cowboy and Native American relics, are quite reasonable. Moreover, with the exception of the extremely popular Wells Fargo items, neither reproductions nor fakes are a problem. However, obtaining desirable items can be, as few dealers outside the Western states handle mining memorabilia. Most local collectors make their finds near to home: in old mining camps, second-hand stores, attics, and even abandoned mining sites. Those who do not live in the West are best advised to either make contact with local dealers or "go west" on a buying trip or two.

Mining Equipment

Just as the gear used in mining silver, gold, and other Western metals ranged from the simple to the complex, the small to the very large, so the interests of collectors range from pocket-size objects to those which require barn-size storage. Equipment size also reflects changes that took place as prospectors exploited the "golden lands" of the West.

The first men into the mother lode sought placer gold, loose flakes of "color" which could be sifted by use of a pan from streambeds. As this source dried up, picks, shovels, and crowbars were used to attack the "dry diggings," rock outcrops which held veins of precious metal. Once these too were gone, it was necessary to seek underground with drill and dynamite and to employ a variety of machinery to convey, crush, and sort the ore.

Pick, shovel, and miner's pan: pick, wrought steel with hardwood handle, 31 inches long; shovel, steel with hardwood handle, 47 inches long, pan, sheet tin, 13 inches in diameter; all California; c. 1920–1935. Pick, $25–35; shovel, $20–30; pan, $35–50.

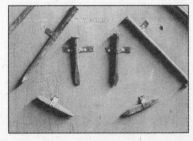

Miners' hand-held drills, wrought steel, 6 to 18 inches long; Nevada; c. 1880–1910; $10–15 each.

Every piece of equipment utilized at each stage of the process, including the items employed by the assayers who determined gold content, is in theory collectible. However, larger, bulkier machinery usually finds its way to museums or historic reconstructions rather than into the home of the average collector. Moreover, such pieces come on the market so seldom that it is difficult to fix firm price guidelines.

Price Listings—Mining Equipment

Miner's pan, tin, 11 inches in diameter; c. 1860–1880; $30–45.

Miner's pan, tin, 12.5 inches in diameter, embossed "Henderson's Patent"; c. 1870–1900; $70–95.

Miner's pan, copper, 12 inches in diameter; c. 1870–1890; $80–120.

Crow or pry bar, wrought iron, 28 inches long; c. 1900–1920; $45–60.

Crow or pry bar, wrought iron, 29 inches long, impressed "Shaft #3"; c. 1910–1930; $75–100.

Pneumatic drills, steel, 3.5 to 5 feet long; Utah; c. 1900–1920; $400–600 each.

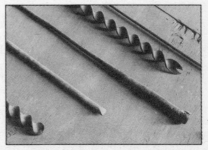

Drill bits for pneumatic drills, steel, 12 to 24 inches long; Utah; c. 1900–1920; $15–30 each.

Arrasta ore mill or crusher, steel and iron, 39 inches high; Colorado; c. 1880–1890; $1,100–1,400.

Hand-powered ore mill or crusher, iron and sheet steel, 28 inches high; Colorado; c. 1900–1920; $750–900.

Crow or pry bar, wrought iron, 27.5 inches long, impressed DUNN; c. 1900–1920; $55–70.

Pickax, wrought steel with wooden handle, 30 inches long, two sharp ends; c. 1920–1930; $30–45.

Pickax, steel with wooden handle, 29 inches long, one sharp end and one blunt; c. 1910–1930; $40–55.

Pickax, steel with wooden handle, 28.5 inches long, hammer form with tapering point; c. 1920–1930; $40–55.

Ore bucket, sheet and wrought iron, 21 inches in diameter; Nevada; c. 1900–1920; $115–140.

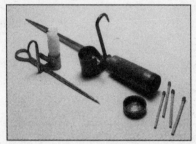

Miners' candle holders. Left: wrought iron pricket or "Sticking Tommy," 6 inches long; right: rare iron and brass hanging candle holder combined with match safe, 9.5 inches long; both Colorado; c. 1875–1900. Left, $90–120; right, $175–225.

Shovel, sheet steel with wooden handle, 39 inches long; c. 1920–1930; $20–30.

Shovel, sheet steel with wooden handle, 37.5 inches long, branded "Cripple Creek"; c. 1910–1930; $70–95.

Hand-held drills, steel, 6 to 12 inches long; c. 1880–1900; $10–15 apiece.

Pneumatic drill, steel, 5 feet long; c. 1920–1930; $350–550.

Air pump which supplied energy for pneumatic drills, iron and steel, 5 feet long; c. 1930–1950; $1,600–2,200.

Blasting powder box, wood, 11 inches high, stenciled DANGER/RESTRICTED; c. 1920–1940; $60–90.

Dynamite box, wood, 9 inches high, stenciled DYNAMITE/DANGER; c. 1920–1940; $50–75.

Candle holders. Left: "Sticking Tommy," wrought iron, 5.5 inches long; Nevada; c. 1880–1900; $75–95. Right: Rare hanging or standing holder, wrought iron, 8 inches high; California; c. 1850–1870; $200–275.

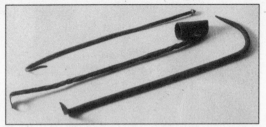

Miners' lighting devices, top to bottom: hanging candle snuffer, 9.5 inches long; hanging candle socket or holder, 13 inches long; hanger for kerosene lamp, 11.5 inches long; all wrought iron; all Colorado; c. 1860–1890. Top to bottom: $70–95; $100–135; $55–75.

Oil can, sheet metal, long-necked, 14 inches high, stenciled "Benton Mine"; c. 1900–1920; $65–90.

Oil can, galvanized metal, 12.5 inches in diameter, barrel form with loop handle; c. 1910–1930; $35–50.

Ore mill (so-called Chilean or Denver quartz mill), iron and steel, 42 inches high; c. 1900–1910; $900–1,300.

Ore bucket, sheet iron with wrought iron handle, 19 inches in diameter; c. 1890–1910; $125–150.

Miners' cap lamps, sheet steel with wrought iron hooks, 2.5 to 7 inches high; Colorado; c. 1870–1900; $40–80.

Early safety lamp, punchwork-decorated sheet brass, 5.5 inches high; Utah; c. 1870–1890; $80–110.

Miner's safety lamps, brass, glass, and brass wire screening, 7.5 inches high, used throughout the West; c. 1900–1930;

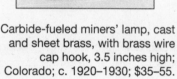

Carbide-fueled miners' lamp, cast and sheet brass, with brass wire cap hook, 3.5 inches high; Colorado; c. 1920–1930; $35–55.

Ore sample bag, canvas, 12 x 8 inches, stenciled "Boulder"; c. 1900–1920; $40–65.

Ore sample bag, canvas, 11 x 8 inches, stenciled "# 1"; c. 1910–1930; $25–35.

Stamps, iron with wooden handles (for stamping identifying letters and numbers on machinery and ore bags), 6 to 9 inches long; c. 1910–1930; $10–15 each.

Candle holder, wrought iron pricket or "Sticking Tommy" type, 6 inches long; c. 1870–1900; $80–120.

Candle holder, wrought iron folding "Sticking Tommy" type, 5.5 inches long, impressed RICE PAT.MAR.29,'81 (Colorado patentee); c. 1881–1900; $200–275.

Candle holder, wrought iron rod with hanging hook and candle socket, 11 inches long; c. 1860–1890; $100–135.

Candle holder, wrought iron with adjustable ratchet, hanging hook, and candle socket, 13.5 inches long; c. 1860–1880; $150–200.

Betty lamp, cast iron with wrought iron hanging hook, circular reservoir, 4 inches in diameter; c. 1850–1870; $135–185.

Front: miner's helmet in composition material with battery-powered electric headlamp, 7.5 inches high; rear: two kerosene lanterns, sheet iron and glass, 10 to 11 inches high; all Colorado; c. 1920–1930. Helmet with lamp, $100–135; lanterns, $35–45 each.

Miner's cap lamp, sheet steel, 3.75 inches high, teapot shape with wrought iron hook which attaches to cap; c. 1870–1900; $45–60.

Miner's cap lamp, sheet steel, teapot shape with wrought iron hook, impressed C.CLANTON/MFR./WASHINGTON CO.PA.; c. 1880–1900; $75–100.

Miner's safety lamp, brass and glass, 6.5 inches high, tubular form, impressed AMERICAN SAFETY LAMP/MINE SUPPLY CO./SCRANTON,PA.; c. 1900–1920; $90–120.

Mining helmet of steel-reinforced composition material with brass carbide lamp, 6 inches high; Nevada; c. 1920–1940; $85–120.

Mining surveyor's transit in carrying box, brass and sheet iron, 14 inches long; Colorado; c. 1880–1910; $235–285.

Miner's carbide lamp, brass with round reflector and cap hook, 4 inches high; c. 1920–1930; $35–55.

Mining helmet, sheet steel, 10 inches long; c. 1900–1910; $90–120.

Mining helmet, heavy composition with steel reinforcement, 10.5 inches long, marked NO. 3 SHAFT; c. 1920–1930; $75–100.

Mining helmet, heavy molded plastic, 11 inches long; c. 1950–1970; $25–35.

Sign, painted wood, 2 x 3 feet, "R. TALON/ASSAY OFFICE"; c. 1920–1930; $150–200.

Sign, lithographed sheet steel, gold and white on black, 2.5 x 4 feet, "JOHN MATTHEWS/ASSAYER & BULLION BUYER/FT.COLLINS"; c. 1900–1920; $300–450.

Assayer's scales, brass and iron in mahogany and glass case, 12 x 20 inches; made by Philadelphia manufacturer; c. 1910–1920; $300–450.

Assayer's scales, brass and iron, portable in 4 x 8 inch pine case; c. 1890–1910; $50–75.

Sign for assayer's office, lithographed sheet tin, 28 x 12.5 inches; Boulder, Colorado; c. 1910–1924; $250–325.

Mine office sign, lithographed sheet tin, 42 x 18 inches; Stratton Mine; Cripple Creek, Colorado; c. 1900–1910; $275–350.

Assayer's or bullion buyer's scales, brass in mahogany and glass case, 20 x 13 inches; manufactured in Philadelphia, used in Nevada; c. 1890–1920; $350–450.

Portable assayer's scales, brass and iron in glass-fronted walnut box, 16 x 10 inches; Colorado; c. 1870–1890; $275–350.

Prospector's portable scales, brass in walnut case, 8 x 3.5 inches; Alaska; c. 1890–1910; $110–145.

Mortar and pestle, cast iron (for crushing ore samples), 6 inches in diameter; c. 1870–1890; $75–100.

Assayer's slag mold, cast iron with 25 round depressions, 10 inches square; c. 1910–1930; $80–110.

Assayer's slag mold, cast iron with handle and four cone-shaped depressions, 12 inches long; c. 1900–1920; $65–90.

Assayer's crucibles, stoneware, 3 to 5 inches high, beakerlike receptacles used in melting ore samples; c. 1890–1920; $20–35 each.

Mortar and pestle used in grinding up ore samples, cast iron, 9 inches high; Nevada; c. 1920–1930; $75–110.

Assayer's crucible holder, pincerlike wrought iron tool, 14 inches long; c. 1920–1940; $65–95.

Assayer's ladle, cast iron spoon for pouring molten ore, 12.5 inches long; c. 1900–1930; $45–65.

Assayer's screen for straining rough ore samples, sheet iron and iron wire, 14 inches in diameter; c. 1900–1920; $50–65.

Mining telephone, bakelite phone in cast iron wall case, 14 inches square; c. 1920–1940; $185–245.

Mine elevator with passenger cage, iron and steel, iron wire mesh, 10 feet high; c. 1910–1920; $2,200–2,800.

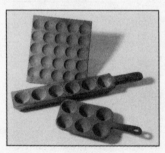

Assay office slag molds, cast iron, 9 to 15 inches long; Colorado; c. 1920–1940. Top to bottom: $75–95; $90–120; $85–110.

Assayer's equipment. Top: set of three crucibles, stoneware, 2.5 to 5 inches high; bottom: slag mold, cast iron, 12 inches long; all used in Colorado or Nevada; c. 1910–1930. Top, $20–35; bottom, $70–90.

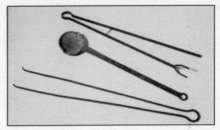

Assayer's tools, top to bottom: crucible holder, 14 inches long; molten metal ladle, 13 inches long; pincers, 17 inches long; all wrought iron; used in Colorado; c. 1920–1940. Top to bottom: $65–90; $40–55; $55–75.

Assayer's equipment, top to bottom: sample splitter, sheet iron, 11 inches square; screen for straining rough ore samples, sheet iron and iron wire, 10 inches in diameter; bag for ore samples, canvas, stenciled SLIDE MINES/BOULDER COLO, 16 x 12 inches; all used in Boulder, Colorado; c. 1910–1930. Top to bottom: $80–100; $65–80; $50–75.

Mine shaft telephone, brass telephone in cast iron wall-mounted case, case 12.5 inches square; Nevada; c. 1915–1930; $225–285.

Ore car, wooden body, cast iron wheels and braces, 4 x 6 feet; c. 1900–1920; $750–900.

Ore car, cast iron and sheet steel body, 4 x 5 feet; c. 1925–1935; $500–650.

Slag car, cast and wrought iron, cone-shaped body 3 feet in diameter mounted on two wheels; c. 1880–1900; $500–750.

Mining elevator bell, stainless steel, and bell instruction sign, lithographed sheet tin. Bell, 4 inches in diameter; sign, 12 x 6 inches; both Colorado; c. 1920–1940. Bell, $200–250; sign, $175–225.

Electric motor-driven engine which pulled trains of ore cars through mines, iron and steel, 5 feet long; c. 1920–1930; $1,500–2,000.

Mucker, steam-powered iron and steel device which shoveled ore from mine floor into ore cars, 10 feet long; c. 1920–1940; $2,500–3,500.

Steam boiler (used to generate power for drills and mine elevators), sheet and cast iron, 14 feet long; c. 1890–1900; $5,000–6,000.

Prospector's mule pack saddle frame, wrought iron, leather, and wood, 26 x 14 inches, used in California's Sierra Nevada; c. 1870–1885; $185–265.

Horse or donkey collar, sheet steel and leather, 23 x 16 inches, used on horses that pulled ore cars from Colorado mines; c. 1900–1920; $70–95.

Ephemera

The mining industry generated a great deal of paper goods from stock certificates, checks, and land deeds to advertising pieces promoting local mines and businesses. There are also interesting photographs of miners and mining sites. All are collectible, most are moderately priced, and a few are extremely attractive. Best of all, unlike much mining memorabilia, they are highly portable, easily displayed, and comfortably stored.

Price Listings—Ephemera

Stock certificate, chromolithographed paper with mining scenes; Wyoming Gold Mining Co.; 1901; $20–30.

Stock certificate, chromolithographed paper with mining scenes; Colorado Mining Co.; Cripple Creek; 1905; $25–35.

Stock certificate, chromolithographed paper; Nevada Silver Mining Co.; Tonopah; 1891; $10–15.

Stock certificate, chromolithographed paper, hand-stamped BUSTED; Windward Mining Co.; Moab, Utah; 1910; $20–30.

Mining stock certificate, lithographed paper with scene of underground mining, 10 x 7 inches; Cripple Creek, Colorado gold mining district; 1903; $20–30.

Mining stock certificates, lithographed paper, 10 x 7 inches; all from Colorado mines; c. 1895–1905; $15–25 each.

Detail of vignette from mining stock certificate, lithographed paper, 10 x 7 inches; Wyoming gold mine; c. 1890–1900; $20–30.

Deed to forty-acre mining tract in northern Arizona; 1890; $3–5.

Deed to the "Painted Post Mine"; Colorado, 1886; $6–9.

Deed to "mineral rights" on twenty-four acres in eastern California; 1907; $5–7.

Deed to the "Texas Claims," one hundred twenty acres in Nevada; 1912; $5–7.

Statement of deposits and coinage; U.S. Branch Mint; Carson City, Nevada; February 1872; $30–45.

Check drawn on Gould & Curry Silver Mining Co.; Virginia City, Nevada; illustrated; 1868; $20–25.

Check drawn on Monitor Gold Mining Co.; San Francisco, California; 1864; $10–15.

Check drawn on Virginia City, Nevada, bank; 1879; $8–12.

Deeds to mining claims, printed paper, 9 x 5 inches; Colorado mines; c. 1890–1910; $5–9 each.

Seals used to stamp mining stock certificates and company documents, cast iron, 6 to 8 inches long; Nevada corporations; c. 1900–1920; $15–25 each.

Broadside advertising illustrated lecture about gold miners in Alaska, chromolithographed cardboard; c. 1900–1910; $200–275.

Broadside seeking miners to work in Nevada mines, promises "fair wages," undated; early 1900s; $300–400.

Magazine, *Gold*, various issues dealing with mining; c. 1970–1972; $2–3 per issue.

Daguerreotype, quarter-plate, two miners with tools and guns; c. 1850–1860; $1,300–1,800.

Daguerreotype of the mining town of Grizzly Flat, California; half-plate; from an important collection; c. 1845–1855; $3,500–4,200.

Photograph of a group of hard-rock miners, treated paper, 7 x 5 inches; California; c. 1900–1910; $125–165.

Ambrotype, eighth-plate, of building with sign "Miners' Supplies"; c. 1850–1860; $250–350.

Tintype sixteenth-plate, miner with pick beside stream; c. 1860–1870; $125–175.

Tintype, eighth-plate, view of ore crusher and other mining equipment; c. 1870–1880; $90–120.

Tintype, sixteenth-plate, view of town with mine tipples in background; c. 1870–1880; $80–110.

Stereo view, men panning for gold in stream; c. 1890–1910; $20–30.

Photograph of a horse-drawn train of ore cars, treated paper, 7 x 5 inches; Colorado; c. 1920–1930; $60–80.

Reverse glass painting of mine shaft scene, oils on glass, 10 x 8 inches in wooden shadow box frame; Western states; c. 1940–1950; $300–400.

Stereo view, group of miners climbing in snow over Alaska's Chilkoot Pass; c. 1900–1910; $15–20.

Stereo view, worker operating a mining sluice on California river; c. 1870–1880; $30–45.

Stereo view, panorama of Virginia City, Nevada; c. 1870–1880; $65–95.

Stereo view, main street of unidentified mining town; c. 1880–1900; $25–35.

Miscellaneous Collectibles

Due to the general fascination with mining lore, a wide variety of souvenir objects relating to the field has been produced. These pieces, which range from nineteenth-century silver spoons to mid-twentieth-century whiskey bottles, often bear the names of mining towns or commemorate important events in the West's mining history. They are, for the most part, quite affordable.

Price Listings—Miscellaneous Collectibles

Occupational shaving mug, hand-painted picture of miner with tools on white earthenware mug, 4 inches high; c. 1890–1900; $250–320.

Occupational shaving mug, hand-lettered BENTON'S MINE within floral wreath, white earthenware, 4 inches high; c. 1900–1910; $90–120.

Whiskey flask, porcelain, representation of miner panning gold, 10 inches high; Old Bardstown; 1978; $25–35.

Whiskey flask, porcelain, representation of miner panning gold, 9 inches high; by Potters; 1979; $30–40.

Whiskey flask, porcelain, in form of prospector, 10.5 inches high; Ezra Brooks; c. 1970; $20–25.

Whiskey flask, aqua glass, on one side miner with backpack and phrase FOR PIKES PEAK; on other, hunter shooting deer; 7.5 inches high; c. 1860–1870; $90–110.

Souvenir spoon, sterling silver, handle finial terminating in Alaska state seal and miner's pan, 6 inches long; c. 1900–1910; $75–100.

Souvenir spoon, sterling silver, bowl inscribed with representation of Colorado capital, handle terminates in miner's windlass, pick, and shovel; 5.5 inches long; c. 1900–1910; $80–120.

Souvenir spoon, sterling silver, handle in the f rom of standing miner with pickax, 6.5 inches long; c. 1900–1920; $60–85.

Souvenir spoon, sterling with gold wash, shovel form bowl inscribed "Goldfield/Nev.," handle terminates in miner's pan backed by crossed pick and shovel; 6.5 inches long; c. 1880–1900; $100–135.

Souvenir spoon, sterling silver, handle engraved with miner's pick, shovel, and pan; 6 inches long; Sonora, California; c. 1890–1910; $80–110.

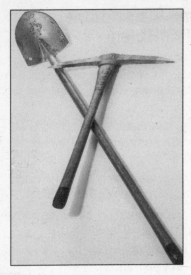

Commemorative pick and shovel set, brass-plated steel with wooden handles and logo of mining company, 37 to 43 inches long; Colorado; c. 1930–1940; $500–600 the set.

Souvenir spoon, sterling silver, bowl with engraved representation of ore-dredging machine, 6 inches long; Oroville, California; c. 1920–1930; $50–75.

Miniature pick and shovel, sterling silver commemorative piece, 6 inches long, with engraved date 1906 and name of mine official; $250–350.

Pin, crossed pick and shovel, sterling silver, 2 inches across; c. 1920–1940; $40–60.

Pin in form of miner's helmet, silvered pot metal and enamel, 1.5 inches across; c. 1930–1950; $25–35.

Watch fob in form of pure gold nugget on silver chain, 13 inches long; c. 1890–1900; $450–600.

Inkstand in form of miner with pick and shovel, cast lead, 3.5 inches high; c. 1900–1910; $45–60.

Figurine, hand-painted porcelain figure of comical miner waving shovel, 3.5 inches high; Japan; c. 1930–1940; $20–30.

Figurine, miner pulling reluctant burro, 4 inches long; Japan, c. 1930–1940; $25–35.

Wells Fargo Memorabilia

Much of the gold and silver that came out of the West traveled via the Wells Fargo stage line. The battles between that company's employees and outlaws seeking to steal its strongboxes are an important part of Western lore, and items associated with the Wells Fargo name have an avid collector following.

This popularity, however, has also led to the manufacture of numerous reproductions as well as things which were never issued by Wells Fargo but simply bear the firm's logo. Among the fakes to watch out for are belt buckles, badges (often embossed "Special Agent"), watch fobs, and luggage tags. It should also be noted that in 1973, Wells Fargo issued its own brass buckle reproduction, and this is now considered collectible.

Price Listings—Wells Fargo Memorabilia

Express company sign, WELLS FARGO & CO., polychrome-painted wood, 46 x 14 inches; c. 1900–1910; $1,000–1,400.

Mail bag, canvas and leather, stenciled W.F. & CO., 24 x 20 inches; c. 1890–1910; $250–350.

Pommel bag, leather pouch that held rider's valuables, marked WELLS FARGO & CO., 9 x 12 inches; c. 1870–1890; $1,000–1,400.

Stagecoach strongbox, ironbound wood marked WELLS FARGO & CO., 18 x 14 x 10 inches; c. 1870–1890; $4,000–6,000.

Strongbox padlock, steel, embossed W.F. & CO., heart-shaped, 4 x 2.75 inches; c. 1870–1900; $800–1,000.

Strongbox key, brass, stamped W.F. & CO., 2 inches long; c. 1870–1900; $200–300.

Employee's badge, brass, shield-shaped, impressed W.F. & CO., 2 inches high; c. 1900–1920; $70–100.

Medal, sterling silver, engraved with employee's name, issued in 1902 for fiftieth anniversary of Wells Fargo; $900–1,300.

Horse blanket, wool, stenciled W.F. & CO., 4 x 5 feet; c. 1900–1910; $200–300.

Pass, printed cardboard, entitling bearer to ship personal belongings free of charge on Wells Fargo vehicles; 3 x 2 inches; 1903; $70–95.

Express frank, stamplike sticker of lithographed paper entitling bearer to ship 50 pounds of cargo via Wells Fargo, 2.5 x 1 inch; 1906; $30–45.

Ticket, printed paper entitling the bearer to ride both Wells Fargo stage and Union Pacific Railroad, 3 x 2 inches; c. 1900–1910; $45–65.

Annual free pass for travel on the Northwestern Stage Co., a Wells Fargo spur line, 3.5 x 2.5 inches; 1878; $100–150.

Time table for Wells Fargo & Co. Western routes, printed paper, 8.5 x 5 inches; 1868; $200–300.

Brass buckle, Wells Fargo & Co., on reverse "Copyright 1973" and serial number; with original belt; $30–45.

Hunting and Trapping Memorabilia

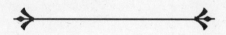

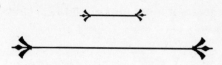

An area of interest to a limited but growing number of collectors is memorabilia associated with the hunters and trappers who first explored the West and exploited its natural resources. Initially there were the French coureurs de bois, or "woods runners," who sought furs for a growing European market. When French power waned in North America, these were replaced by American and British trappers seeking primarily the beaver skins used in hat manufacture. By 1840 the beavers were gone, but there was still bison to kill. The opening of the transcontinental railroads in the 1860s led to an influx of "buffalo hunters" who supplied the Eastern markets with hides for use as both leather and carriage robes. When the bison, too, were extirpated in the 1880s, the hunters and trappers passed from the scene, leaving behind but a few mementos of their passing.

From the trappers we have acquired the steel traps they used in seeking beavers, fox, and mink; the trade hatchets they employed both to cut wood and to defend themselves; and the gear, such as snowshoes, used to sustain them during long months in the woods. From the hide hunters we have skinning knives, hide scales, and, most important, the old single-shot, heavy-caliber Sharps or Henry rifles used to bring down their shaggy prey.

Some of these items, like traps, are easy to find; others, such as rifles, are harder to acquire. In all cases there are questions of authenticity. Were these really used in the West? In no area is it more important that a collector have documentation.

Price Listings—Hunting and Trapping Memorabilia

Rifle, single shot, .45/.90 caliber short barrel breechloader; manufactured by Christian Sharps; c. 1850–1870; $800–1,200.

Pennsylvania half stock .36 caliber muzzle-loading percus-

Detail of breech and stock of single shot .50 caliber rifle by C. S. Welles; Evansville, Indiana; c. 1850–1865. Though slow-loading, these heavy rifles were accurate and favored by buffalo hunters; $800–1,100.

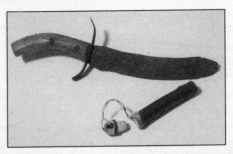

Above: Skinning knife, steel with deer horn handle, 11 inches long; c. 1840–1860; $80–120. Below: scent container, black birch with carved wooden plug, 4 inches long; c. 1880–1900; $45–60.

Skinning knife, steel blade marked "J. Russell & Co./Green River Works," wooden handle with brass ferule, 11.5 inches long; John Russell; Green River, Massachusetts; c. 1850–1870; $185–265.

Left to right: powder measure, carved wood, 2.5 inches long, $20–25; shot pouch, leather, 8 inches square, $175–250; powder horn, cow horn with leather carrying thong and carved wooden stopper, 10.5 inches long, $65–85; all Colorado; c. 1840–1870.

sion rifle; manufactured by Joseph Golcher; c. 1860–1865; $1,500–2,000.

Powder horn, carved cow horn 10 inches long with leather carrying strap and wooden stopper; c. 1850–1870; $50–75.

Powder horn, brass with embossed floral decoration, 6.5 inches long; c. 1860–1870; $60–85.

Powder horn, copper with embossed hunting scene and name of American manufacturer, 7 inches long; c. 1860–1880; $90–110.

Shot pouch, buckskin with carved wooden stopper, 6 inches long; c. 1850–1880; $45–65.

Skinning knife, steel with a stag horn handle, 9 inches long, c. 1850–1870; $65–85.

Trade ax, wrought iron with steel edge, hardwood handle, 16 inches long; Colorado; c. 1840–1860; $180–230.

Skinning knife, steel blade marked "J. Russell & Co./Green River Works," wooden handle, 10.5 inches long; by John Russell of Green River, Massachusetts, one of the most famous makers of knives used in the West; c. 1855–1885; $150–200.

Skinning knife, steel blade made from blacksmith's file, buffalo horn handle, 9.5 inches long; c. 1860–1880; $125–175.

Beaver trap, sheet and spring steel with wrought iron link chain, 10 inches long; c. 1840–1860; $75–100.

Bear trap, sheet and spring steel, 21 inches long; c. 1860–1880; $400–550.

Trapper's scent container, carved pine cylinder with wooden stopper, used to carry scented bait for traps; 4.5 inches long; c. 1860–1880; $65–95.

Traps. Above: Bear trap, cast and sheet steel, 26 inches long, Oregon; c. 1870–1890; $500–650. Below: Beaver or small game trap, sheet steel with iron link chain, 9 inches long; c. 1880–1900; $50–65.

Hide scales, tension type, brass and iron, 4 inches across; c. 1860–1880; $50–75.

Hunter's game bag, heavy canvas with brass fittings, 12 x 14 inches; c. 1880–1900; $70–95.

Trapper's pack basket, woven splint, with leather harness, 21 inches high; c. 1870–1900; $225–300.

Trapper's pack sled, hardwood with wrought iron runners, 40 inches long; these small sleds were used to hand-drag furs and supplies across ice and snow; c. 1840–1870; $350–475.

Snowshoes, bear paw type; rawhide in a bentwood frame, decorated with tufts of red trade cloth; 19 inches long; c. 1870–1890; $200–275.

Fire striker, wrought iron, U-shaped, used with flint to kindle fires, 3 inches long; c. 1850–1870; $30–50.

Cooking pot, cast iron with three legs and wrought iron wire bale handle, 8.5 inches in diameter; c. 1860–1880; $80–110.

Frying pan, sheet iron, 8 inches in diameter; c. 1880–1900; $30–45.

Snowshoes, buckskin thongs on a bent hardwood frame, leather straps, 35 inches long; c. 1880–1900; $170–220.

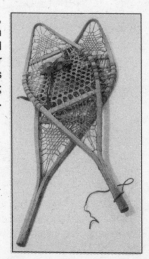

Frying pans,
sheet iron,
7 to 8 inches
in diameter;
c. 1860–1890;
$30–45.

Set of Western deer
horns mounted for
display, 28 inches
across, $85–115.

Knife and fork, steel with pewter inlay on wooden handle, 7.5
to 8.5 inches; c. 1860–1890; $8–12 each.

Drinking cup, carved from hardwood with stub handle, 3.5
inches high; c. 1850–1870; $100–125.

Drinking cup, enameled tin, 4 inches high; c. 1870–1900;
$15–20.

Cabinet photo of two buffalo hunters with rifles and large pile
of skins, treated paper, 4 x 6 inches; c. 1870–1890;
$165–235.

Western Logging Memorabilia

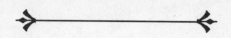

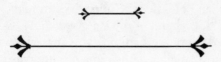

Everyone likes to be first into a new field of collectibles, and if there is anything new and hot in Western material right now, it's lumbering gear. Of course, timber cutting was important in other areas (Paul Bunyan came from Minnesota), but it was in the West, particularly California, Oregon, Washington, and British Columbia, that the big trees were found. And it was there that logging reached its apex in the late nineteenth and early twentieth centuries.

Many different specialists worked in the woods, each with his own equipment. High riggers lopped off the tops of giant firs, cedars, and spruces, often 150 feet high and 12 feet in diameter. Fallers brought down the giants, and buckers cut them into manageable sizes. That was the easy part! Getting massive loads of timber out of the forest required the services of bull skinners with their teams of oxen, choker setters to handle the drag chains, and a host of other skilled workers.

Much collectible gear, like axes, saws, ox yokes, chains, and peaveys, is small enough to be readily collected and displayed. But some of the most interesting items—donkey engines and specialized logging trucks, for example—are so large that few private collectors can hope to own more than a single example.

That's the bad news. The good news is that in this newly discovered field, much desirable material may still be found stored away in old barns, garages, and abandoned company buildings. Collectors can really get in on the ground floor here, and it's a good thing, as few auctioneers or dealers are handling this material. Moreover, prices for most smaller items remain quite reasonable.

Price Listings—Western Logging Memorabilia

Falling ax, single bit, steel, 6-inch head; c. 1880–1900; $45–60.

Falling ax, single bit, steel, 6.5-inch head; c. 1900–1920; $65–90.

Falling ax, double bit, hardened steel, 9.5-inch head; c. 1890–1910; $110–130.

Falling ax, double bit, steel, logging company brand, 9-inch head; c. 1900–1920; $100–125.

Falling ax, double bit, steel, 9-inch head; c. 1880–1900; $55–75.

Wedge, wrought iron (used to widen cut in tree), 7.5 inches long; c. 1890–1910; $25–35.

Wedge, wrought iron, 9 inches long; c. 1900–1920; $20–30.

Wedge, wrought iron, 6.5 inches long; c. 1900–1920; $15–25.

Mallet, oak head and handle (used to drive wedges), 10 inches long; c. 1900–1920; $15–20.

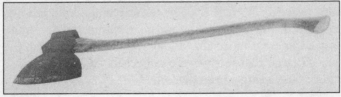

Falling ax, single bit, steel with hardwood handle, 6.5-inch head; c. 1880–1900; $55–75.

Pinch or crowbar,
wrought steel,
19 inches long;
c. 1900–1920; $15–20.

Mallet, oak head, maple handle, 12 inches long; c. 1890–1910; $20–30.

Pinch or crowbar, wrought steel, 23 inches long; c. 1910–1930; $15–25.

Pinch or crowbar, wrought steel, stamped OAKLAND, 27 inches long, c. 1920–1940; $30–45.

Crosscut saw, steel with maple handles, 10 feet long; by Simmonds Manufacturing Co.; c. 1900–1910; $170–240.

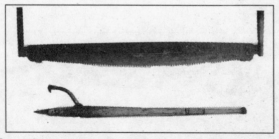

Top: Two-man crosscut saw, steel with maple handles, 7 feet long; c. 1870–1900; $145–185. Bottom: Peavey or pike pole, steel head with hardwood shaft, 5.5 feet long; c. 1890–1910; $40–60.

Saws used in lumbering, top to bottom: One-man crosscut saw, steel with pine handle, 4 feet long; c. 1870–1880; $65–95. Ripsaw, steel with pine handle, 4 feet 6 inches long; c. 1890–1910; $40–65. Pruning saw, 3 feet 9 inches long, steel with hardwood handles, c. 1900–1930; $25–35.

Crosscut saw, steel with hardwood handles, 16 feet long; by Atkins Manufacturing Co.; c. 1890–1910; $250–350.

Crosscut saw, steel with hardwood handles, 12 feet long; by Disston Manufacturing Co.; c. 1900–1920; $200–250.

Gasoline-powered drag saw (crosscut saw), iron and steel, 6.5 feet long; by Wade Manufacturing Co.; c. 1900–1910; $1,000–1,500.

Gasoline-powered drag saw (crosscut saw), iron and steel, 6.5 feet long; the Arsenam Bow Saw; c. 1923–1928; $750–1,000.

Steam-powered drag saw (crosscut saw), iron and steel, 7 feet long; by Ransom Manufacturing Co.; c. 1880–1890; $2,000–2,700.

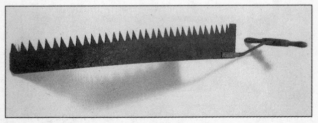

Open pit saw, steel with hardwood handle, 9 feet long; c. 1870–1880; $170–210.

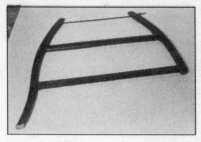

Bucksaw, steel with hardwood frame, 36 inches across, used to trim smaller branches on fallen trees; c. 1900–1930; $30–45.

Oil can, sheet metal with iron wire bale handle, 15 inches long; c. 1920–1940; $25–35.

Circular saw blade, steel, 34 inches in diameter; c. 1900–1930; $90–130.

Circular saw blade, steel, 46 inches in diameter; c. 1910–1930; $175–250.

Oil bottle (for saw blades), glass with tin spout, 8.5 inches high; c. 1900–1920; $20–35.

Oil can, tin with wire bale handle and pouring spout, 10 inches high; c. 1880–1910; $35–55.

Saw-sharpening frame, wood and iron, 3 x 4 feet, c. 1880–1900; $275–350.

Machine for sharpening tools such as axes and scythes, cast iron, steel, and grinding stone; c. 1890–1910; $80–120.

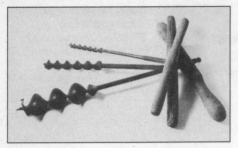

A group of augers used to drill holes for fixing lines to trees, steel with hardwood handles, 12 to 22 inches long; all c. 1880–1910; $15–35 each.

Ox yoke, oak and cedar with wrought iron fixtures, 61 inches long; c. 1880–1900; $110–160.

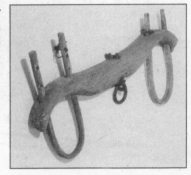

Peavey or pike pole (used to handle logs in water), steel and hardwood, 5 feet long; c. 1910–1930; $45–65.

Peavey or pike pole, steel and hardwood, marked PORT GAMBLE, 5.5 feet long; c. 1890–1910; $100–135.

Pair of logger's studded or "cork" boots, leather, size 9; c. 1910–1930; $40–60.

Pair of logger's studded or "cork" boots, leather, with bunk number, size 10; c. 1900–1920; $65–90.

Branding stamps (to mark logs), wrought iron, 3 to 7 inches high; c. 1890–1920; $10–15 each.

Blocks (used in moving logs), ironbound hardwood, 8 to 20 inches long; c. 1880–1920; $35–55 each.

Block and tackle, ironbound hardwood, 9 to 14 inches long; by the Lamb-Gray Harbor (Washington) Co.; c. 1910–1920; $50–95 each.

Ox shoes, wrought iron, 4 to 6 inches long; c. 1870–1890; $5–7 the pair.

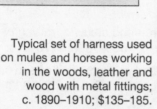

Typical set of harness used on mules and horses working in the woods, leather and wood with metal fittings; c. 1890–1910; $135–185.

Logging chain, wrought iron, individual links 3 to 9 inches long; 1870–1910; $3–5 per link.

Ox yoke, oak and maple, 64 inches long; c. 1870–1880; $125–175.

Ox yoke, cedar and maple, 55 inches long; c. 1880–1900; $100–150.

Ox goad, hardwood with pointed wrought iron tip, 4 feet long; rare; c. 1880–1900; $165–235.

Ox shoes, wrought iron (in two parts for cloven hoof), 4 to 7 inches long; c. 1870–1900; $5–7 a pair.

Shingle cutting tools, c. 1880–1910. Above: froe club, turned maple, 11 inches long, $12–16; below: two froes, steel with maple handles, 13 to 14 inches long, $30–45.

Triangle (used by cooks to call men to meals), wrought iron, 12 inches on each side; c. 1880–1910; $150–200.

Gut hammer (for striking triangle), wrought or cast iron, 9 inches long; c. 1880–1910; $75–90.

Froe, wrought iron blade with hardwood handle (for shingle cutting), 9-inch blade; c. 1900–1910; $35–50.

Froe club, turned pine (used with froe), 11 inches long; c. 1900–1910; $15–25.

Screw or pump jack, cast iron and steel (for raising or turning logs), 2 to 4 feet high; c. 1880–1910; $175–375.

Logging wheels, hardwood and wrought iron (to keep moving logs off ground), 8 to 10 feet in diameter; c. 1880–1900; $800–1,200.

Donkey engine, iron and steel, steam driven (to move logs), 10 to 12 feet long; by Murray Brothers; San Francisco; c. 1890–1910; $4,500–6,000.

Blacksmith's anvil, wrought iron, 28 inches long; every logging camp had a blacksmith to shoe animals and repair equipment; c. 1900–1920; $200–250.

Blacksmith's pincers and hooks such as those used by logging crews; all wrought iron; c. 1880–1900. Pincers: 15 to 19 inches long, $30–45 each; hooks: 5 to 8 inches long, $10–15 each.

Donkey engine, iron and steel, steam driven, 12 to 14 feet long; by Washington Iron Works; c. 1900–1910; $3,700–4,500.

Lumber piler, iron and steel, 3 x 6 feet; by Hilke Manufacturing Co.; c. 1920–1930; $1,200–1,800.

Logging engine, iron and steel, steam driven, 16 feet long; by J. I. Case Co.; c. 1905–1915; $3,400–4,200.

Tractor, McCormick-Deering Trac Tractor, iron and steel, gasoline powered, 13 feet long; c. 1910–1930; $5,000–6,500.

Tractor, International, T-20, iron and steel, gasoline powered, 14 feet long; c. 1930–1935; $3,000–4,000.

Photograph, loggers with saws and axes, black and white, 6 x 8 inches; c. 1900–1920; $40–65.

Photograph, river filled with logs, black and white, 5 x 8 inches; c. 1920–1940; $25–35.

Photograph, logger standing by large, partially cut through tree, black and white, 6 x 9 inches; by well-known logging photographer Darius Kinsey; c. 1900–1910; $300–450.

Gambling Devices

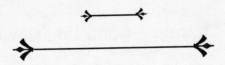

Though gambling was hardly confined to the West, it was (and is) very much a part of Western life, and most collections include some gambling paraphernalia. Moreover, many of the region's most dramatic events are associated with games of chance. Wild Bill Hickok met his end while playing poker in a Deadwood, South Dakota, bar; and one of the numerous charges lodged against the infamous Billy the Kid was ". . . keeping a gameing table . . ."

Collectible gambling devices cover a wide range, from large objects such as the floor-standing roulette wheels used in casinos and the "money wheels" common to carnivals, to decks of cards, dice, and dice cups. A particularly fascinating (and quite pricey) area is that of gamblers' "cheats," tools such as card shavers and "cold deck" trays which were designed to provide the professional with an illegal edge on the competition.

Provenance is a major problem in this field. Few gambling items bear any indication of where they were used, so if you want to collect only those with a Western history, you must rely on some prior owner's statement that they actually have a Western origin. A few items, such as dice cups, were designed for communal use in a bar or casino, and these may bear an owner's mark, always a big plus.

The high end in gambling equipment is the cheating tools. Some may bring prices in the thousands, and there have been reports of reproductions or made-up pieces.

Price Listings—Gambling Devices

Gambling or money wheel mounted on base containing table and storage areas, polychrome-painted wood, cast iron, and brass; 5.5 feet high; California; c. 1910–1920; $7,000–8,000.

Gambling or money wheel, polychrome-painted wood and cast iron, wall mounted, 47 inches in diameter; c. 1920–1940; $550–700.

Gambling or money wheel, polychrome-painted wood and iron wire, mounted on wooden tripod stand, 4 feet high, 30 inches in diameter; c. 1930–1950; $350–500.

Roulette wheel, table mounted for a casino, mahogany with ebony inlay, brass, and steel; 4 x 6 feet; from a casino in Broadmoor, Colorado; c. 1885–1895; $8,000–11,000.

Gambling or "money" wheel, painted wood and iron, 35 inches in diameter; made from a wagon wheel; Colorado; c. 1900–1910; $200–300.

Casino roulette wheel, inlaid mahogany with decorative chrome pillar, 30 inches in diameter; Nevada; c. 1890–1900; $4,000–5,500.

Tabletop roulette wheel, ebonized wood and chrome, 14 inches in diameter, Western; c. 1900–1910; $300–400.

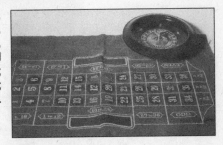

Portable roulette wheel, bakelite and chrome, 9.5 inches in diameter, with green baize printed layout, Western; c. 1920–1930; $125–185.

Serving tray in the form of a roulette wheel, lithographed tin, 14 inches in diameter; from a Nevada casino; c. 1935–1945; $100–150.

Roulette wheel, tabletop form, ebonized wood with anodized aluminum fixtures, 20 inches in diameter; c. 1910–1930; $400–550.

Roulette wheel, miniature traveling form, ebonized wood with chrome-plated fixtures, 11 inches in diameter; in original carrying case; found in Wyoming; c. 1900–1920; $750–950.

Roulette wheel, for home use, plastic and pot metal, 8 inches in diameter, with felt laydown, all in original box; c. 1930–1950; $30–45.

Poker chip holder, laminated wood, with colored clay chips, 9 x 6 inches, Western; c. 1920–1940; $65–95.

Gaming chips. Left: Ivory roulette chips, 1.5 inches in diameter; Nevada; c. 1900–1910; $5–8 each. Right: Faro chips, bakelite, .75 x 1.75 inches, Western; c. 1920–1930; $3–5 each.

Faro counting rack, mahogany with steel spools, 25 x 34 inches; made by a New York box manufacturer for a Western casino and extremely rare; c. 1870–1880; $1,600–2,200.

Poker set, cardboard playing cards, clay chips, in an inlaid wooden case, 20 x 13 inches; Nevada; c. 1900–1910; $700–850.

Poker chips, ivory, with colored motifs, umbrella, fan, hat, etc., 2 inches in diameter; c. 1900–1920; $4–6 each.

Poker chips, colored clay, 2 inches in diameter, marked EL PASO SALOON; Texas; c. 1915–1925; $12–18 each.

Faro chips, bakelite, oblong, in solid colors, .75 x 1.75 inches; c. 1920–1930; $1–3 each.

Boxed whist set, colored
cardboard cards in
walnut and brass box,
14 x 9.5 inches;
c. 1860–1880;
$400–550.

Faro chips, composition, oblong, 1 x 2 inches, marked
LONG'S CLUB; Nevada (?); c. 1910–1930; $4–7 each.

Casino faro table setup including abacuslike card counter,
felt and wood layout, cards, card holder, chips, and baize
top walnut table; 6 x 4 feet; all from c. 1880–1900
Colorado saloon; $3,500–4,500.

Poker chip holder, bakelite with brass handle, 6.5 inches
high; c. 1920–1940; $20–35.

Poker chip holder, wood with ebonized wood lift, 8 inches in
diameter; c. 1890–1910; $125–175.

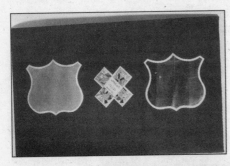

Card game layout for
the game of red and
black, baize, 32 x 20
inches; rare example
by a New York
manufacturer for a
Colorado casino;
c. 1880–1900;
$900–1,200.

Card game
layout for the
game of high-
low, baize,
38 x 20 inches,
Western;
c. 1890–1900;
$600–850.

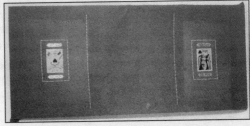

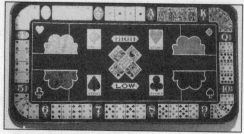

Card game layout for the game of Diana, baize laid down on walnut, 56 x 25 inches, Western; c. 1870–1880. Only two copies of this layout are known to exist; $5,500–6,500.

Set of playing cards, hand-colored cardboard, 4 x 3 inches; manufactured by Thomas Crehore; Dorchester, Massachusetts; c. 1840–1845; $700–800.

Set of playing cards, cardboard, bearing photographs of Western Indian tribes by San Francisco and Los Angeles photographers, 4 x 3 inches; c. 1900–1905; $1,400–1,700.

Set of playing cards, cardboard, with lithographed Western scenes, 4 x 3 inches; c. 1930–1950; $70–95.

Set of playing cards in original lithographed cardboard box, box marked STEAMBOAT PLAYING CARDS, 4 x 3 inches; c. 1900–1910; $65–95.

Card case, fitted leather and brass case to hold single deck of playing cards, 5 x 6 inches; c. 1890–1910; $75–100.

Roulette layout, baize laid down on hardwood, 70 x 34 inches; Nevada; c. 1890–1900; $700–950.

Card press, mahogany with iron screw mechanism, 13 x 5.5 inches, Western; c. 1880–1900; $200–300.

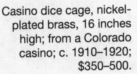

Casino dice cage, nickel-plated brass, 16 inches high; from a Colorado casino; c. 1910–1920; $350–500.

Dealer's box for use in card games, chrome-plated steel, 4 x 5 inches; c. 1900–1920; $130–180.

Card press, walnut, branded "Nevada City/No. 9," 5 x 12 inches; c. 1900–1920; $165–235.

Faro case, square walnut box with built-in spools used by gamblers to keep track of card sequence in faro game, 19 x 21 inches; c. 1890–1910; $750–950.

Roulette wheel layout, felt dyed in various colors, for use in placing bets, 60 x 35 inches; c. 1900–1920; $350–500.

Gambling hall layout, polychrome-painted wood, for various nineteenth-century card games, 50 x 30 inches; c. 1890–1910; $600–750.

Gambling hall layout in painted felt for the card game of high-low, 34 x 19 inches; c. 1900–1930; $400–550.

Pair of dice, ivory; c. 1900–1920; $10–15 the pair.

Pair of dice, bakelite; c. 1920–1930; $10–15 the pair.

Pair of poker dice, bone or ivory; c. 1890–1910; $30–45 the pair.

Home dice cage, aluminum, 12 inches high, Western; c. 1900–1910. Though designed for "friendly" competition, these were often used by gamblers; $125–175.

Gambler's bubble-topped dice shaker, chrome with clear glass cover, 7 inches high, with magnet used to control fall of dice; Nevada; c. 1900–1920; $250–375.

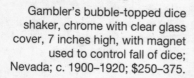

Automatic draw poker dice box, walnut and steel with ivory dice, 20 inches long; Colorado; c. 1890–1900; $700–950.

Dice cup, leather embossed with geometric patterns, base stamped "Hanley's/Silver City," 5 inches high; c. 1880–1900; $100–135.

Dice cup, leather, undecorated, 4.5 inches high; c. 1900–1910; $20–35.

Dice cage, chrome-plated wire cage mounted on wooden base, contains pair of bakelite dice, 12 inches high; attributed to a Reno, Nevada, gambling house; c. 1920–1940; $300–400.

Bubble dice shaker, turned wooden base with clear plastic

Tavern dice gambling game, "Win A Beer," anodized steel, chrome, and glass, Western; c. 1935–1945; $300–400.

Revolving casino dice bowl or "Hieronymus Tub," walnut, 18 inches in diameter with ivory dice 2 inches across; South Dakota; c. 1870–1880; $1,400–1,900.

cover over pair of bakelite dice, 7.5 inches high, c. 1920–1940; $225–275.

Dice drop, round chrome, steel, and glass tube with interior baffles, 9 inches high; c. 1930–1950; $125–165.

Dice drop, turned and faceted mahogany tube, 7 inches high; c. 1880–1900; $175–250.

Dice game layout, green and orange felt with numbers 1–12, 28 x 9 inches; c. 1910–1930; $240–320.

Magnet for use in controlling the fall of dice which have been

A group of professional gamblers' dice drops, walnut and glass, 10 to 12 inches high, Western; c. 1870–1890; $150–300.

Dice game layout, baize, 36 x 14 inches; used in a California gambling house; c. 1890–1910; $550–700.

"loaded" with tiny bits of metal, 4 x 3 inches; c. 1890–1910; $75–100.

Gambling tops or teetotums, brass with impressed numbers, 1.5 inches high; c. 1920–1940; $30–45 each.

Card trimmer, brass and steel mounted shears used to trim edges of cards so gambler could recognize them, 10 x 5 inches; c. 1880–1900; $1,200–1,600.

Early chuck-a-luck layout, baize laid down on wood, 34 x 13 inches; made in Chicago for use in Colorado; c. 1870–1890; $600–800.

Gambling tops or teetotums, brass and bakelite, 1.5 inches high; used in various games throughout the West; c. 1880–1920; $20–45.

Lottery tickets, printed paper, 4.5 x 2 inches; for the Louisiana Lottery drawing in Kansas City, Kansas; 1894; $30–45 each.

Gambler's shears type card shaver, brass and steel mounted on wooden base, 13 inches long, Western; c. 1880–1890; $1,700–2,200.

Gambler's corner trimmer, brass and steel, 7 x 5 inches; used to reshape corners of cards after they had been trimmed; Colorado; c. 1870–1880; $2,000–2,700.

Card trimmer, steel knife blade hinged to walnut base, 7 x 4 inches; c. 1880–1910; $900–1,200.

Gambler's "holdout," two-piece sheet steel and wire spring device designed to slip card into player's hand from deck concealed in shirt or vest; rare; each unit approx. 9 x 7 inches; c. 1900–1920; $2,500–3,000.

Gambler's "cold deck" machine, sheet tin, iron wire, and canvas, 9 x 7 inches, Western; c. 1900–1910; $1,800–2,200.

Gambler's "holdout," spring-loaded sheet steel, 7 x 10 inches; designed to be worn under vest (produced the winning card on order!); California; c. 1900–1910; $2,200–2,800.

Books on card playing, all c. 1870–1910. Left to right: *The Card Player*, $50–75; *Card Sharpers*: *Their Tricks Exposed*, $75–125; *Whist*, $15–25.

Gambler's "cold deck" apparatus, spring-loaded sheet steel device which enables player to slip new deck of fixed cards into game, 7 x 6 inches; c. 1915–1935; $2,000–2,800.

Gambler's ring, silver finger ring with built-in knife edge to mark cards during card game, 1 inch in diameter; c. 1880–1910; $200–300.

Pamphlets on gambling, both c. 1890–1900. Left, "The Thompson Street Poker Club," $100–150; right, "Why Gamblers Win," $75–100.

Tobacco humidor with gambling scenes, painted chalkware, 7.5 inches high; c. 1900–1910; $250–350.

Print, lithographed paper, 14 x 10 inches, scene of dogs gambling, typical of Western gambling house "art"; c. 1910–1920; $75–95.

Advertisement for Cyrus Noble whiskey featuring scene of gamblers at Old Orient Saloon; Bisbee, Arizona; lithographed cardboard, 26 x 16 inches; c. 1890–1900; $350–475.